T0246115

10 9 8 7 6 5 4 3 2 1

Permissions:
University of North Texas Press
1155 Union Circle #311336
Denton, TX 76203-5017

The paper used in this book meets the minimum requirements of the
American National Standard for Permanence of Paper for Printed Library
Materials, z39.48.1984. Binding materials have been chosen for durability.

  Library of Congress Cataloging-in-Publication Data

Hoover, Timothy R., 1959– author.
  Soul serenade : King Curtis and his immortal saxophone / Timothy R. Hoover.
    Pages cm
  Includes bibliographical references and index.
  ISBN-13 978-1-57441-881-1 (cloth)
  ISBN-13 978-1-57441-887-3 (ebook)
  1. LCSH: Curtis, King, 1934–1971. 2. Saxophonists—United States—
Biography. 3. Rhythm and blues musicians—United States—Biography.
4. LCGFT: Biographies.
  ML419 .C87 H66 2022
  788.7/165092 [B]–dc23
                      2022017129

Number 17 in the North Texas Lives of Musicians Series

The electronic edition of this book was made possible by the support of
the Vick Family Foundation.

Typeset by vPrompt eServices.

Contents

Illustrations

Preface

H e won first prize twice in a row at the Amateur Night at the Apollo Theatre. Buddy Holly insisted on paying the airfare and fees so they could record together at Buddy's studio in Clovis, New Mexico. His sound was so crucial to the Coasters that he was considered by many to be "The Fifth Coaster." His solo on their hit "Yakety Yak" revolutionized the role of the saxophone studio musician. He befriended, recorded, and toured with Sam Cooke. He opened for the Beatles at Shea Stadium and supported them the rest of their 1965 tour, backed by the same band that would soon include Jimi Hendrix. Aretha Franklin was his unofficial "little sister" at Atlantic Records. He should have been on Otis Redding's plane the fateful day it crashed. He brought Donny Hathaway to Atlantic Records. He became a very close friend and mentor to Duane Allman. He won a Grammy Award. And he was inducted into the Rock and Roll Hall of Fame but tragically never lived to accept his award.

During the incendiary music revolution that began in the 1950s and lasted into the early 1970s, "King Curtis" Ousley was in the middle of everything. Not only was he talented, having played some of the most memorable saxophone solos in music, but he was also one of the most prolific artists of his generation, recording with well over two hundred musicians during an eighteen-year span. He was a major influence on a great many young aspiring musicians and, later, producers. Yet, while he is well known in the industry, he remains relatively unknown outside the music business.

Would the Coasters have been a success without King Curtis on so many of their hits? Probably. Would Sam Cooke's raucous *Live at the Harlem Square Club, 1963* album and subsequent tour have been as entertaining and energetic without Curtis? Undoubtedly. Would Aretha Franklin have been any less successful had she not met her "big brother" and bandleader at Atlantic Records? Would her interpretation of Otis

Redding's "Respect" have been any less impactful as a revolutionary feminist anthem without his timeless solo? Not likely. Would Donny Hathaway have been discovered and signed to a major recording label without King Curtis? Someone most certainly would have discovered his talents at some point around that time.

Would Sam Moore's debut solo album for Atlantic Records have been possible without Curtis's tough-love production abilities? Now there's a fair question, for Sam will admit that Curtis brought out something in him that he didn't know he had inside. The two would argue day and night about what material to record, but by the end Sam acquiesced and covered songs that challenged him like never before. And Sam told me he is eternally grateful.

From the beginning of her stint at Atlantic Records until the end of their time together, Aretha Franklin always felt more comfortable, more at ease onstage or in the studio with King Curtis backing her. Not only was Curtis note-perfect, his bands were, too. Others discovered this as well. At the Montreux Jazz Festival in 1971, try as he might, bluesman Champion Jack Dupree, with all his limitless ability to deviate from a standard twelve-bar blues format, could never shake King Curtis and the Kingpins loose when they were backing him. They meticulously stalked his every move the entire concert—with virtually no rehearsal.

King Curtis's large frame housed an immense talent harnessed into a subtle ability that seemed to make every artist and every song better. He was universally accepted in an era characterized by segregation, even in music. Many times, he was the only Black musician in the recording studio. His skill, physical stamina, and chameleon-like ability to adapt instantly to any musical genre while working with any musician or producer would separate him by a wide margin from any other saxophone player of his time. He also evolved his headlining career into a significant portfolio of soul, pop, blues, and jazz. I don't know of any other artist of his generation that was more influential, or unrecognized.

While searching for a soul saxophone artist to listen to, I had settled on the bluesy Eddie "Cleanhead" Vinson (his live collaboration with Etta James is outstanding). It wasn't until 1994 that I started on my quest to write this book after seeing David Sanborn perform King Curtis's hit "Soul Serenade" at Northrup Auditorium in Minneapolis. It blew me away. At that moment I knew I had to learn everything I could about King Curtis Ousley.

While working for orthopedic surgeon (and favorite music maven) Dr. Terry Gioe, I asked why nobody had written King Curtis's biography and wondered aloud about pursuing it. Knowing I had played college soccer, his response was classic Terry: "Hoover. The day. The DAY you write a biography is the day I play for the United States Men's National Soccer team!" Challenge accepted.

Interviewing people can be exciting and unpredictable, and I had plenty of large and small adventures along the way. My first interview in 2001 was with retired vice president of Atlantic Records Jerry Wexler. My initial call to him was answered in a gruff voice, and he quickly told me to call him back in three weeks. Three weeks later I called him again and he asked me to call him back in an hour, then quickly hung up. An hour later, unsure where this interview would go, I called again and Jerry answered the phone. He couldn't have been more gracious and supportive. He was so excited to hear I was writing Curtis's biography that he asked me to use his name to influence any potential future interviewees. He also happily volunteered a few personal photos. I was overwhelmed by his support.

Ahmet Ertegun, former president and co-founder of Atlantic Records, was still on a flight back to New York City from Detroit when I called for our scheduled interview. His secretary, Francis, gave me Mr. Ertegun's apologies and said he still very much wanted to keep our appointment to speak about Curtis that day. She called me back two hours later after Mr. Ertegun had landed and quickly made his way to the Atlantic offices, where he gave me a marvelous interview.

I tried for almost a year to reach Sid Bernstein, the promoter who brought the Beatles to New York's Carnegie Hall in 1964 and Shea Stadium in 1965. Like water being consistently dripped on his forehead, I doggedly called him on the first of every month and left a message saying how much I would like to talk to him about why he had handpicked King Curtis and his band to be one of the opening acts for the Beatles at their Shea Stadium concert. After ten months, as I was taking my seven-year-old daughter into St. Paul Children's Hospital for some elective surgery, my phone rang. It was a New York City area code. Thinking it was one of the sales representatives for the medical company I worked for, I answered the call in a casual manner. I will never forget the very New York accent on the other end of the line, nor the thrill of hearing the voice it belonged to say, "Tim Hoovah … are ya sittin' down? This is Sid Bernstein."[1]

I had hoped to interview Isaac Hayes after his April 15, 2002, concert with the Cyrus Chestnut Quartet at the Naples Philharmonic Center in Naples, Florida. The head usher, Nancy Andrews, had said she would pass my request along to Mr. Hayes. At concert's end, many other performers had come back onstage to visit with members of the audience, but no Isaac Hayes. He was nowhere to be seen. Disappointed, I started to leave my seat, when I noticed Nancy in the aisle at the end of our row. She beckoned me to come with her. I turned to my friend, Lance Provance, and said triumphantly, "You are going to meet Isaac Hayes!" Isaac Hayes is the only artist I've interviewed that had me completely intimidated. Backstage, as he rounded the corner into the reception room, resplendent in an African outfit and hat, he took my breath away. Isaac Hayes, writer for Stax Records, solo artist, movie star, and voice of Chef on "South Park." Wow. I was nervous. During the post-concert meet-and-greet, Mr. Hayes couldn't have been more cordial, and we had a nice chat.

I learned later that during the interview, one of the guitar players in the band had leaned over to Lance and asked, "Hey, what's that guy talkin' to Isaac about?"

Lance replied, "Oh, he's interviewing him for a biography that he's writing about King Curtis."

The guitarist replied, "Man! That guy writin' a book about Curtis? Man, that's cool. That is COOOOOL." His enthusiasm for this project still makes me smile. It was a small yet wonderful moment of support that has continued to reinforce my determination to write King Curtis's story.

It took me over three years to finally locate Mickey Baker, who had expatriated to France in the mid-1960s. Mr. Baker was incredibly important to filling in the early-to-mid-1950s era of King Curtis's career. We emailed back and forth to schedule a phone interview. When I called on the agreed-upon date and at the designated time, his wife answered, saying that he was unavailable, as he was taking a nap. Disappointed, I sent off an email to try to reschedule. A very apologetic Mickey Baker emailed back to me immediately, asking me to call him at once for he had told his wife to be sure to wake him when I called.

Curtis's girlfriend, Modeen Brown, maybe the most critical person to this story, was a challenge to locate, like many others. One night I got a call from King Curtis film documentarian Dennis O'Keefe, saying, "I think I found Modeen!" When hearing about the discovery of Modeen's whereabouts, my dear friend Roy Simonds of Surrey, England, emailed across the Atlantic Ocean an excited "ABSOLUTE MAGIC!" After sending her a letter and then a follow-up phone call, I was sitting in Modeen's kitchen with my tape recorder on, one of many visits to her home. She is an amazingly gracious woman, and we have been fast friends ever since.

Acknowledgments

I owe a tremendous debt to so many who were involved in this project. After years of off-and-on research, in 2000 I found the author of *King Curtis, A Discography*, Roy Simonds, in Surrey, England. His effort was a startling piece of dogged determination requiring over thirty-five years of work. His publications, interviews, connections, and discography were essential to this book. I can't state that firmly enough. Without Roy's help, support, and friendship, there would be no biography. His devotion to King Curtis motivated me, and we quickly were emailing or calling each other at least once a week, a pattern that continued for the next twelve years. Plans to finally meet face-to-face for the first time in England were tragically interrupted by his untimely death in December 2012. I miss him terribly.

Rob Hughes worked closely (and tirelessly) with Roy Simonds, and his resolute research cannot be understated. Rob's determination has led to incredibly essential material, and I am beholden to him for all his hard work.

Modeen Brown, Curtis's girlfriend/fiancée, has been such a wonderful supporter and her enthusiasm, grace, and friendship have been my rudder for over twenty years. She's taught me much about life and love. She's a dear friend, and I treasure every moment we can spend together.

Dennis O'Keefe began an unfinished King Curtis film documentary in 1986. He was deeply important to this work, as his connections helped source many participants in this book. I deeply appreciate his support and wry humor over these many years.

Thanks to George Massey in Switzerland, who has also been helpful with his previous interviews and unwavering enthusiasm for this project.

The people at *Hittin' the Note* magazine (with editors Pete Sienkiewicz and Bill Ector) created my first opportunities in writing, publishing articles I wrote about King Curtis and Delaney Bramlett. Their interest in this project always spurred me forward.

Authors John Broven and Tom Wilk have contributed mighty reviews and opinions that kept me focused and were so very helpful. John also performed

Roy Simonds (November 29, 1944—December 1, 2012). For Roy: the best friend I've never met. *Courtesy of Vicky Smith / The Simonds Family.*

a very necessary and extensive fact-check on my material. I deeply appreciate of all their efforts to stay in touch and cheer me on.

Red Kelly (the "Soul Detective") contributed some needed insights into Fame Studios in Muscle Shoals and American Sound Studios in Memphis that were very helpful.

The people at independent publishing website Reedsy have been a significant resource for me, helping me find Elizabeth Evans, my first professional editor. I am grateful for her interest, competence, and energy. She gave me some much-needed inspiration early on. Copyeditor Aja Pollock (another Reedsy talent) contributed crucial polishing to the manuscript, and I'm still amazed at her exacting review. Who knew she and her husband had the band play "Memphis Soul Stew" at their wedding reception? What a crazy coincidence.

I am also deeply indebted for the patience and faith that everyone at the University of North Texas Press has put into this project, particularly editors Ron Chrisman, Karen DeVinney, and Carolyn Elerding. I am thankful for their guidance and wisdom. Their feedback has always been patient, helpful, and kind. I'm thrilled this book will be a part of their significant Lives of Musicians series. I've really enjoyed the long journey with them.

Thanks to WJFF Radio Catskill's Jonathan Mernit for his support on his radio shows and his enthusiasm for King Curtis over the years. It's much appreciated.

There were a number of businesses and people that gave their support for the photos used in this book. Among them were Modeen Brown, Jerry and Paul Wexler, Richard Weize and the Bear Family Records Archives, Getty Images, PoPsie Photo and Artizen Photo Printing.

Grateful acknowledgment is made for permission from Alfred Music Publishing to reprint lyrics from "Soul Serenade," by King Curtis and Luther Dixon (Soul Serenade Words and Music by Luther Dixon and Curtis Ousley Copyright © 1964 EMI Longitude Music and Kilynn Music Publishing, Inc. Copyright Renewed All Rights for EMI Longitude Music Administered by Sony Music Publishing (US) LLC, 424 Church Street, Suite 1200, Nashville, TN 37219 All Rights for Kilynn Music Publishing, Inc. Administered by Warner-Tamerlane Publishing Corp. International Copyright Secured All Rights Reserved Reprinted by Permission of Hal Leonard LLC). The many, many artists, agents, producers, collaborators, and friends of Curtis Ousley who contributed to this work in one shape or form, opening their hearts and many times their homes, have overwhelmed me with their sincerity and kindness. Thank you.

So many memorable phone and personal interviews. Everyone I've spoken to was universally excited to talk about King Curtis, which has always been incredibly gratifying. Thanks to Ahmet Ertegun, Jerry Wexler,

Delaney Bramlett, Bonnie Bramlett, Ruth Bowen, Cornell and Erma Dupree, Jerry Jemmott, Chuck Rainey, Bernard Purdie, Carl Gardner, Joel Dorn, Isaac Hayes, Sid Bernstein, Arif Mardin, Tom Dowd, Sam and Joyce Moore, Norman Dugger, Shirley Alston Reeves, Gene Chrisman, Bobby Wood, Mickey Baker, Barbara Castellano, Clarence Clemons, Jimmy Douglass, Gene Paul, Bobby Elliot, Wayne Jackson, Michael Lydon, Thomas "Curly" Palmer, David Sanborn, Jimmy Smith, Trevor Lawrence, Cissy Houston, Tyree Glenn Jr., Paul Wexler, and Bobby Whitlock. Their honest recollections were incredibly helpful, and their respect and love for the talent and the man that was Curtis Ousley is still palpable and deeply reverent.

I also would have been lost were it not for my family and friends who supported me when I needed strength and motivation. My wife Teresa; our children, Sophie Strauss (and husband Danny), Izzy and Sam Hoover, and Tyler Clevett; my parents, the Rev. Dr. Henry and Jean Hoover, and Carol and Ed Kuehnel; as well as my sister, Martha; brother Matt and his gal Chris Christian-Vint; "Second-Mom" Barbara Christensen; niece Becky Krocak Costigan (who did some proofreading on early drafts); and cousins Heidi and David Samuels along with Molly Cottle and the Nelson and Schroeder families, have all been wonderful champions. Dr. Terry Gioe has continually challenged me while cheering me on, and I particularly appreciate his sharp wit, sarcasm, and friendship over the years. Other important people supporting this project were Paul Wiese, my many friends at Arthrex Inc. and St. Anthony Orthopaedic Clinic, Dr. Jim Gannon, Mike Clark, Greg Guederian, Lance Provance, Jim Fil, Anne Labonte, and Carrilee Kelley, who have all been so uplifting. Thank you all for your love and friendship.

The people who knew Curtis Ousley over fifty years ago still mourn their loss to this day. I hope the following pages give them pause to reflect, remembering Curtis with a smile, maybe a tear, as his long-overdue story is finally being told. They have all touched me with their sincerity, spirit, and infectious energy regarding this book. While many of the people interviewed here can be classified as a "who's-who" of the rock and soul music eras, I have never been met with anything less than warmth, unequivocal support, and hospitality. This book would have been impossible without their personal contributions and honest efforts.

Chapter 1

Behind the Eight Ball

A t the moment of his birth, Curtis Ousley had towering odds against any potential success. Born on February 7, 1934, he was named Curtis Montgomery, the lovechild (born out of wedlock) of African American parents: the Rev. I. B. Loud, a prominent (and very married) Dallas, Texas, minister and sixteen-year-old Fort Worth housecleaner Ethel Montgomery, tangled in the throes of a torrid affair. Curtis was put up for adoption by his mother soon after birth and was given his adoptive parents' last name. He was raised in rural Mansfield, Texas, some twenty miles southeast of Fort Worth, by his new parents Josie and William Ousley, who also raised another adopted child, Josephine. It was here among the rural farm fields that Curtis Ousley's initial musical influence may have been his adoptive father, who played guitar in the local church every Sunday.

In Dennis O'Keefe's documentary in progress, *Soul Serenade: The King Curtis Ousley Story (as told by those who knew and loved him)*, Curtis's little sister, Josephine, notes their unremarkable existence:

> Curtis and I were raised down there in Mansfield, Texas, down there on a little farm. We were adopted by Josie and William Ousley. William Ousley, he played guitar, I don't know, Curtis, he was a

smart young man, he just picked up music. They bought him his
first little saxophone. We grew up in a nice house, back then there
wasn't any telephone or electric lights. We cooked on wood stoves,
and we read and studied our lessons by oil lamps. There wasn't
any television back then, we had radio. I remember listening to
Minnie Pearl; we used to listen to her on the radio [on "Grand Ole
Opry," Radio WSM, Nashville, Tennessee]. We used to listen to the
Joe Louis fight; he used to come on the radio. We had chores to do,
we fed the hogs, we fed the chickens, and we milked the cows, we
picked watermelon. We had a little of everything to do on the farm.
We didn't raise cotton or anything.[1]

By the time he was eleven years old, Curtis Ousley was dreaming—
dreaming of being the next Louis Jordan. But by 1945 who *wasn't* influenced
by the likes of Jordan? Virtually every young saxophone player of the day
aspired to be the next great horn player, the next new "jump" music feature.
In 1945, Louis Jordan was it.

The theatrical saxophone player had created an extensive string of hits,
beginning with "I'm Gonna Move to the Outskirts of Town" in 1942. Jordan
and his label, Decca Records, scored an amazing fifty-seven hits that domi-
nated the *Billboard* "race" and R&B recording charts over the next nine
years. He was easily one of the most successful and influential early pioneers
of what is widely labeled today as "rhythm and blues" music. Speaking with
author Mike Hennessey many years later, Curtis confirmed his major influence: "It was Louis Jordan playing alto saxophone. I heard it on the radio and
told my mother that I wanted to play that instrument more than anything."[2]
Young Curtis Ousley, too, hoped to become the next charismatic musician
to take the country by storm. Many of his fellow hopefuls would ultimately
succeed due to either opportune or financial means. With major obstacles in
his way, young Curtis had neither. But as you will hear from his schoolmates,
teachers, and friends, Curtis, as friend Nathaniel Scott put it, "Had some
natural ability that [fellow students] didn't have, or that we hadn't found yet,
but he found his pretty early."[3]

From these humble and isolated beginnings came the additional
weight of being Black in the Deep South. Segregation was without question the code of the day and had been for generations. But God-given

The Ousley Family in their Sunday best: William, Josie, Josephine, and Curtis. *Courtesy of Modeen Brown.*

musical talent could many times transcend even Jim Crow. Curtis rode a bus to James E. Guinn Elementary School in Fort Worth, Texas, with his sister, Josephine, and friend Nathaniel Scott. Despite the lack of quality facilities, instruments, or training (status quo for the majority of Black schools at the time) Curtis's penchant for music emerged early at James E. Guinn. Nathaniel Scott remembered: "Curtis and I attended the same elementary school together. At that particular time, any of the individuals going to school started music in the fourth grade. That's where we both started. We were all somewhat at the same level, music-wise, but the only one who was ahead of the whole deal was Curtis Ousley. I don't know—we all practiced, but it seems as though Curtis had some natural ability."[4]

Even then, Curtis was large for his age group and towered over most of his fellow classmates. In grade school his unmistakable physical presence, however, belied his quiet demeanor. Scott continued: "He didn't talk much; he did the majority of talking through his horn. He didn't have anything: he had his horn, he had himself, and that was it. And he felt as though that was all he needed, and he had confidence in himself."[5]

Did Curtis throw himself into music, and particularly the saxophone, for comfort from the potential alienation, abandonment, and insecurity he had regarding his adoptive family situation? Was it an emotional escape from his mundane rural homelife? A temporary respite from the stigma of being of color in the Deep South, a diversion or reprieve from the reality of the deep-seated humiliation of segregation? The answers are best left to armchair psychoanalysts to debate. It is noteworthy, however, that while sister Josephine has said that Curtis received his first saxophone from his adoptive parents, the Ousleys, years later his girlfriend Modeen Broughton (later Modeen Brown) steadfastly maintained that Curtis reconnected with his birth mother, Ethel Montgomery, at a young age and that she was the one who provided his very first horn. There is significant evidence that Curtis established strong relationships with both his adoptive parents and his birth mother early in his upbringing, a particular grounding that many adopted children are not accorded. Curtis would maintain close ties to both his birth mother and adoptive family, visiting them often. Regardless of who gave it to him, Curtis always remembered the specific date he received his first saxophone: May 12, 1945.[6]

Curtis wanted to expand his musical education, and it was impossible to accomplish this in the farming community of Mansfield. Curtis moved some twenty miles away to Fort Worth and maintained an apartment with his birth mother so he could more easily attend I. M. Terrell High School, also in

Curtis and school friends from I. M. Terrell High School.
Courtesy of Modeen Brown.

Fort Worth, a better school academically as well as musically. Most importantly, Terrell High had Mr. Gilbert Baxter.

I. M. Terrell High School was named after Isaiah Milligan Terrell.
In 1882 he was one of the first four Black teachers to be employed by the
Fort Worth public school system. He became principal of East Ninth Street
Colored School, which was renamed the North Side Colored School No. 11,
and served there until 1915. In 1921, in honor of its former principal,
North Side Colored School No. 11 was renamed I. M. Terrell High School.
The school was moved to its final location of 1411 East Eighteenth Street,
site of a formerly white elementary school. Isaiah Terrell later became an
active leader in the Houston, Texas, Black community and remained so until
his passing in 1931 at the age of 72.[7]

I. M. Terrell High awakened the sleeping musical giant that lay within
Curtis Ousley. Having produced famous musical alumni such as saxophone
player Ornette Coleman and guitarists Cornell Dupree and Ray Sharpe,
I. M. Terrell provided Curtis Ousley with his first advanced music training.
His self-confidence in his abilities was bolstered by a very special music
teacher: Gilbert Baxter.

Nathaniel Scott followed his grade school chum to I. M. Terrell High
and also never forgot the positive impact Mr. Baxter's music classes made
on the lives of all the students there. It was much more than just the
"gospel of music" the dynamic Baxter preached to his rapt charges; it was
a philosophy of life: "That's the one thing Mr. Baxter used to tell the
guys in the band: 'I can't have more confidence in you than you have
in yourselves,' ... And Curtis took that very seriously. And that was his
complete bag: music, music, music."[8]

Curtis took his instructor's words to heart, quickly forming a band of
fellow musicians from high school and hitting the local Fort Worth music
scene with a vengeance. Curtis's belief in his music was on an upward trajec-
tory and now his personal self-confidence began to grow. Talent-wise, he
had already separated himself from the other horn players in his high school
music class, and he now aimed at distinguishing himself from the rest of
the local professional competition. His solution was a tireless work ethic,
playing long hours after school to outwork everyone in his path. But just

working hard did not seem to be enough; somehow, something was missing. He needed a "catch" to hook the fans, giving them another way to remember him in addition to his exhaustive performing effort. Curtis felt that a colorful stage name was necessary to increase his visibility around the community. The self-christened title, though hatched at a young high-school age, would serve him well for the rest of his life. Curtis Ousley was now King Curtis.

It's interesting that many years later in 1959, the liner notes by author Joe Muranyi for Curtis's first solo album for the Atlantic Records subsidiary Atco, *Have Tenor Sax Will Blow*, noted a different version of this self-coronation. Muranyi described how, when Curtis later settled in New York, "he received his sobriquet 'King Curtis.' His agent, who was looking for a name to put on some newly cut records that Curtis had made, thought Curtis Ousley too cumbersome; so he dubbed Curtis 'King' in the time-honored tradition that has made dukes, counts, sirs, lords and princes out of so many musicians in the jazz world. The name stuck, and his fans and the trade know him best as King Curtis."[9]

Muranyi's version is heartily disputed by Nathaniel Scott, Curtis's boyhood pal, who claims the most accurate knowledge of the real story behind the evolution of Curtis's moniker:

> He [Curtis] originated that; King Curtis, nobody gave it to him, he did that himself. I'm sure that he didn't do it out of cockiness, because he just wasn't that type of individual. He had his own band, but the guys who played with him in high school, they really wanted to listen to him. He played so hard until the young guys in high school, we gave him a name: 'Juicy Lips.' Curtis was the type of individual, that when he did play, he put everything into his playing that he could. In other words, if he didn't come out wet with sweat and open himself up, so far as his clothes etcetera, etcetera, to get some air when he got through playing, then he didn't feel as though he had satisfied the guys that were listening, the guys that were playing, and even himself.[10]

This tireless work ethic was akin to James "Godfather of Soul" Brown's act to perform (whether exaggeratedly or not) to the point of abject physical collapse—all to the delight of his rabid audiences. Fans loved witnessing a performer who would give his all and leave it right there onstage, to the point of sheer exhaustion, for all to witness and cherish. At some point late in the show, giving in to the fatigue and weight of the moment, Brown would suddenly concede defeat and be unable to continue, weary and vanquished by the effort of entertaining. Wrapped up in a robe like a boxer and slowly led away offstage by a consoling band member, looking like a vanquished fighter guided back to his dressing room, Brown appeared engulfed by despair, inconsolable that he let his fans down and was unable to finish the show. The moment had seemingly gotten the better of him and he was now at an unfortunate, albeit magnificent, end.

Suddenly getting his second wind, Brown would immediately about-face and lurch back towards the front of the stage, fighting off the support of his assistant and limp forward, against total collapse, straining to get back to the microphone. Returning to his rightful place at center stage, he would triumphantly throw back his robe and squeeze a few more phrases out for his adoring fans, continually trying to give them more effort against insurmountable fatigue. The crowd's reaction was always predictable: absolute hysteria.

The music fans in Fort Worth similarly loved and respected magnificent musical effort and would take note of their young local's physicality with his saxophone. His insistence on giving his all to his fans and pushing his own physical limitations to new heights—straining to hit the last high note, interacting with his audience, honking his horn, chest heaving for breath and drenched in sweat, shirt ripped open and clinging to his exhausted body— would win over crowd after crowd, night after night.

Showtime was serious time. Curtis was a stickler for every detail of performing onstage, from making sure his band was well prepared for a specific locale, down to the particular uniform the band would wear. He insured all band members were immaculately dressed and as focused as possible, and he would not settle for anything less. This early concentration on professionalism never left his fans disappointed with any King Curtis performance.

With his music teacher's charge to have self-confidence still ringing in his ears, Curtis challenged himself and looked to branch out into guitar as well as singing. To get started, he sought out Ray Sharpe, a fellow I. M. Terrell

The new "King of Fort Worth," King Curtis. *Courtesy of Modeen Brown.*

High classmate (whose 1959 hit song, "Linda Lu," would reach number 11 on the Billboard Top R&B chart and number 46 on the Top 100). Though younger than Curtis by a few years, Sharpe had already set about mastering the instrument with his friend and classmate, Cornell Dupree. Speaking to writer Adam Komorowski, Sharpe noted:

> When King was here in Fort Worth, he started playin' clubs, you know, same thing as I did. One time he expressed an interest in wanting to play the guitar and this is when I first met him. He went to the same school as I did, but he was in the graduating class two years ahead of me. I was still in school, still learning how to play the guitar. Of course, I had sort of gotten some publicity with the kids at school, performing on talent shows and things like this, and he came to me to teach him some lessons, you know, how to learn to play the guitar because he was very interested in doing it.[11]

While more well known for his saxophone prowess, King Curtis became accomplished enough to later record numerous songs featuring his guitar playing.

In the 1940s, the Fort Worth music scene was red-hot, with clubs springing up all around town and the local populace streaming in to hear artists perform night after night. Amid all the well-established talent, young King Curtis fit right in. Recalling Curtis's early influences, Nathaniel Scott noted:

> In Fort Worth, there were quite a few excellent musicians, and we even had professional artists come through the Jim Hotel, that was where a lot of up-and-coming musicians would go. Curtis was one of the first individuals that they let sit in at a set and let him play. His style was unique; he listened to quite a few musicians that were very good, like Ornette Coleman, Gene Montgomery, Bobby Simmons, Red Connor— he listened to them, not to find out what they were doing, but he wanted to create within himself his own thing. He didn't want to sound like Charlie Parker or Gene Ammons, he listened to them. He didn't want to sound like Red Connor or Gene Montgomery; he wanted to sound like Curtis Ousley.[12]

His early talent and strenuously physical work ethic led young Curtis and his band to become the house band of an all-white nightclub. Years later, he recalled to author Mike Hennessey his wonder at the fact that he could at that time make two hundred and forty dollars a week playing local clubs: "More,' he reminisced with a proud grin, 'than the principal of the high school."[13] Curtis had quickly leapfrogged the color barrier of the Deep South with his honking horn and physical performances. In the face of this extraordinarily early acceptance from the white music entertainment market of Fort Worth, the musical man-child would forever maintain his devotion to the Blacks of his community. He never forgot or discarded his roots. This personality trait—that of deep loyalty to his people, his beginnings, and his friends—would stay with Curtis for a lifetime and make an indelible impression on all those he befriended. These people still speak of him today with the deepest of reverence.

In spite of his busy schedule at the all-white club, Curtis was still drawn to hanging around the hottest Black venue in the city, the Paradise Club.

Every Sunday he would show up in hopes of sitting in with the house band, not only to play, but also to demonstrate and maintain his deep commitment to the real music fans of the area—*his* people—and the struggles they all shared. With Curtis, it was always about giving something back. The Paradise was his opportunity and outlet to display his solidarity. Little did he know that his early interest and support of the local Black populace through the Paradise would be a critical component to his future local and global success.

The Paradise was owned by Aaron and Robbie Watkins, who were husband and wife as well as the ambassadors of the local Black Fort Worth music scene. They remembered to documentarist Dennis O'Keefe their impressions of the young "Big Man": "Aaron and I had a club on New York and Irma, the Paradise," Robbie Watkins recalled, "and we had a small band, and this guy would come in and sit with our house band. Every week, on Sunday evenings, he'd come in and he'd pack the house, and he played real well, and we fell in love with him."[14]

Aaron concurred, astounded at the immediacy of King Curtis's popularity as well as the significant income he generated for their club:

> Curtis's club, they closed early on Sunday. He was the house band out there; his main club job was a white club, and the only Black club he would come and play in was the Paradise. Because he wanted to let his people know some of the things that he could do. Every Sunday, everybody looked for King Curtis to come, and he would come, and we were charging twenty-five cents in and twenty-five cents out. There wasn't any stamps on your hand, or anything like that; when you went out, and you came back, you paid twenty-five cents. And believe it or not, we had a club that would hold about a hundred and thirty people, and at the end of those three hours, when we counted the money, we always had a hundred and twenty-five dollars, sometimes a hundred and fifty dollars. At a quarter a head, it almost seems impossible, but it was really true.[15]

Everyone in Fort Worth, Texas, would storm the Paradise Club, crowding it to the rafters, anytime King Curtis and his band were the featured artists for that Sunday evening.

Curtis now added tenor saxophone to his musical arsenal. His influences grew as he listened to Gene Ammons, Dexter Gordon, Lester Young, and Sonny Stitt. He remembered: "I also dug Ben Webster and Coleman Hawkins for ballads, [Stan] Getz for his facility, [Charlie] Parker for technique and phrasing. I also loved Arnett Cobb, a very fine tenor player. Another guy who influenced myself and Ornette Coleman was a Texas tenor man named Red Connor. He was a Coltrane ahead of his time. I used to argue that if I could play what these giants were playing, then I must be as good as they were. I know different now. They had to think of it first!"[16]

If the goal was to be an eclectic and innovative artist, Curtis quickly realized, there were also obvious drawbacks. For such a young musician, he had a remarkably savvy perspective regarding the potential for mainstream success: "I saw that the music was dividing and I had the commercial business sense to realize that way-out jazz wasn't getting to the public. I realized that, good as those big-name musicians were, they would always be coming out to where *I* was working."[17] His early appreciation of the music market would guide Curtis in the many difficult business decisions he had to make for his future.

The affable Curtis didn't play the Paradise Club every Sunday just because he was looking for extra work or increased local exposure. He also went to the Paradise because he was lonely. "He was never expected—when he came in, it was just something he wanted to do, not because of pay or anything," Robbie Watkins said with a smile, "It was just that he didn't have anything left to do where he was working, and he'd come by to spend the evening with us."[18]

Regardless of the motivation behind his appearances at the Paradise Club, Curtis always gave the crowd maximum effort, and his fan base continued to multiply. Curtis realized there was more to performing than just blowing the roof off the nightclub. He had to continually entertain his devoted audiences. From the start to finish of every set, the Paradise's patrons witnessed Curtis's coming of age, evolving and redefining his music and stage presence, all the while saving something for the final song. "His last number would always be 'Night Train,'" noted Aaron Watkins, "and I had a thirty-foot bar, and at the end of the song, that last song, he'd walk the floor and go around to everybody's table and blow. We had chairs, so he could get up on the bar. And that's the way he ended his show: walking down the bar, blowing 'Night Train.'"[19]

By early 1952, Curtis was a high school senior. His early experiences of successfully crossing over well-established color barriers night in and night out—switching back and forth, chameleon-like, with white crowds one night, Black crowds the next (and many times both within the same day)—would begin to set Curtis Ousley apart from other, even older, horn players in Fort Worth, in spite of his youth. Couple this performance knowledge with his keen business interpretation of the market, then add his significant size, stamina, and musical personality, and you had the makings of a star. His innate ability to immediately recognize, define, diagnose, and perform well in every musical environment and genre (even at such a young age), from club dates to later recording sessions and concert stages, would be Curtis Ousley's defining trait as a professional musician. But was Fort Worth, Texas, big enough to contain all this explosive young talent and moxie?

Chapter 2

A Small Bite of the Big Apple

In the summer of 1952, high school senior Curtis Ousley went to visit an uncle, the brother of his birth mother, in New York City. While vacationing there, he was blown away by the city and its opportunities. He had become well established in the Fort Worth, Texas, music scene and now the sheer scale of the New York music market instantly got under Curtis's skin. Right away he felt that he fit in. He belonged in this city. Suddenly, in his mind Fort Worth, Texas, had become increasingly smaller and more limited compared to the new challenges and endless possibilities available in New York City. Now grown to six feet, two inches tall and weighing over two hundred pounds, the Texas-sized farm boy had also grown confident enough that he was not intimidated by the new big-city surroundings and fast-paced lifestyle. Curtis wanted to see how he stacked up against the established New York competition. What better way to find out than entering Ralph Cooper's Amateur Night at the famous Apollo Theatre?

Opened on January 26, 1934, the Apollo Theatre in the Harlem area of New York City had initially been the Hurtig and Seamon's New Burlesque Theatre, a venue for whites only—white-only entertainment supported by white-only employment. The theater was not only off-limits to Black patrons, but also would not hire African Americans for even the most menial of labors. So, when Hurtig and Seamon's closed and the owner, Sidney Cohen, charged Morris Sussman to change the theater's name to the Apollo, a theater that hired Black entertainment for the Black populace, people took notice. As its location on 125th Street was in a predominantly white part of town at the time, catering to the Black customer with Black entertainment in this area was deemed by many to be pure folly.

Near the end of 1934, Ralph Cooper, who had worked closely with producer Clarence Robinson at the Lafayette Club, was hired to be the master of ceremonies for a talent contest for amateurs to be held every Wednesday night at the Apollo. If the crowd disliked you, they would boo lustily and fill the air with catcalls and insults. The poor performers would be excused from the stage, to the ravenous delight of all but the performers themselves, humiliated beyond words. While having fun at the expense of a few hopeful artists may have seemed rich entertainment by many customers, master of ceremonies Ralph Cooper was more than a little concerned with maintaining a positive tone to the evening, and he searched for a way to sensitively excuse a contestant who was being roundly booed off the stage. Enter Norman Miller.

Cooper had previously discovered Miller back at the Lafayette Club working as a stagehand. The short, pudgy man had a heart of gold and a real gift: he could instantly put people into stitches with his backstage antics. Coworkers had affectionately dubbed Miller "Porto Rico" because the energetic man also had a particularly portly profile. Cooper immediately hired him for the audition night at the Lafayette. The roly-poly Miller would dress up in hysterical costumes and kindly shoo inferior Lafayette contestants off the stage, all to the delight of the patrons (and especially to Miller, himself) while brilliantly dispersing any negative energy from the crowd.

Ralph Cooper had tremendous empathy for all contestants on the Apollo stage, but most specifically for the less gifted. His answer was as easy to see as Norman Miller's ample silhouette: Cooper hired Miller to reprise his successful Lafayette Club court-jester role at the Apollo Theatre.

Cooper described his appreciation for Miller along with his sympathy for the situation: "Porto Rico put a full head of creativity into his crazy costumes. He'd dress up like a hermit and chase people with a pitchfork; he'd be a farmer with a shotgun or an old lady with a broom. He'd always do a funny little dervish, and he brought the house down every time. But he never 'hooked' the contestants or pushed them. I don't believe he ever even touched them. And this was an important thing—because one thing that I didn't want was for it to be a humiliation contest. Years later, when they were about to reopen the Apollo in 1983, someone asked me what kind of hook I was going to use to yank losers from the stage. 'We're not going to use any kind of hook,' I said. 'When we started Amateur Night years ago, we didn't use a hook. I doubt we need one now.'"[1]

Contestants realized that if the rabid crowd at the Apollo liked what they heard they would cheer loudly and you could win serious prize money for the evening. And if you won four weeks in a row, you would be rewarded with a week's feature booking at the Apollo, suddenly making a significant name for yourself in New York. Walking onstage into this virtual lion's den would cause the cockiest contestant's blood to curdle. Along with supreme ability, you had to be damn brave to enter this talent contest. Amid the cheers, jeers, insults, and tears, the Amateur Night at the Apollo Theatre was born.

By the time King Curtis entered the scene in New York City in 1952, many a star had been born from the stage of the Apollo, and not just performers that won the coveted four-weeks-in-a-row grand prize. Sarah Vaughan won just one Amateur Night at the Apollo, launching her towards becoming one of the great jazz vocalists of all time. Others who achieved greatness from the humble (and humbling) stage of the Apollo were such luminaries as Ella Fitzgerald, Ruth Brown, Pearl Bailey, and Billie Holiday, followed later by James Brown, Gladys Knight, Wilson Pickett, and Dionne Warwick. Luther Vandross was booed off the stage four weeks in a row before he won the first-place prize on his fifth try, a supreme exercise in courage and fortitude that then spawned a marvelous career.

It's little wonder, then, that eighteen-year-old Curtis Ousley quickly set his sights on the Apollo Theatre to explode (or implode) his career. To enter this roiling sea of rabid opinion, however, Curtis needed more than just the optimism of youth. Being cagey enough to enter the Wednesday amateur talent-night contest also required significant courage. You can imagine the terror he and his fellow hopefuls must have faced, sitting below the stage in the green room before his first performance, elbow to elbow with the three dozen other hopefuls in the cramped and overheated waiting area, nervously pacing back and forth like too many cattle shuffled into an overly narrow corral (with many soon heading to the proverbial slaughter). Nerves fraying while staring at each other, listening to the boisterous crowd overhead launching or evaporating careers with each passing breath.

Ralph Cooper had this perspective on why performing in the Amateur Night show was so difficult for young and upcoming artists: "There's always a truckload of reasons why amateurs fail. They can go off-key. They can lose the beat. They can forget the words. They can sweat so bad that they freeze. Whatever happens, they're probably just scared to death."[2]

When Curtis finally emerged onstage, the crowd did not care that he was adopted or had persevered against monumental odds to come all the way from Fort Worth, Texas, to play for them. They were not sympathetic to the significant financial challenges and long travel necessary just to get to New York, nor concerned with his ability to turn a Texas bar crowd (Black or white) into a raucous musical event, holding the audience in the palm of his hand. They only cared that he could take their breath away at the Apollo Theatre and entertain them at that specific moment in time.

Curtis won the Amateur Night at the Apollo an impressive two weeks in a row. He also paired this sizable effort by sitting in on his very first recording session in New York City, in November 1952 for the Bob Kent Band on the Par label (a very short-lived subsidiary of Prestige Records) playing on "Korea, Korea" and "Oh! Baby." In just a matter of weeks after arriving in New York, Curtis performed well at the Apollo Theatre and now had his first studio recordings under his belt. Not bad for an eighteen-year-old high school senior coming to town for a visit.

Instead of thrilling Curtis, however, his monumental wins at the Apollo and his first studio recording experience created more problems, confounding his choice of career path. This early success in New York created a raging internal conflict between attending college to study music in Texas after graduating high school or immediately embarking on a professional career in New York City. His head told him school was the logical and correct direction he should take, but the New York music scene had ignited something new and passionate inside his heart. The weight of this critical decision sat heavily on Curtis as he returned home to Fort Worth from his extended New York City vacation.

Having had such an exciting and positive initial recording experience in New York, Curtis focused on aggressively pursuing studio work while back home in Fort Worth. He found his way into a local recording studio in 1953, backing four songs by jump blues artist Melvin Daniels (the first two for RPM Records, the latter two for Crown Records): "I'll Be There," "Boogie In the Moonlight," "If You Don't Want My Lovin'" and "Hey Hey Little Girl." Curtis also cut two feature sides under the title King Curtis and His Tenor Sax with Orchestra for the Gem label in the summer of 1953, with Melvin Daniels returning the earlier favor to support Curtis on "Tenor in the Sky" and "No More Crying On My Pillow." Curtis had mastered the Fort Worth club scene and began achieving some early status in the local recording venues. Now back home, life was good and, understandably, he suddenly thought to himself, "Why not stay here in Texas after all?"

It's no generalization to say that any successful artist must have some good luck at some point early in their career, and Curtis's first break came to him when he was back on his home turf. After returning from New York City, Curtis heard that Lionel Hampton and his band were on tour throughout the Southwest. While stopping over for a performance in Fort Worth, the band's saxophone player took ill and Curtis's name was suggested to the bandleader as a replacement. When Lionel Hampton came calling, Curtis leapt at the opportunity to sit in with the band, fitting in so well that he finished the remaining national tour with Hampton over the next three months.

Between his brief but successful stay in New York, his positive Apollo Theatre experience, and his astoundingly good fortune to tour with Lionel Hampton, coupled with all the excitement of experiencing both New York City and Fort Worth recording studios, Curtis faced a critical decision. The challenges of deciding the direction of his career were suddenly harder, not easier. Curtis's talents had attracted music scholarship offers from Wiley College and Bishop College, both historically Black colleges in Marshall,

High school graduate, Curtis Ousley. *Courtesy of Modeen Brown.*

Texas, and Curtis was thrilled. Yet, New York City beckoned him to come north. Strategic decisions had to be made regarding education versus music career, studies versus employment, and Texas versus New York City. Although he was making decent money, enough to live in Fort Worth, the cost of traveling to and living in New York City was significantly greater than his earning capabilities, which acutely limited *any* possibilities to the point of near despair.

When Curtis returned to Fort Worth from the Lionel Hampton tour, Aaron and Robbie Watkins, who had become Curtis's "big brother and sister," observed his anxiety and indecision. Aaron recounted:

> When he finished high school, we would talk. He would say, 'Aaron, I really wanna make it in music.' 'Long John'—he'd say, Long John, he called me Long John—'I'm gonna make it,' he said, 'but there ain't but one thing holding me back. I know I got the talent; I know I got the get-up in me, but ...'
> I said, 'Well, what's holding you back?'
> He said, 'I just don't have the finances.'
> So, I asked him, I said, 'Well Curtis, what do you want to do? Do you want to go back to school and go to Wiley with all your friends?'
> He said, 'No, I wanna go to New York.'
> Robbie chimed in, "He was talking about going to New York and furthering his education in music, and we encouraged him. But, seemingly, he was kind of vague, about, you know, 'I would go if—finances were a little better.' So, we encouraged him; we thought we had a little we'd share with him. The sky was the limit as far as we were concerned. His music was his life.[3]

So, it was decided. Curtis would set aside his initial dream of a formal college music education and leave Fort Worth for New York City.

How many gifted people fall short of following their dreams due to something as basic but critical as financing? How many talented artists are ultimately constrained, not to mention strangled, by their wallet? Yes, Curtis had decided to go to work in New York City. But how to pay the rent, put food on the table, or even get him from Fort Worth to the Big Apple? Curtis moved in with the Watkins family to cut costs, but it still did not allow him to save enough money to enable any hope of going anywhere, much less New York City. However, "Long John" Aaron and Robbie Watkins would stand for nothing less than getting their beloved prodigy to New York by any means possible. They wracked their brains and bank accounts to try and make Curtis's dream become a reality.

Aaron remembered the deep emotion and angst of the moment: "I said, 'Well, Curtis, what do you have to offer for borrowing four or five hundred dollars?' And he looked at me, and that's kinda the hurtin' part when he said, 'Nothin' but my face!' I'll never forget it, that's when we both looked at each other and began to cry."[4] After much soul searching and discussion, Aaron made sure his "little brother" would be taken care of:

> But it all worked out: I got the money, I let Curtis have the money. Before that, we went out and bought an old '46 Ford coupe—gave three hundred dollars for it, which I didn't tell my wife about that. But that's what he left in, that old '46 Ford coupe, with his pound cake sitting on the seat, a box of fried chicken—my wife fixed him a hell of a lunch. He drove all the way to New York; it was about a week when he called. He said, 'Whatever you all need, I'm just as close to you as your telephone.' And he really meant that.[5]

Legend has it that young King Curtis, all six feet, two inches, and two hundred pounds of him, could often be seen walking the streets of Harlem carrying his saxophone in a large brown paper bag, the two of them inseparable.

Now that he was in New York, an epicenter of the music world with limitless opportunities for live performing and for recording studio work, Curtis did not want to ignore his musical education. In early 1954, he sought out noted New York saxophone teachers Garvin Bushell and Joe Napoleon. Bushell recalls in his autobiography his first conversation with the young saxophonist:

> One day the phone in my studio rang. The voice said, 'My name is Curtis Ousley. I live in Fort Worth, Texas and I'm coming to New York City and I want to study with you.'
> 'Fine, be glad to have you.'
> 'Where's your studio, on 49th and Broadway?'
> 'Yeah.'
> 'I'll be in to see you Monday morning about 11 o'clock.' This was tenor saxophonist King Curtis. Sure enough, he showed up and began studying with me five days a week for about a year. I felt proud of him, since he was one of the students I turned out early on in my teaching.[6]

Fellow musician Tyree Glenn Jr., whose father played for many years in the Duke Ellington band, also took lessons from Bushell shortly after Curtis did, from 1955 to 1957. He told me about the early evolution of Curtis's style:

> Garvin mentioned to me that when King Curtis was a young man, Curtis had called him a few years earlier from Texas and asked if he could study with him in New York. He [Bushell] always said with a smile that King was playing a style of saxophone that they used to call 'chicken saxophone' back in the twenties and thirties. This was a very heavy staccato style of soloing that King made famous on so many hits. Boots Randolph, a very fine saxophone player more known for the country and western scene, also had this style of saxophone. Curtis, however, was more associated with this style in the rock and soul era.[7]

Bushell enjoyed his new student from Fort Worth, but something else caught his attention and his concern. Although polite, talented, and confident, Curtis infrequently showed a short fuse: "King Curtis was a big, strong kid and had a temper he couldn't control. He knew his size, and he didn't let anybody tell him anything."[8]

Curtis quickly found work with the society bands of Lester Lanin and Art Mooney. Speaking years later to liner notes author Dale Wright for Curtis's Tru-Sound album, *Old Gold*, Curtis recalled: "Art's was the first big band I worked with after coming to New York from Texas. We played weddings, hotel dates and college proms and I was forever squelching a desire to let go."[9]

Once successfully relocated to the New York environment and continuing in his music studies, Curtis hit the club audition scene, not only to pay the bills but to get his "chops": the necessary experience and exposure of practicing and playing anywhere (and with anyone) to get his face, and more importantly his sound, noticed. Yes, King Curtis had succeeded at the Apollo Theatre, but the process of building one's musical pedigree and reputation could be painfully slow and challenging. In Atlantic Records president Ahmet

Ertegun's autobiography, Atlantic Records producer Arif Mardin shared but one example:

> King Curtis told me a story which I think every musician should know. He came from Texas up to New York, and one night there was a jam going on at Birdland. A group of wonderful musicians were playing 'Cherokee,' which ordinarily is played in the key of B flat. Curtis was watching all these great musicians and finally they said to him, 'Okay, boy, come on then, you can come up and play.'
>
> So he took his saxophone, got up, hit one note, and it was the wrong key. They were playing in B major, which is very difficult for saxophones or B flat instruments. Furthermore, it's a very complicated song, so the chords were extremely difficult. Curtis looked around and one of the older men turned to him and said, 'Why don't you learn to play in all keys and then come back here?' Curtis told me, 'I thought I was pretty good. I'd been playing around, I could play and I could honk,' but he went back home, practiced some more, and then came back.[10]

It was not uncommon to catch Curtis playing at the many Harlem clubs in the area, from the Apollo Theatre to Small's Paradise to the Baby Grand on 125th Street. Tyree Glenn Jr., fellow student of Garvin Bushell and leader of Tyree Glenn Jr. and the Fabulous Imperials featuring Wayne Bartlett, described what it was like for a struggling local artist jumping from club to club in New York at the time:

> The club scene was very different then from now. Back then, you got a gig to play, say for ten days to two weeks in a club. Nowadays, as I understand it, the most you can get, if you are lucky, is two to three days. Most of them now are just for one night. To do a one-nighter in a club back then, you had to have a big name or a hit record. We were lucky in that we played in Trudy's and the Peppermint Lounge in Manhattan, where you could go into the club for up to two months at a time.
>
> We were a downtown band, so we did not play at Small's or Baby Grand. I would go down there on my day off and see all the bands in Harlem. It was during this time I got to know King somewhat. As we were a very popular band in New York, he knew who I was of course (also through the name of my father). I would go to see him every now and then when he was playing somewhere.

He was—as well as for many other young saxophone players of the day—my idol. When he was at the Apollo, I would stop by backstage and say 'hello.' I had been backstage at the Apollo as a seven- or eight-year-old many times, as my father played there very often with Duke Ellington at that time.[11]

Glenn only came to know King Curtis after Curtis's early struggles had led to recognition around town. Glenn would soon realize that, in addition to his mountain of talent King Curtis possessed a similarly monstrous weakness for gambling:

I still remember one time going to see King backstage right before the show and being amazed at all that was going on back there. It was a madhouse! Most of the acts had a big craps game going on in the corner. It must have been about five minutes before showtime, and King and most of the others were still standing around in their *underwear*! I also remember that King had a valet/roadie who (of all things!) put his sax together for him before the show. Wow, I thought, that was really something, but I also thought that I never wanted to get so famous—or so old—that someone has to put my sax together for me.

Anyway, it was almost showtime, and I said goodbye to King and all the others there and left through the stage door at the back of the Apollo and went around to the front so I could see the show. The whole time while I was walking around to the corner to the front of the Apollo, I was wondering, 'How in the hell is King and all the others going to be on time for the show?' Well, the theme music from the Apollo started, the emcee said his introduction, and the curtain opened; there was King, looking great, playing his opening song, and the people were going wild! I thought to myself, 'If the crowd had seen everyone backstage at that craps game in their underwear five minutes before, what would they have thought?' To this day, I still don't know how King got onstage ready to play in such a short time. I guess you have to have a good valet![12]

Curtis had quickly refined his abilities and survived his initial foray into the New York City music world. He could not only acclimate to any musical environment or audience, but he could also change seamlessly from a nearly naked backstage dice-thrower into a polished featured musical headliner in a matter of seconds. His Apollo experience opened a few new doors, and he

Ever the dapper performer, young Curtis was always
immaculately dressed. *Courtesy of Modeen Brown.*

formed a band with Osie Johnson on drums and Horace Silver on piano
(who were later replaced by Lenny McBrowne and Joe Knight on drums and
piano, respectively).

Eighteen-year-old "King Curtis" Ousley now had his ample foot and
commensurate frame in the door of the local New York City music scene.
And, unbeknownst to anyone at the time, even Curtis himself, he was due to
kick that door right off its hinges in very short order.

Chapter 3

The Doc and the Guitar

Curtis had met the songwriter Doc Pomus while getting his feet wet in session work around town and, especially, recording with producer Bob Rolontz for the Groove label, a subsidiary of R.C.A. Victor Records (Rolontz was the label head and, previously, had become well known as a perceptive *Billboard* magazine reporter). Pomus, whose real name was Jerome Felder, had written and sung blues music in the 1940s and was concentrating more on writing in the 1950s. He partnered with Mort Shuman to form one of the most prolific and successful songwriting teams in popular music history, on par with the duo of Jerry Leiber and Mike Stoller. Together, Pomus and Shuman penned such classics as the Drifters' "Save the Last Dance for Me," "This Magic Moment," and "Sweets for My Sweet," as well as over twenty memorable Elvis Presley songs, including "Viva Las Vegas," "Little Sister," "(Marie's the Name) His Latest Flame," and many other hit tunes.

In 1954 Pomus had heard about a new, charismatic young saxophone player from Fort Worth, Texas, that had come to town. He sought Curtis out to play in his band and, later, to record on a few songs with the Doc Pomus All Stars in 1955 and 1956. The group recorded "Work Little Carrie"

Once settled in New York City, King Curtis sent this portrait to
his parents, signed "To my darling Mother and Dad,
Love Always, Curtis." *Courtesy of Modeen Brown.*

and "The Last Blues" on the After Hours record label. Pomus formed a band
with both Curtis and R&B guitar virtuoso Mickey Baker. On playing in
Pomus's band, Baker told me: "Doc Pomus was a Jew that sings like he's
king of the blues."[1]

Pomus recalled:

In 1956 I was singing at the Club Musicale. It was located at West
70th Street off Broadway in New York City directly underneath the
Stratford Arms Hotel. The band on weekdays would be the Morty
Jay Trio. It was composed of Morty on piano, Carl Guy, an excellent
guitarist, and John (his second name eludes me) on bass.

On weekends it was different. It was jazz and low-down blues and
an audience of aficionados who scraped their hard-earned daytime gig
bucks together and got out one or two nights over the weekend to howl

or stomp at the righteous sounds. The band consisted of Mickey Baker on guitar; King Curtis on tenor saxophone; Jimmy Lewis on bass; on piano was Reggie Ashby or Herman Foster and the drummer was Eddie Dougherty or some other great percussionist.

The Musicale was a white club, and consequently much of that material that I sang at black clubs and which was easily recognizable to a black audience would be left out of my repertoire at the Musicale. I sang three or four forty-five-minute sets during the week and weekends at the Musicale and did the same kind of thing two or three times during the matinees. I emceed everything and featured Curtis and Mickey at show time doing wild, long solos. Sometimes, when it got real good to them, they'd carry on for ten or twenty choruses and the crowd would hoot and holler 'til it sounded like the Wednesday night Amateur Show at the Apollo.[2]

Pomus was always friendly and supportive of Curtis. Years later, while talking to their mutual friend the Atlantic Records producer Joel Dorn, Pomus confided that he had shared Garvin Bushell's concerns regarding Curtis. Dorn told me: "Pomus told me that he said to Curtis, 'That temper of yours is gonna get you killed some day.'"[3] While uncommon, Curtis lost his cool often enough for friends and acquaintances to take notice and share their worry.

Although the finished product of these early efforts with Doc Pomus, both in the recording studio and onstage, was far from earth-shattering, the biggest benefit to Curtis was meeting his future mentor in guitarist Mickey Baker. McHouston "Mickey" Baker is so revered in the music industry, so widely regarded as one of the great visionaries of his time, that he is commonly credited, along with Bo Diddley and Chuck Berry, to be among the most influential guitar artists of the 1950s rhythm and blues era. The reason why his fame isn't comparable with that of the other members of this elite guitar triumvirate is obvious: he recorded primarily as a studio artist backing other headliners. Low profile aside, Mickey Baker has garnered worldwide industry respect for his talents. Baker seemed amused by this popularity, but he also recognized his own innovativeness, when he told me:

One thing I found out in life: you can never go back to doing anything. Time passes. By the time I got back to Atlantic Records after a long tour, everybody was trying to play the guitar like me. They finally realized in those days, especially with guitar players, they were laid back—with [a Gibson] L-5 guitar or L-7 guitar, trying to play like Charlie Christian—everything is cool. I just bought a fifties guitar and started to make all kinds of noise on it, and everybody said, 'He plays music with a stick, how can you make music with a stick with strings on it?[4]

What King Curtis would soon bring to the saxophone session world with his innovative interpretations, Mickey Baker had at that time already made well established for the guitar. Both artists would amass a staggering level of recording work as well as shining later as featured artists. From the 1950s to the 1960s, if you wanted the best guitarist in all of New York backing you in the studio, you called Mickey Baker. At that time Baker achieved a level of respect in the industry such that he was given a most understated moniker by his peers. Though plain, its simple eloquence summed up the high level of reverence fellow artists held for the abilities of Mickey "Guitar" Baker.

The recording session musicians of the era were not merely an after-thought to a musical production, simply regurgitating written notes from a fixed, stagnant position facing a music stand rather than an audience. They were much more critical to the finished production, and the main artist's success depended on their personal interpretation of the basic melody in the studio. Many times, a hit record was won or lost on the successful collaborative creativity of the studio backing group, which was given broad parameters by the featured artist and producer on what and how to play. Once in the studio, session players often had surprising freedom for personal interpretation in what they played. And if the studio engineer, producer, or singer did not like that interpretation, the offending session player wouldn't be invited back; it was too costly to the success of the song and the career of the artist. Baker had this overview of the studio environment:

In those days, with most of the recordings, there were hardly ever any arrangements made—they had lead sheets. On these lead sheets, they would write the bass lines for the bass player, and the guitar player would just go crazy doing what the hell he wanted to do. The saxophone player followed the lead sheet. All he would have in front of him was the lead sheet with breaks. They had the breaks written when you had to make breaks on the instruments. Otherwise, most of that music was done what I call 'liperallously'; just do it by your lip. In fact, those people that wrote music had no idea of how to write music like that; they just depended on certain musicians, and I happened to be one of them.[5]

Mickey Baker knew that while talent was one thing, being creative with that talent was another entirely.

Baker, who in 1954 was already well entrenched in the New York City club and recording business, would become much more than just a friend and business acquaintance to King Curtis. He had a keen eye for young talent and was adamant about nurturing new artists, putting them into positions to help them to grow and succeed. After just one recording session with Curtis, Baker was sold on the young Texan's talents. Regarding his initial meeting with King Curtis in the studio in 1954, Baker said: "I met King Curtis from that record—he was very dynamic. I know he was working at a little club in Harlem called the West Side Club. I worked there because he was also working the club. I had a jam session with him a couple of times."[6]

The torch that Aaron and Robbie Watkins had carried so faithfully for Curtis back in Fort Worth during his musical awakening was now picked up and held firmly aloft by Mickey "Guitar" Baker. Baker steered Curtis toward opportunity, giving him direction, support, and a mature voice of experience in the industry, which Curtis deeply respected (and desperately needed). He was increasingly deliberate in putting Curtis into positive environments. The two became very fond of each other, and Baker would be instrumental in guiding the inexperienced Curtis from recording studios to club engagements that would become the springboard for his New York City session work career.

While Curtis was becoming known on the stages of New York, he was still anonymous in any recording studio. As both markets were quite different from each other, this was a major problem for Curtis. Baker remembered, "I was a very popular studio guitarist at the time in New York, and I couldn't get anybody to give him [Curtis] a gig on many record sessions because nobody knew anything about him [in the recording industry]. At the time, sax men Sam Taylor and Jesse Powell were doing all the recording sessions. Since I was already making that kind of noise on a guitar, they always used me."[7]

Although getting his friend King Curtis more studio and club work was initially difficult, Baker noted that everywhere the young man followed him, he always left a distinct impression, even on his competition: "I remember that [saxophonist] Jesse Powell told me, 'Wow, he came here really with the right name; he is going to become king of the saxophone."[8] Curtis could always create memorably positive musical experiences with anyone who met him, including skeptical, well-seasoned studio stalwarts.

In 1955, Mickey Baker was introduced to Barbara Prior (who later became Barbara Castellano), who quickly became his manager. After a few years, the two were wed in 1957. Barbara easily adopted Mickey's firm platform of encouraging and supporting young and talented artists in New York. Barbara's professional involvement with Curtis was just as critical as Mickey's recording studio–wide promotion of his young friend; she became the young Texas tenor's first manager. Barbara recounted to me:

> I loved rock and roll, and I worked at the Gale Agency. I moved from there to work for a man named Bob Shaw. I was working at the Shaw Agency when I met Mickey in 1955. Mickey and I would go to dinner very often to a place called Frank's down on 125th Street, which was one of the classier, better restaurants of the era. There was a club across the street, and Curtis worked there.
>
> Curtis was such a dear, dear friend of ours. I met Curtis with Mickey, and he was a charming young man. We were all what I would basically say was just friends. Mickey wanted to help him, and he helped him into recording sessions and I was trying to get him a record deal.
>
> Basically, he was a very, very young man when we met him, and he was a very sweet, loving person. It's strange, but he bought us a housewarming gift when we got an apartment on Central Park West. It was so cute, because this was something people don't think of nowadays. He bought towels for the bathroom, very fancy. He always had good taste, and he was a very caring young man.[9]

Mickey grabbed his young protégé and the two backed the Sparks of Rhythm band on four tracks for the Apollo record label in July 1955. Recording together began in earnest in November and into December, when the two supported some of the earliest Solomon Burke tunes (Apollo), along with the Nitecaps and Mr. Bear and His Bearcats (both for the Groove record label). While none of these recording opportunities were commercially successful or achieved any notoriety for Curtis, he continued to focus on getting his name out around the Manhattan recording community.

New York City clubs in the 1950s looked for ways to entice their clientele in addition to the entertainment offered by the house band. "Every gin mill, every nightclub in town, for whatever reason, had a small stage, a 'shake dancer,' and a three- or four-piece band at the back of the lounge," Barbara explained to me. "'Shake dancer' is another name for those girls that slither around the brass poles in clubs these days. I never quite understood why this was so in vogue at the time, but it was."[10]

Curtis was not immune to the charms of the fairer sex, particularly the wiles of the shake dancers of Harlem. As most every club there employed this additional entertainment to accompany their house band, Curtis had significant, up-close exposure to many of these very provocative performers. In this environment, Curtis would meet someone whose relationship with him would become more than just casual: Ethelyn Butler.

Originally hailing from the Caribbean, the attractive and imposing six-foot-tall Butler made her living as a dancer working in Harlem. She was plenty familiar to the many who read *Jet* magazine, a weekly publication begun in 1951 to specifically target Black readers. Ethelyn appeared consistently in Major Robinson's "New York Beat" gossip columns for many years. In the July 16, 1953, *Jet* issue, Robinson noted, "Ethelyn Butler, the six-foot shake dancer, claims to be a direct descendant of Africa's Watusi tribe."[11]

Ethelyn Butler met Curtis at one of the many Harlem clubs he worked at and frequented in 1954, and Curtis fell hard. After dating briefly, Curtis was so smitten with the comely, statuesque Butler that the two quickly became engaged, as the August 12, 1954, edition of *Jet* magazine noted: "Bandleader

King Curtis and shake dancer Ethelyn Butler announced their engagement. She will retire after the wedding to open a dress shop."[12] Following up, Robinson also discussed Butler in his September 30 *Jet* column: "Since she inherited $75,000 from an aunt's will, Ethelyn Butler is giving up shake dancing. She has enrolled in a ballet school because, she says, now that she is rich, she wants to become a cultured artist."[13] Nine months later, the May 12, 1955, *Jet* magazine followed up on the couple, noting that while the marriage had not yet occurred, it would soon: "King Curtis says he will wed after he returns from tour."[14]

The Bakers, among others, were completely astounded and deeply taken aback by their friend's relationship with Butler. "She was just generally unlikable," said a nonplussed Barbara during my interview with her. "Yes ... Ethelyn was very strange and very jealous. Curtis tried to be generous with her, but I don't think she cared about anything but herself. He wanted a loving relationship, and she would always push it away. They never really got along."[15]

Mickey was equally unimpressed and more than a little concerned for Curtis: "I do know she was a headache. She kept telling King Curtis what to do. She wanted a record session singing herself. Shake dancers in New York, I remember a lot of them, but I don't remember seeing her any time onstage. She was very pertinacious, in my opinion. She gave me the impression that she wasn't interested in what King Curtis was doing at all. I went to see him to bring him a Christmas present once with Barbara, and that's when I met this girl. She was so out-of-sight. He was a very nice guy. She would dominate him."[16]

Based on the Bakers' observations, it's no surprise that the relationship between Curtis and Ethelyn became a stormy one, as Major Robinson's gossip column would bluntly opine nine months later in the February, 9, 1956, issue of *Jet*: "The once hot romance between bandleader King Curtis and shake dancer Ethelyn Butler has cooled off."[17] Despite the instability in their relationship, the two would form a publishing company together called Kilynn Music Publishing. The ever-chivalrous Curtis wanted to be sure he took care of her, giving his future wife rights to many of his songs.

Socially, the Bakers and Curtis would often go out on the town for dinner, drinks, and fun, especially after a nightclub performance. Ethelyn was conspicuously absent from Curtis's side on these frequent nightly excursions. That was just fine with the Bakers. "I didn't enjoy being in her company, and we did not socialize on a regular basis," noted Barbara. "Curtis came over on his own."[18]

Chapter 4

The Solo Heard around the World

Thanks to the Bakers, King Curtis was now well integrated into New York session work while he continued to pursue the many nightclub opportunities around town, always dedicated to expanding his footprint in the city. His next big break came in 1954, and, as many do, it came unexpectedly— so much so that at first, he didn't believe it when it happened.

Curtis recalled to author Charlie Gillett in a 1971 interview:

I was just playin' in a club one night and a guy happened by there, says 'What are you doing playing here?' you know, 'You shouldn't be playin' here.' I was making about seventy dollars a week, a little less than that take home. I had a guitar player, no; I had a drummer and a piano player, no bass. I'd play 'Flyin' Home,' 'Rock Around the Clock,' stuff like that, you know, honkin' and playing and getting tips and stuff like that. This guy [Jesse Stone from Atlantic Records] walks in there one night—you hear this all the time when you're playing in gin mills like that, you know, 'What are you doing playing here,' 'You're too good,' 'You shouldn't be playing here'—shut up and listen! This guy come up to me this night and he didn't have any teeth, he'd just had all his teeth pulled, and I think he'd been drinking some of everything—wine, whiskey and beer, and you know, just looked like just a normal fellow, except he was a little loaded, and you know, like he'd been drinking all this, and the aroma from his breath was enough to kill you! And he says I'm this and I'm that, and I can do this and I can do that. So, I always listen to, you know, I always got a minute to listen to people, you know. You never know when one is for real.

The next day this guy brought a guy down from RCA Victor. The next day I got a contract with RCA Victor, and the next, no, the same day I made eighty-two dollars and fifty cents for four-and-a-half hours work. And here I was working six days, seven hours a night. Forty-two hours and I was only making that. So I said that's for me! This was during the era when they didn't make rock and roll records without a saxophone.[1]

Ultimately, the individual most responsible for King Curtis's break into major-label recording-session work was Ahmet Ertegun, founder and president of Atlantic Records. It was Ertegun who had dispatched producer Jesse Stone to review a new young saxophone player in town from Texas. Legendary for his late-night prowling of the New York music scene, ever searching for the next big national talent, Ertegun always had his fingers on the pulse of the city's musical heartbeat. He vividly remembered stumbling across a tremendous young artist who would eventually become a very dear friend:

I discovered King Curtis, who was playing in a bar on Eighth Avenue, across the street from the old Madison Square Garden. When I saw him at that club, I think he had just come up from Texas at that time. I walked into the bar and was very much impressed by the way he played. I thought, "Hey—this guy is a great player." Here is this guy all the way from Texas (I think his nickname was actually ":Tex") who is a *terrific* saxophone player. I think that King Curtis was underrated as a great saxophone player. Had he just played with jazz groups, he would be considered a great jazz saxophone player. Everybody was scuffling [for work], and he took whatever jobs he could, and he played R&B better than anybody. There was Willis Jackson who played that R&B saxophone, who was also like a jazz player. I think that Curtis was a better player.[2]

In his autobiography, Ertegun was no less effusive: "His tone was so big, and he played so beautifully. I said, 'My God! This is the man we need for our records; we've got to get him!' He was really just superior to anyone else around in playing rhythm and blues."[3]

After one look at King Curtis, Ertegun had dispatched music director Jesse Stone to introduce himself. The day after Stone's visit, Bob Rolontz, producer for Groove Records, approached Ertegun for help finding any new horn players available (a common collaborative practice for record labels in town) and Ertegun immediately had the answer. Rolontz stated to author Roy Simonds:

> Now the reason I used Curtis, reason I found Curtis, was because I was unable to get a tenor man to play on a date I had coming up and I called Ahmet Ertegun, and I said, 'Do you have any ideas on any new young people I should use?' He said, 'Yes, there's a young kid from Texas playing in a bar on 8th Avenue.' I went to see him and it was Curtis and I liked him, gave him my card, he didn't believe me. He finally showed up at the studio rather late and said, 'I didn't really believe this was real,' and that's how it got started. Then Ahmet called me, asked how he was, and I said he was great. From that point on I used him a lot.[4]

Curtis quickly went from six-day, forty-two-hour work weeks onstage to working more than sixteen recording dates a week, an astonishing pace. *Star Date* magazine's August 1955 issue observed that Curtis, by that time, had played on about thirty records for various labels of the time such as Gem, RPM, Modern and Prestige.[5] The reasons why King Curtis became so popular in the recording studio so quickly were blatantly obvious to Rolontz: "First, he was damn good. Secondly, he was very bright, so he understood what people wanted him to do. You know, they didn't have arrangements. Most of them were lead arrangements and he could … he was creative. He was also strong physically; he could do a lot of dates in a day and it wouldn't wear him out. He had a good lip."[6]

Session work in New York City was extremely difficult to break into, as the bulk of the work went to the select few who had carved out a name or niche. The man on saxophone in New York recording sessions at the time was the aptly named Sam "the Man" Taylor. Curtis quickly recognized the top-level competition in town and went to work to break Taylor's stranglehold on the local recording market. Ahmet Ertegun remembered Taylor as "Atlantic's most reliable honker. He was a very self-effacing, nice man who always came through."[7]

Early on, Bob Rolontz realized significant contrasts between the two horn men:

> He [Curtis] was more inventive than Sam, and after a certain point you do two-hundred records ... it's difficult to sound different on each of them. So Sam's style became ordinary because he had done so much, not because he was ordinary. But you heard him so much that Curtis brought a fresh style, fresh sound and all. I remember King Curtis was an affable, agreeable man who was sometimes the only Black player in the backup band, which placed him in the position of being the resident Black player at rhythm-and-blues.[8]

Clearly Curtis's early experiences in Fort Worth—as the only Black artist playing in a white band in a whites-only establishment one night and in a Black band in a Black establishment the next—led him to be completely comfortable playing in any recording studio environment, even if he was the only person of color present.

Jerry Wexler, vice president of Atlantic Records, who was credited with coining the phrase "rhythm and blues" for the roots music of the day, gave me this perspective on the changing of the guard among saxophone players in New York City: "Before Curtis, the hot session man was Sam 'The Man' Taylor. The way these things go, ... one guy gets all the work. One player becomes the favorite, and he was the one that gets all the work. He [Taylor] was 'the Man' and along came Curtis and just eclipsed him."[9]

Rhythm and blues continued to evolve in the industry, in spite of the early perception some had of the new, earthy music. Bob Rolontz recalled, "Although some of us must have felt superior to the primitive 'street sound' the producers were striving for, we took our work seriously and I know for a fact that no matter what kind of session we were all involved in—sometimes a vanity production with hopeless material and an untalented soloist—King Curtis never gave it less than his best shot, even though that sometimes meant camping it up to get that 'loose-as-a-goose' [light-hearted barnyard] feel."[10] Some producers and arrangers were still getting used to their discomfort with the unstructured style that was inherent in the genre.

While he had deep respect for his competition (and Taylor specifically), Curtis told author Charlie Gillett that he bemoaned the musical quality resulting from the quick pace of recording that was in vogue at the time. What distinguished the Texas tenor from the current New York studio musicians on sax was that while everyone else recorded quickly, Curtis wanted to take his time creating:

> Oh yeah, I still admire him [Taylor], sure. He's one of the great saxophone players. Well, he just don't make, he's another guy who's not really interested in [working a long time on developing a recording], you know, they just record. They go in the studio, and with no preparation in mind, with a guy telling them [guidelines of what to play]. I cut an album in like a session with an hour's overtime. I mean, how much preparation can you give an album like that? No matter how good you are, you don't get no second chance to compete with the people out here who really know how to make records. I mean, you take Sly [Stone], he takes months to finish one album. Months, in the studio. I know the Rascals used to book a studio for a month, six weeks, to do one album.[11]

The music scene in New York, and across America, was evolving at an incredible pace. Music historian Peter Grendysa wrote that the change in the hierarchy of New York City saxophone session work was also due to the continually maturing R&B style: "The rhythm and blues scene in 1955 was in a state of rapid change as rock and roll began taking over the hearts and pocketbooks of white teenagers. Nothing more than jump R&B in the beginning, rock'n'roll relied on fast, danceable rhythm numbers with simple and understandable, youth-oriented lyrics. The old-line sax men who had ignited the fuse to this revolution, Sam 'The Man' Taylor, Big Al Sears, Jay McNeely, and Hal Singer, were very busy in the studio, but record companies scrambled to find players with fresh, youthful and different sounds."[12]

King Curtis had planted himself in the minds and the ears of virtually every record company needing a new saxophone player and new sound in the studio, yet he still struggled to ascend to the next level in his career. Would he end up like Sam "the Man" Taylor and soon be eclipsed by a younger, more innovative studio saxophone player? Or was there yet another elevated level that he could achieve? Mentor Mickey Baker continued to try to spread the gospel of King Curtis to anyone that would pay attention. Curtis had gained critical early acceptance into the New York City recording studios with his sound, talent, and focus. Was there a path to even greater success and notoriety, or would this young man's legacy become just another solid, albeit unremarkable, career?

Although Curtis had been "discovered" by Ahmet Ertegun and then contacted by music director Jesse Stone in 1955, he did not record on any Atlantic sessions until 1956. Continuing his efforts to participate in a hit recording, on May 13, 1956, King Curtis played on three singles by the Tibbs Brothers, who were known for their urban blues for the Atco label, a subsidiary of Atlantic Records created as an alternative label to be run by Herb Abrahamson, who had returned from his two-year service in the military. Coincidentally, these songs were written by the duo of Curtis's friend Doc Pomus and Pomus's partner, Mort Shuman. Unfortunately, like many of the early recordings featuring Curtis, these tracks did not amount to any critical acclaim.

The following year brought Curtis back together with his friend and mentor Mickey Baker, who had formed a group called Mickey and Sylvia with one of his music students, Sylvia Vanderpool. Recorded on the Groove label, the duo's first album session (with Curtis backing on sax) produced their biggest hit, "Love Is Strange," in March 1957, which soared to number 1 on the *Billboard* R&B chart and number 11 on the pop music chart. This shocked Mickey Baker, because the catchy call-and-response duet almost did not happen.

Sylvia's future husband had been promoting his girlfriend aggressively and Mickey felt that letting Sylvia record with him would mollify Joe Robinson. Barbara Castellano had this perspective: "Her boyfriend was very dollar-oriented, and he was a very bright man. Joe also wanted to start a publishing company, and when Mickey met me, [Joe] said, 'If [Sylvia] becomes part of your organization, I will start a publishing company.' And that's how we started our publishing company."[13]

"I started Mickey and Sylvia basically as a joke," laughed Baker.[14] Barbara concurred, "Sylvia was a beautiful girl, she looked like Elizabeth Taylor to me. Sylvia dated Joe Robinson [whom she married in May 1959], and after Sylvia had taken music lessons from Mickey, Joe was insistent on Mickey recording with Sylvia. Mickey acquiesced and formed Mickey and Sylvia more as a joke than anything else. Mickey was doing it to help Sylvia."[15] Mickey and Sylvia's mixture of blues, playful lyrics and light-hearted pop music banter won over the public to the stunned amazement (and amusement) of the Bakers.

When Mickey hit the studio with Sylvia, there was no question that he would include Curtis on any recording session he possibly could. However, as he explained, "I couldn't get started with King Curtis because at the time I was working real hard to try to make a duet with Sylvia."[16] With Mickey and Sylvia an unexpected success, Baker could now refocus on his protégé's career. In addition to supporting Curtis in the studio, Baker insisted that when Mickey and Sylvia performed live they use Curtis for their opening act. "When we did the first Mickey and Sylvia show at the Apollo Theatre, we staged it where we opened with 'Honky Tonk.' and we had Curtis onstage opening with the saxophone solo from 'Honky Tonk.' It was really awesome. It was a great opening act," remembered Barbara. "One thing I can say was, he was always sharp, and he looked like a star. He always dressed well."[17]

For the next year and a half, Curtis would record with everyone from Mickey and Sylvia to the Willows, Joe Turner, Solomon Burke, and Chuck Willis. All told, historian Roy Simonds counts seventy-five recording sessions during these early eighteen months in Curtis's career, a vivid illustration of Curtis's immediate popularity in the studio, as well as a true testament to the big man's stamina. Everyone now knew that, as producer Bob Rolontz noted, King Curtis "had a good lip."

Curtis worked directly with Ahmet Ertegun and his right hand man, Jerry Wexler, for the first time in a January 22, 1958, recording session for Big Joe Turner. This session with the two Atlantic Records giants would spawn working relationships and deep personal friendships that would quickly transcend the ethnic and economic barriers of the day. But then again, Atlantic Records was run like no other record label in town.

The story of Atlantic Records had begun in 1947 when a young Ahmet Ertegun was looking for work. When his father, the Turkish ambassador to the United States, passed away three years earlier, he decided he had better make something of himself. He eventually chose to pair with his friend Herb Abramson, an avowed jazz and R&B record collector and music producer from New York who had produced Clyde McPhatter, Big Joe Turner, the Ravens, and others. Together they launched Atlantic Records. And while Atlantic was similar to many of the independent labels of the era in that it "arose out of an enthusiasm, a passion, really, for music," Atlantic was also very different.[18] Author Peter Guralnick elaborates:

> Unlike many of its contemporaries, Atlantic was nurtured by a combination of creative enterprise, cultural sophistication, business acumen, and a good taste that would be rare in any field but that has been practically unheard of in the music industry. Rather than simply following whatever trend happened to pop up or flooding the market with an undifferentiated flow of 'product,' hoping something would stick, Atlantic went its own idiosyncratic way, drawing on the jazz inclinations of both its owners, the gospel and R&B practical experience that Herb Abramson brought to the company ... and the persuasive charm of Ahmet Ertegun, one of the wittiest and canniest men in the business.[19]

A few years later, in 1953, Ertegun and Abramson approached a mutual friend of theirs, Jerry Wexler, when they decided they needed someone to run the music publishing side of their company. While working for *Billboard* magazine in 1949, Wexler had coined the phrase "rhythm and blues" to label the Black music of the time. Wexler had previously done work as the promotions director for the publishing house of Robbins, Feist, and Miller, which involved promoting Atlantic's music around town. While successful, the ebullient Wexler felt constrained and unhappy in his work, something he confessed to his fellow jazz club fans Ertegun and Abramson during their many forays into the New York City music scene. Wexler longed for a position producing albums, not shilling written songs to record labels. When Wexler was approached by Ertegun to come to Atlantic, he felt exhilarated but also uncomfortable with the prospect of working for friends. He suggested that he would, however, be open to being a *partner* at Atlantic. Ertegun's immediate reaction to his friend's aggressive play? He laughed in his face.

In his autobiography, Wexler recalled his personal shock at his own outlandish proposal: "I'm not sure where I got the balls to ask for equity. After all, Atlantic was already in motion. They'd hit with 'Drinkin' Wine Spo-Dee-O-Dee,' Ruth Brown's 'Teardrops from My Eyes,' Joe Turner's impossibly beautiful 'Chains of Love,' (written by Ahmet himself) in addition to just signing a young, blind blues singer named Ray Charles. Where the hell did I come off asking for a piece of the pie? I wasn't surprised when Ahmet turned me down."[20]

Although disappointed with what he perceived as a lesser offer from Atlantic, as well as the rejection of his counteroffer, Wexler resumed his job and would be amply, indeed stunningly, rewarded for his audacity one year later. When Herb Abramson went into the Army for a two-year stint, Ertegun had a change of heart and approached his friend Wexler to revisit working for Atlantic, this time as his partner. With Wexler's acceptance, the main ingredients were finally coming together that would make Atlantic Records a force in the industry. This recipe of Ahmet Ertegun as president and Jerry Wexler as vice-president would lead Atlantic Records to the pinnacle of R&B and soul music success, taking it from neophyte recording label to major industry giant. The marked differences in style between Ertegun (the smooth, resplendent and urbane music ambassador) and Wexler (the hip, no-nonsense, aggressive, roll-your-sleeves-up producer) would form a friendly union that would succeed for the next twenty-two years.

By 1955, Atlantic had taken a keen interest in the group the Robins, based on the recommendation of Ertegun's older brother, Nesuhi. Nesuhi had been impressed with the songwriting partnership of Spark Associates, who also produced the group. The writing company featured Mike Stoller, Jerry Leiber, and Lester Sill and had written some minor hits for the Robins on the Spark Records label. Leiber and Stoller would later end up writing "Hound Dog" and "Love Me" for Elvis Presley, as well as eventually writing most of the songs for Elvis's movies *Loving You* and *Jailhouse Rock*.

When offered an Atlantic contract, the Robins' Carl Gardner and Bobby Nunn didn't hesitate to jump ship to Atlantic. The remaining Robins,

Ty Terrell, along with Billy and Roy Richard, aligned with their manager, Gene Norman. Gardner and Nunn recruited Leon Hughes, Billy Guy, and Adolph Jacobs; they renamed the group, and the Coasters were born. The final iteration of the group was Gardner, Guy, Cornell Gunter, and Dub Jones.

A month after Curtis had recorded his first Big Joe Turner tracks with Ahmet Ertegun and Jerry Wexler, Jerry Leiber and Mike Stoller needed a saxophone player for their upcoming Coasters recording sessions. As Stoller recalled to authors Rob Hughes and Roy Simonds: "I think the first time we met King was either on a session that we had put together—I'm trying to remember what session it was. It was a studio thing, and King was in the horn section. It might have been something Jesse Stone might have had arranged, or it might have been a chart I did. When we first arrived in New York to stay, because Jerry [Leiber] and I started in L.A., we didn't know all the players in town. People at Atlantic would help by recommending different people."[21] For the Coasters sessions, Ahmet Ertegun quickly recommended the new sax man at Atlantic, King Curtis.

The first song King Curtis recorded with the Coasters was "Zing! Went the Strings of My Heart" in May 1958. He would soon become critical to the Coasters' sound, to the point that years later Bill Millar, Coasters biographer, would dub King Curtis "The Fifth Coaster." As Jerry Leiber noted to Millar, "King was a fantastic musician who was great to work with because he knew almost instantaneously exactly what we were looking for."[22] "He did exactly what we said," echoed partner Mike Stoller. "Jerry and I would write saxophone parts that repeat themselves between phrases and we would tell King exactly what we wanted the solos to be. Y'know, sometimes Jerry would be whispering in his ear while he was playing, singing little phrases to him during the solo break."[23]

Millar's comparative analysis of other session horn players is no less effusive, but Curtis still stands out: "The buzzsaw phrases of Gil Bernal or Plas Johnson had their own appeal. Like the walls of 'Smokey Joe's Café,' they were dirty, coarse, and greasy. King Curtis was clean, note-perfect and his solo breaks on the Coasters records had no equivalent in rock. His tone—deep, fruity, and round with a characteristic burr that slides into a growl or stutter—and his facility—memorably impressive figures and inflections—combine in under twenty seconds to create a unique statement full of charm and utility not once but over and over again."[24]

During that initial recording session, Mike Stoller recalled stumbling upon the sound that would define the Coasters as well as their innovative sax player: "We first heard King playing a little of this what we'd call 'chicken scratch' at the end of a session while he was packing up, and it was kinda like a bluegrass fiddle player, and we just loved it … so we hired him for the very next Coasters session that we had."[25] Indeed, Leiber and Stoller chose to feature Curtis on the very next song. After Leiber and Stoller gave King Curtis the basic song sheet guidelines for Curtis's famous riffs, Curtis relied on his own talent and years of experience to translate their recommendations into the final result. And the role of saxophone studio musician in rock and roll would change forever.

The song was "Yakety Yak." A horn player now set a new precedent by carrying the lengthy break (which is two verses long) all by himself. Curtis's signature "chicken scratch" staccato style in the song gives the tune unforgettable energy and country flavor, all the while sassing back to the adult rules heard in the song. The Coasters were noted for their humorous and irreverent lyrics, which many times pushed the envelope of youthful disobedience to parental authority. "Yakety Yak" was, as Mike Stoller recalled to Millar, "really the first song that had to do with children, with teenagers, so to speak. I don't know how consciously it was angled in that direction because I remember writing it with Jerry and Jerry shouted out the first line and I shouted the second line right back at him. I started playing piano and we wrote the song—the rest of the lyrics are Jerry's—from there, very rapidly."[26]

When asked how the public responded to Curtis's interpretation of the saxophone break in the song, Ahmet Ertegun remembers the hysteria: "Well, he played that 'chicken thing'—people were crazy about what he was doing!"[27] And it wasn't just the local New York recording studios or the American music scene that took notice. As an amused King Curtis proudly recalled to author Charlie Gillett, "[Atlantic Records] got a letter from some big person in Europe that wrote to Jerry [Wexler] about this record. And they wanted to know who the saxophone player was. Some big high official in Europe when this record came out. And that's what they wanted to know, who was the saxophone player."[28]

Jerry Wexler had this analysis of one of the most recognizable sax lines in pop music history: "But he (Curtis) had an antecedent in a sense on certain tunes, who was Gene Barge. Do you remember Chuck Willis in 'C. C. Rider'? Gene Barge plays on it. After that, King Curtis came along, and he became the soloist on 'up' tunes as well as ballads. And there was a Gene Barge lick, 'da-da-dooey-it-da-da-doy,' that became King Curtis, who expropriated it. And you can hear that on such records as LaVern Baker's 'I Cried a Tear' and on Ivory Joe Hunter's 'Since I Met You Baby."[29] Curtis had also taken his youthful influence, Louis Jordan, applying Jordan's "Ain't Nobody Here but Us Chickens" style to bring the same rural humor and irreverent feeling to his "Yakety Yak" work. The resultant solo is timeless. As even Curtis himself noted, everyone around the world wanted to know, who was that saxophone player?

Years later in his autobiography, the Coasters' lead singer, Carl Gardner, remarked upon how seamlessly King Curtis fit in with the Coasters on these early recording dates:

> Out of those sessions came 'Three Cool Cats,' 'Zing Went the Strings of My Heart,' 'Yakety Yak' and 'Charlie Brown,' with the fantastic King Curtis on sax, playing brilliantly for us.
> King Curtis was sometimes known as the fifth Coaster. He was a sensational musician and worked with the greats. But when he was around the Coasters, it seemed like he could just feel our bodies and the direction of our music better than any musician that ever lived. He played on every one of our New York recording sessions. He was one of the greatest freelance studio musicians. He played with so many greats to list them here would require a whole chapter of its own. His performances were always impressive, clean and note perfect. His solo breaks on all the Coasters records have no equal in rock to this day.[30]

Curtis approached every recording session with the a philosophy of defining and interpreting differing styles: "I think you first have to get enough knowledge of your instrument, and then enough knowledge about music to be able to subconsciously display whatever you feel, the way you would sing it. That's the way I play, like I just check the horn, to see if it was in tune, but I can play the same thing that's there, doesn't matter if it's not [in tune], long as the horn is tuned from say 'E' to the other 'E'. If that's the key it's in, I can play it even though it should be an E flat if that's a B flat instrument, you see."[31]

On "Yakety Yak," Curtis's horn was not only perfectly tuned, but his solo style hit the song's bull's-eye dead center. Curtis explained his creation of the down-on-the-farm translation of the song that exploded his career: "Once you become aware of the mechanism of the instrument, then you can totally put yourself in the vernacular of whatever. Nothing else would have fitted 'Yakety Yak,' it's that type of song. When I was playing that because it fitted that solo, I wasn't trying to establish myself as playing that type of saxophone. I would get sick of hearing that on every song. I mean, can you hear me playing 'Body and Soul' like that?"[32]

Curtis's friend and mentor Mickey Baker had left town to go on tour for an extended period. Upon his return, he learned that King Curtis was now an international success. While not at all surprised at his friend's level of talent, Baker was nonetheless startled by how quickly Curtis had rocketed into the global consciousness during his absence. "Man, I left on tour for a while, I come back, and Curtis was a star!"[33]

Chapter 5

To Clovis and Atlantic

With the impact that "Yakety Yak" made on the youth of 1958 and the global popularity of the record, King Curtis became a household name. Curtis would reprise his saxophone studio role for the Coasters again and again for such hits as "Charlie Brown" (number 2 on the *Billboard* R&B chart and number 2 on the Top 100), "Poison Ivy" (number 1 on the *Billboard* R&B and number 7 on the Top 100), and many others. Yet he still differentiated his horn's voice from song to song rather than contenting himself with a consistent "chicken-scratch" platform for every Coasters track. While roaring with rollicking solos on "That Is Rock and Roll" and "Run Red Run," he modified his expression into a plodding, smoky, steamy solo in "Smoky Joe's Cafe." Years later, when Leiber and Stoller felt as though the Coasters had reached their zenith and the song writing duo moved on, Curtis even stepped in to produce the group.

As the saying goes: be careful what you wish for, because your wish just might come true. While Curtis was thrilled with his newfound international success, his Coasters work quickly caused deep personal alarm. Yes, Curtis was now a star. But he was also concerned that his Coasters "Yakety Yak" barnyard style would pigeonhole him into a sound that carried an extremely limited market, a musical niche that could marginalize and narrow his talents and even put an eventual choke hold on his ability to generate revenue and broaden his career. Even during his early years in the Fort Worth music scene, Curtis had been astute enough to realize the commercial value of having a broad base of material and the ability to adapt his style for different audiences and songs. He was also keenly aware of the New York recording session scene's penchant for milking the current "new style" to death, along with the potential negative consequences that were soon to follow when that new style quickly flamed out. He voiced his anxiety years later to Charlie Gillett: "Sometimes I don't know if that record did me good or did me bad, you know what I mean? ['Yakety Yak'] definitely established me but then I had to tell people I could play other ways, you know?"[1] Curtis loved to play jazz, soul, blues, and R&B music and wanted to be able to record all genres during his career, not be forced to maintain a single style or sound to survive.

Much to Curtis's relief, then, Ahmet Ertegun refused to brand Atlantic's newest horn sensation as the Texas Tenor with the "Yakety Yak" sound, much less categorize him as *just* an R&B artist:

That was just a thing he [Curtis] did, like, in the beginning. He has a beautiful tone. He can play ballads beautifully. The jobs cased you into whatever you had become. He chose to play whatever he could play where he could make a living. He became the *great* saxophone in the R&B style. There were a whole lot of people that preceded him. Lionel Hampton's band developed Illinois Jacquet, Arnett Cobb, Johnny Griffin—they all played R&B honk. At the same time there were a whole lot of other saxophone players around who were playing screaming saxophones. That was very popular with Black people in those days. There was some jazz saxophonists who sold very well: John Hardee, Don Byas. King Curtis was a very warm player—played with a great deal of emotion and he was a very outgoing personality. Saxophone was a big instrument, preceded by guitar as a great solo instrument that people bought in large quantities. Curtis could have been a great jazz saxophonist had he played only in jazz groups and jazz clubs. We still think of him as jazz as well as an R&B player.[2]

Curtis formed a band with notable members Herman Foster on piano, Al Casey on guitar, Jimmy Lewis on bass, and Belton Evans on drums.

King Curtis and Bobby Darin. *R. H. Andreas/Bear Family Records Archives.*

Throughout the year he also supported songs by Ruth Brown, the Drifters, Neil Sedaka, Brook Benton, Joe Turner, Chuck Willis, Bobby Darin, Mickey and Sylvia, Clyde McPhatter, LaVern Baker, Don Covay, and many others. According to King Curtis discographer Roy Simonds, Curtis recorded on at least *seventy* recording sessions during the year, an incredible workload for any studio musician.

In 1958, King Curtis became a celebrity. His band signed on with the Small's Paradise nightclub to be the house band. This netted Curtis a consistent ten weeks of work a year in stints of one week at a time, providing a predictable income. It was also tremendous exposure. Small's would play an integral role in Curtis's professional stage life.

Curtis's sizable personality was not just limited to the stage—he wanted to enjoy the fruits of his new success and loved to maintain a high profile around New York City, living large and playing the role of man-about-town bandleader, wearing expensive furs, driving huge cars, always sure to have his trademark gold wristwatch exposed just past his left shirt cuff for all to note.

Doc Pomus's songwriting partner, Mort Shuman, recalled Curtis's metamorphosis from farmhand to polished New York City musician on BBC Radio London: "King Curtis playing sax with that inimitable chicken-scratching style from Texas, where King was absolutely unbelievable. He would come in with those mohair suits, you know, like you could see him three blocks away on a foggy London night! I mean, it would just shine out there! You know, on this big beautiful black cat coming in, always had these Caddys about eight miles long. He was a great, great, great fella, King."[3]

During this explosive year for Curtis, he would be hired to play in the massive music show productions of Alan Freed. These star-studded musical happenings would provide the network for Curtis to make intimate and lasting friendships with fellow artists who would eventually become the who's who of the rock and soul music genre: Sam Cooke, Ben E. King, Otis Redding, and others. His ability to quickly make contact and establish deep-seated personal, as well as exacting professional, rapport with any artist he met would win over and impress even the most cynical of famous artists. The first "big name" act to make Curtis's acquaintance and befriend him at one of these Freed shows? None other than Buddy Holly and the Crickets.

The icebreaker for King Curtis and Buddy Holly had nothing to do with music and everything to do with Curtis's predilection for gambling. J. I. Allison of the Crickets told Dennis O'Keefe:

> The first thing I remember about King Curtis was the Brooklyn Paramount, in the fall of '57. We did a show with Little Richard and probably twenty acts on the show. The only thing we had happening at the time was 'That'll Be the Day.' King Curtis was in the band, 'Big Al'

Sears, Sam 'The Man' Taylor—it was the Alan Freed Show. Our dressing room was right next to King Curtis, and before anything, we got
involved in a dice game with him. Buddy and I and Joe B. [Maudlin] all
played a game called, 'four-five-six.' We got to hanging out and being
good friends and noticing how good he played saxophone in the band.
He was really good.[4]

Curtis and Holly hit it off from the start, both personally and professionally.
That initial meeting would be the catalyst for Holly to invite Curtis to fly to
Clovis, New Mexico, to write and record songs with Holly. Personnel would
also include a young guitar player in Holly's band who, like Holly, also hailed
from Curtis's home state of Texas, Waylon Jennings.

Buddy Holly later called Curtis to revisit his previous invitation to come
to Clovis. The commentary about this conversation in *Jet* magazine specu-
lated that the compensation was a strong reason for Curtis's excitement to
record with his new friend: "Bandleader King Curtis, much in demand at
recording sessions, was flown to Clovis, N. M. by white singer Buddy Holly.
He got $1,000 and expenses just to blow his sax for a [single] record date."[5]
Other sources maintained that the phone negotiations between Buddy and
Curtis went something like this:

"That'll be five hundred dollars and plane fare," Curtis said.
"Ain't that a little high?" Buddy asked.
"You're making yours all the time and I gotta make mine," Curtis
    replied. "You send the money up to New York."
"No," Buddy argued, "if I was to send you five hundred dollars and
    the plane crashed, I'll lose my money and my sax player."
"Mr. Holly, just send the money and don't talk like that."[6]

Regardless of the specific arrangements, on September 9, 1959, Curtis
landed at the airport in Amarillo, Texas, just across the border from Clovis,
New Mexico, home of the recording studio owned by Norman Petty, Buddy
Holly's manager. Fourteen-year-old Bobby Keys was waiting for him.

Bobby Keys had grown up in Slaton, Texas, a mere fifteen miles south
of Lubbock. His aunt owned the house across the street from Buddy Holly's
parents' home in Lubbock. Whenever Bobby happened to come up to Lubbock
to visit his aunt, invariably Buddy Holly and his band would be practicing

across the street. Hypnotized by the addictive music wafting throughout the neighborhood from across the way, Bobby Keys went over to the neighbor's garage to investigate. In his autobiography, he noted that he quickly, and unfortunately, realized that he was less than welcome: "Buddy and his band were in high school at the time, maybe six or seven years older than me, which was a big difference at that age. So when I showed up and tried to hang around, I kinda didn't know what to say and got some hard looks. The only way I could think of to keep from getting physically removed from the area was to volunteer to go down to the Hi-D-Ho Drive-In and get french fries, burgers, Cokes and the like for everyone."[7]

Keys' initial ploy to infiltrate Holly's band practices by "buying" his way in had one significant problem—at thirteen years of age, he had no money:

> Of course, I didn't have the money to do it, but I was determined, and it didn't take long for me to find a way. My grandmother, I knew, collected S&H Green Stamps and put 'em into books, and there was an S&H stamp redemption center not far from my aunt's house, so I sorta light-fingered a couple books of Green Stamps during the week [at home in Slaton] and then, when we got to Lubbock, I took 'em down to the redemption center and turned 'em in for cash money. After loading up at the Hi-D-Ho, I went back to the garage and said, 'Hey, here you go, burgers, and Cokes, now can I stay?' I had to pay my way, but I was in.[8]

Once he made it to high school, Keys began playing baritone saxophone in the school band, as it was the only instrument the school had left that was not taken. He instantly fell in love with the tone of the horn and running his fingers over the keys. That initial infatuation with the saxophone led later to touring with Holly's band (after Holly's tragic death on February 3, 1959). This was the first step to a remarkable career, from which he moved on to play sax with Delaney & Bonnie and Friends, ultimately reaching his professional summit as the longstanding saxophone player for the Rolling Stones. Keys is known for solos on such songs as "Brown Sugar," "Waiting on a Friend," "Can't You Hear Me Knocking," and more.

But back to Clovis, New Mexico, where Buddy Holly had invited his friend King Curtis to record a few songs. Buddy needed someone to pick Curtis up at the airport. Now a well-seasoned and well-accepted fourteen years old, Bobby Keys was thrilled to chauffeur King Curtis to the recording studio:

> He was my saxophone hero ... I got a call from J. I. [Allison] because he knew I had a car, a '51 Chevrolet—I was a sophomore in high school, but you could get a driver's license as early as age thirteen in Texas in those days—and they'd come back from New York and gone to Norman Petty's studio in Clovis, New Mexico, where they'd recorded this stuff, about a hundred miles west of Lubbock.
>
> Anyway, they'd hired King Curtis to come to Clovis to play on a couple of Buddy's tracks but there was no passenger service into Clovis, you flew into Amarillo. Well, I forsook my high school basketball game—didn't tell anyone I wasn't gonna show up—and went and picked up King Curtis and drove him to Clovis, drilling him for tips and insights and advice the whole way. When word got around that I wasn't deathly ill and I had in fact gone to pick up a black cat at the airport, that sorta ground my social life in Slaton to a halt. But it didn't matter. Basketball? Pffff. Saxophone, music, chicks, rock and roll? Yeah. I didn't care what anyone in Slaton thought.[9]

When he arrived, Curtis got together with Buddy and lead guitarist Waylon Jennings to do some writing and session work. Reportedly this recording date turned into somewhat of an event, with Sonny Curtis, Bob Montgomery, Jerry Allison, George Atwood, Tommy Allsup, Bo Turner, Waylon Jennings, and Waylon's brother, Tommy, all crowded into the studio.[10]

Curtis, Buddy, and Waylon (along with the other members of Holly's band) recorded four songs together on September 10, 1958. Two tunes featured Holly ("Reminiscing" and "Come Back Baby"), and two others featured Jennings ("When Sin Stops" and "Jole Blon"). Curtis was the one who wrote "Reminiscing." The song features a more refined King Curtis in a swinging style and call-and-response interaction with Holly that, while similar, tries to put establish a mature distance from the previous chicken-scratch, doe-see-doe antics of his earlier Coasters work.

This session was Buddy Holly's first attempt at producing a record, with Waylon Jennings as his first artist. Despite the excitement in the studio over having King Curtis involved, tensions were high. Holly's longtime producer, Norman Petty, was adamantly against Holly getting involved in any music production, possibly fearful of being pushed aside by Holly in Petty's own recording studio. In his autobiography, Jennings had vivid memories of the date:

> Buddy decided he wanted to record me that past summer. He could see how much music meant to me, and maybe he related my yearning desire to himself, growing up in a sunbaked West Texas town with music as an only outlet. On September 10th, he'd taken me out to Clovis to do my first session. It was an unnerving experience. Norman made me feel the most unwelcome I've ever felt in my life. He didn't like me to start with and he didn't want Buddy to get involved in a record company.
>
> "Volare" had been a big hit during the summer for Domenico Modugno, an Italian-language song on top of the American Hit Parade, and that sparked Buddy thinking. He was having King Curtis, the famous R&B sax player who was on the Coasters' "Yakety Yak," fly down to Clovis to play on a couple of his songs, and he thought it might be a nice idea to use him on the classic "Jole Blon" with me singing in Cajun-French. We didn't know the lyrics, so I tried to learn them off the Harry Choates original. By the time we finished, you couldn't understand a word. I just sang gibberish, really. Buddy strummed the guitar, and King Curtis called-and-responded around my fractured French.[11]

Years later, author Perry Meisel wrote about the song and King Curtis's influence on his fellow musicians in Clovis, New Mexico: "'Reminiscing' requires an almost electric crispness from the horn, and Curtis discovers a yakety way to deliver it with a remarkable and surprising freshness, very different from the honk-heavy repetitions of early rock and roll sax, and a style formalized by Curtis's lead horn on the Coasters' hit single 'Yakety Yak' earlier in the same year. To say Curtis dresses up Buddy's sound … is an apt and historically exact metaphor to use to describe both the tune and the larger genesis of Curtis's horn."[12]

Curtis had cemented a close friendship with the bespectacled Holly, even though a white musician associating with a Black musician was taboo for many at the time. But music often seemed to blur the color lines between artists, both onstage and in the studio, despite significant discrimination (and recrimination), particularly in the South. Holly's friendship with Curtis and his friend's subsequent visit to Clovis raised more than a few eyebrows around town.

Indeed, throughout his career Curtis repeatedly found himself to be the only accepted Black man in all-white environments. Even as early as the late 1950s, it was not uncommon for King Curtis to be the only Black musician in the recording studio, always respected by white artists, engineers, and producers. However, while in theory the recording studio had relatively few color barriers, they were there nonetheless, many times simmering below the surface (as would become vividly apparent several years later through Aretha Franklin's experiences at her first Atlantic Records recording session).

Curtis closed out the year by playing in Alan Freed's Christmas Jubilee for eleven days at the Loew's State Theater in New York. The lineup included Chuck Berry, Jackie Wilson, Bo Diddley, the Everly Brothers, Frankie Avalon, Jo-Ann Campbell, Eddie Cochran, the Flamingos, the Crests, the Cadillacs, Dion and the Belmonts, Johnnie Ray, and others.

Just one short month later, on February 3, 1959, Buddy Holly, the Big Bopper (J. P. Richardson), and Ritchie Valens would perform in a concert in Clear Lake, Iowa, and then board a small plane for a late trip to their next stop, Fargo, North Dakota. Guitarist Waylon Jennings had, at the last minute, kindly given up his seat on the plane to the ailing Richardson, who was sick with the flu and anxious to get settled in Fargo to get some rest. Just minutes after takeoff, the plane plummeted to the ground, killing the pilot and all three passengers aboard. One of the songs recorded with Curtis in New Mexico, "Reminiscing," would be released posthumously under Holly's name only in August 1962. This would not, unfortunately, be the last friend and fellow professional Curtis would lose to tragedy, nor to a similarly horrific airplane disaster. After the tragedy, Curtis immediately returned to the studio to back Neil Sedaka, the Drifters, Ruth Brown, LaVern Baker, the Coasters, and many more.

King Curtis was now a well-known musician, had as much consistent recording session work on major hits as he could handle, and was the leader of the house band at Small's Paradise in Harlem. He also continued to make consistent appearances in Major Robinson's "New York Beat" column in *Jet* magazine, with or without his fiancée, Ethelyn, who had no interest in traveling with Curtis when he went on tour or out of town for a recording date. A November 19, 1959, issue snickered this observation: "Bandleader King Curtis almost wrecked his new $5000 car when he swerved to avoid hitting a stray dog and smashed into a tree. To make matters worse, the dog bit him on the leg when he left the car to pet it."[13] Curtis was constantly in the public eye.

After supporting a significant list of artists and blazing through recording session after recording session, in 1959 Atlantic Records was impressed enough by the now established saxophone star and his work for them in the studio to offer Curtis his own solo contract. He jumped at the opportunity. On April 24, 1959, Curtis entered the Atlantic recording studio—for the first time as the featured artist—cutting initial songs for his solo album for their Atco subsidiary. The cover of *Have Tenor Sax, Will Blow* (a possible play on the popular TV series at the time, *Have Gun, Will Travel*, starring Richard Boone as Paladin) shows a doe-eyed and youthful King Curtis cradling his horn, clutching it to his chest as though in anxiety, almost as if it's his security blanket. The innocent expression on his face, coupled with his raised brow, may have suggested to the casual observer (and rightly so) that this must be a first Atlantic solo effort for the young artist, a virtual neophyte to the industry. On the contrary, liner notes by Joe Muranyi gave insight into the maturity of Atlantic's new, yet seasoned, solo artist: "His own playing is quite distinctive; his brassy, round tone with a characteristic burr that sometimes becomes almost a growl, his mesmerizing rhythmic figures and intricate inflections all add up to a style that is original, readily recognizable and easily enjoyed. Indeed, his style has received the sincerest form of flattery from many a tenor man—a note for note copying of many of his style-setting choruses."[14] Atlantic Records held tremendous confidence and optimism for their newly signed solo artist, as expressed by Muranyi: "King Curtis' dynamic music is the kind of American music that in recent years has taken the world by storm. It is easy to understand why."[15]

The album was produced by Ahmet Ertegun's older brother, Nesuhi, who had been hired as the definitive jazz ambassador at Atlantic Records.

Album cover for King Curtis's first solo album for
Atlantic Records. *Atlantic Records.*

Curtis wrote or co-wrote seven of the eleven songs and used his early band
(Al Casey on guitar, Jimmy Lewis on bass, and Belton Evans on drums),
adding Herman Foster on piano, Joe Puma and Jimmy Spruill on guitar,
and Noble Watts on tenor saxophone. It opened with the King Curtis original "Midnight Ramble," reminding the listener immediately of Curtis's
previous Coasters sound, a familiar barnyard staccato style. A cover of Jack
Lawrence's "Linda" contributed a salsa beat, while Curtis also covered a
Latin tune, "Chili," as well as straight-ahead R&B melodies, with the likes
of "Birth of the Blues" and "Jaywalk." Though the album gave a decent
representation of Curtis's broad spectrum of talents and styles and featured

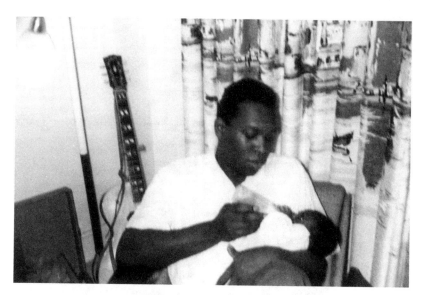

Curtis with Curtis Jr. *Courtesy of Modeen Brown.*

the King Curtis cover of Henry Mancini's "Peter Gunn," the overall sales performance was disappointing and Atlantic soon released Curtis from his contract. Curiously, there was no dedicated single launched by Atco from the album. Undeterred, Curtis was in such high demand from other artists that he was too busy to worry about any negativity generated by his lukewarm initial Atlantic Records solo effort.

Lack of major-label solo success paled in comparison to Curtis's next great event, fatherhood. On September 1, 1959, Curtis and Ethelyn welcomed Curtis L. Ousley Jr. into the family. Curtis couldn't have been more thrilled. This may have been the springboard for the young couple to finally wed. Two months later, on November 5, 1959, Curtis and Ethelyn were married, filing marriage license number 24428 with the Manhattan city clerk.[16]

The relationship between the two had not gone well before Curtis Jr.'s birth due to Curtis's professional schedule. Now came the added emotional stress of parenthood. Curtis and Ethelyn would continue their tempestuous ways for the next five years in a relationship which was doomed from the start. The two would legally separate in early 1964.

King Curtis ended his triumphant 1959 on a high note, supporting Titus Turner, Joe Turner, the Clovers (on several takes for their number 23 *Billboard* hit "Love Potion No. 9"), and the Coasters (on "Poison Ivy"). While continuing to back Mickey and Sylvia, Curtis also co-wrote "Midnight Midnight" with Mickey Baker and registered it with Progressive Music, a publishing division of Atlantic Records, on November 15, 1959. This song is featured on Mickey Baker's album, *The Wildest Guitar,* with Curtis conspicuously absent from the recording session credits. Baker was very matter of fact about the collaboration: "Actually, we didn't write anything. We just went into the studio and started making noise, and we named it after we got through with it. We screamed 'midnight, midnight,' so that became the name of the song."[17]

Still looking to diversify his sound, and not above making an occasional gimmick recording, Curtis played sax on "one-hit wonder" Tommy Facenda's strange recording phenomenon, "High School U.S.A." Previously in Gene Vincent's Blue Caps band, Facenda set out on a solo career in 1958. He first cut the novelty song using names of high schools in Virginia. Atlantic Records picked up the song for national distribution, recording a whopping twenty-eight different state versions. The song achieved an impressive number 28 on the *Billboard* Hot 100 list in November 1959.

In early 1960, King Curtis continued his breakneck recording pace in the studio with Carole King, the Clovers, Clyde McPhatter, Neil Sedaka, and the Coasters. At the same time, Luther Dixon had come to the Scepter recording label and quickly went to work to organize a consistent rhythm section to back his all-girl group, the Shirelles. He wanted a high-end reliable sound using some of the best studio musicians in the business. The standard pool he drew from included King Curtis, Mickey Baker, Panama Francis (drums), Jimmy Lewis (bass), Carl Lynch (guitar), Paul Griffin (piano), and Jerome Richardson (sax). These session artists would give the Shirelles one of the strongest supporting casts in the industry and resulted in the group scoring dozens of hit records, led by their two number 1 hits, "Will You Love Me Tomorrow" and "Soldier Boy."

While Luther Dixon's formula and the group's vocal talents created one of the most successful female bands in pop music history, the group's recording structure did not spawn close relationships between the singers and their studio band. "I never really got to know King Curtis and the other musicians very well," lead singer Shirley Alston Reeves told me. "Luther Dixon would first gather the studio musicians and record the instrumental tracks, then we [the Shirelles] would fly in and record the vocals. But the few times I did see Curtis, he was always funny, always makin' everyone laugh in the studio."[18]

Atlantic Records was not interested in pursuing any more of Curtis's solo work after his underwhelming debut with them. So, King Curtis entered into a recording contract with Prestige Records, recording a number of solo albums for the label as well as their short-lived subsidiary, Tru-Sound. This was Curtis's first significant long-term record label relationship. Prestige also threw everything his way, from rhythm and blues to jazz to straight-ahead blues, on their other brief subsidiary, the Bluesville label (active 1959–1965). His first Prestige work, recorded for their subsidiary New Jazz label on April 21, 1960, was titled *The New Scene of King Curtis* and featured his new band of "Little Brother" Nat Adderley on cornet, Wynton Kelly on piano, Paul Chambers on bass, and Oliver Jackson on drums.

The five tracks on the album enabled Curtis to continue his beloved focus on jazz-oriented recordings, a liberating feeling following his initial disappointments in his solo career. Nat Hentoff was not shy about his praise for Curtis as a jazz artist, nor Curtis in those same notes about challenges with trying to record the genre:

> This is the first straightaway jazz album to have been recorded by King Curtis, a widely popular rhythm and blues performer. The session introduces to jazz listeners a player of uninhibited emotional power with the kind of driving, functional swing that characterized Gene Ammons at his best. 'It's been frustrating up to now,' Curtis explained. 'Although my regular combo plays 60% to 70% jazz—Al Casey, for instance, is on guitar—record companies haven't let me record jazz, because I already had a reputation in commercial music. Now, with this album, I hope to record the way I feel much more often.[19]

Curtis's solo recording contract with Prestige allowed him to support other musicians on other labels as well as record smaller solo projects. After a few sessions for other studios, including backing Little Anthony and the Imperials, Curtis was back in the studio as King Curtis and His Orchestra on July 26, 1960, recording the *Azure* album for the Everest label. An odd and short-lived record company, Everest was founded by electronics inventor Harry Belock and producer-engineer Bert Whyte. The label focused primarily on recording classical music. Created in 1958, the original version of the label would close in the mid-1960s.

Curtis told a number of friends that *Azure*, which included covers of numerous pop song standards of the day, such as "Our Love Is Here to Stay," "Unchained Melody," "Misty," and "When I Fall in Love," was his favorite headlining album. For *Azure*, he traded in his signature hard-driving style for softer, smokier themes, and it's the only album in his career that could be classified as "easy listening."

Reviewer Jason Ankeny had high praise for Curtis's work: "King Curtis' lone LP for the tiny Everest label eschews his signature gutbucket R&B approach in favor of a late-night, bluesy atmosphere that brilliantly captures the unparalleled soulfulness of his tenor sax solos. Ballads and standards spanning from 'Unchained Melody' to 'The Nearness of You' are vividly realized by the lush arrangements of Sammy Lowe, complete with vocal contributions from the Malcolm Dodd Singers. Still, it's Curtis' melancholy leads that command the spotlight, boasting the cerebral intricacy of jazz and the emotional heft of soul."[20] Curtis would eventually record again for Everest when he cut two tracks for the label in late 1960 and into early 1961.

Curtis also branched out into television after meeting the country star and banjo aficionado Earl Scruggs on the set of CBS-TV's "Folk Sound USA," a one-hour special that was telecast in June 1960. Scruggs, not unlike King Curtis, was never afraid of innovation and continued to seek out and experience new genres for his banjo. He was impressed with King Curtis's inventive skill on the saxophone and felt a sense of musical kinship. He told the *Associated Press*: "I remember a network TV program I did with Lester Flatt called 'Folk Sound USA.' They were rehearsing the fire out of it because when that light came on you were live, and if you messed up you couldn't do it again. King Curtis was playing horn on the show and between rehearsals he said, 'Let's pick a tune together.' That was my first exposure to a good horn player. He knew 'Foggy Mountain Breakdown' and we played it and it really turned me on to a brass instrument mixed with country music."[21] Scruggs also recalled to the *Chicago Tribune*: "I'd never played with a good horn player before. I'm always listening for a new sound, so I agreed [to play with Curtis]. I was surprised how well the banjo worked with a saxophone, and that got my attention really fast. I realized the banjo could work in a lot of different situations."[22]

Following studio dates with the Isley Brothers, the Coasters, and Jimmy Jones, Curtis assisted on his first blues album for Prestige's Bluesville label on August 11, 1960, recording with Al Smith. Then it was straight over to Atlantic studio to record with Ruth Brown. Next, the workaholic King Curtis was paired with fellow saxophone players Oliver Nelson and Jimmy Forrest for a Prestige jazz album entitled *Soul Battle*. Recorded on September 9, 1960, with many of the tracks written by bandleader Nelson, the album allowed Curtis to wrestle with R&B styles while maintaining his trend of highlighting the passion for jazz displayed on his previous Prestige/New Jazz solo effort, *The New Scene of King Curtis*. *Soul Battle* featured a support cast of pianist Gene Casey, bassist George Duvivier, and drummer Roy Haynes.

Nelson, who had played with Louis Jordan and Quincy Jones in the 1950s, and Forrest, known for playing with Duke Ellington and Miles Davis as well as for his 1952 number 1 R&B hit,"Night Train," were well established in the jazz genre. Listeners will hear Curtis giving no ground to his experienced jazz cohorts, showing a facility head-to-head with Nelson and Forrest. On the *Soul Battle* album, King Curtis proves that he is not just a honker and a blower, but also a refined and polished jazz musician who can hold his own with anyone.

Opening with "Blues at the Five Spot," the trio shows off a swing style modernized for the times. "Blues for M. F. (Mort Fega)" entertains, as you can pick out each distinctive horn player while the trio slows down to a series of passionate individual runs. Jimmy Forrest opens with a lilting melodic interpretation, deftly handing the baton to Nelson, who follows with a blasting four-note intro to his solo, which listeners would likely

STEREO

SOUL BATTLE
oliver nelson
king curtis
jimmy forrest

prestige
PR 7223

ORIGINAL
Jazz
CLASSICS

Album cover for *Soul Battle. Prestige Records.*

assume to be the big and brassy playing of King Curtis (as opposed to the album's more "refined" jazz artists). Nelson then quickly reverts from his friendly imitation to continue exploring the original melody. Next, King Curtis steps in with a much more polished and urbane jazz sound than what he is known for, ever reminding listeners that he, too, is a surprisingly accomplished jazzman.

"Anacruses" accelerates the album with hectic back-and-forth improvisational play between the three, each challenging the other to step up his game. The cover of the jazz standard "Perdido" continues the previous swing-band pace. With "In Passing," the trio returns to a bluesy R&B feel that adds a bit of jazz experimentation for good measure. A bonus track added to the CD version of the album features Jimmy Forrest's contribution, "Soul Street." Nelson's original solo is tossed skillfully back and forth by Curtis and Forrest in unique, individual interpretations. Curtis's solo lips off to Nelson in an almost voice-like manner, sassing back and forth like an insolent child to an adult, not unlike his earlier irreverent work with the Coasters. Curtis would use this nearly human, vocal horn sound repeatedly throughout his career when covering famous vocalists' songs for his albums, his horn singing the lyrics sung by the original artist.

Though many critics scoff at the consideration of King Curtis as a legitimate jazz artist, Jerry Wexler vehemently challenges this opinion in his autobiography: "He was a saxist—not voguish mind you, just great ... even though *Down Beat* won't give him house room, he belongs forever with Prez [Lester Young] and Sonny Rollins and Trane [John Coltrane]—as well as with Red [Arthur "Red" Prysock] and Jug [Gene Ammons] and Gator Tail [Willis Jackson]."[23]

Playing with Curtis later in another band, King Curtis and the Noble Knights, bass player Chuck Rainey echoed the same respectful sentiments to author Josh Alan Friedman. Rainey had a great appreciation for Curtis's talents as a jazz musician and for how Curtis continually stacked up against the competition:

> King Curtis was known as a rock and roll saxophone player. But during the years I was with him, he did about four or five jazz records. At our matinee shows, he would play all the jazz standards. People like David Newman, Willis Jackson, Red Prysock, Illinois Jacquet, Ben Webster, came to his gigs to get him, to kick his ass, to show him up. Because he'd once been a jazz saxophone player, who now played rock and roll, and they said he's sold out. But to their shock, Curtis ran everybody off the bandstand with his horn. Every living tenor saxophone wished they could play like that and have his tone.[24]

While Curtis was delighted to indulge his love of jazz in these record-ings and continue to strategically broaden his market appeal, he also needed to improve his band and hire someone to oversee his business operations. Another happenstance meeting would add a new and very different, yet vital, component of stability to the steamrolling career of King Curtis. This encounter involved an individual with neither musical talent nor connection to the music industry, but rather a man who simply walked up to Curtis and asked him for a job. Cue Norman Dugger.

Two years earlier, looking for work, Norman Dugger had left Monticello, New York, in the Catskill Mountains for New York City. Dugger told me about finding an early home in Harlem:

> For a couple of years we used to bowl on 125th Street, right by a place called the Record Shack [Bobby's Happy House] near the Apollo owned by Bobby Robinson. There was a fella workin' there named Canada. He was already in the bowling alley, and King Curtis was rehearsin' the band for the Apollo for the upcoming week. He [Curtis] had already won that job (so, if you do a great job, they give you a week). So, during this time, the week he was there, there was a Motown revue: Smokey Robinson, the Supremes—the first time the Supremes ever left Detroit—the Supremes, Chuck Jackson, Sam Cooke on his first show. So, he [Canada] says, 'Well, look, come on, man, come in here, he's [Curtis] downstairs at the Apollo rehearsin' the band, you know, he wants somebody to be his valet, you know, his driver, right?'
>
> So, I had never heard of King Curtis, and I asked, 'Who the hell is King Curtis?' So, I walk up there, right, so he take me down to the rehearsal in the basement. So, Curtis said, 'Uh, we got two more songs to rehearse, then I'll talk to you. In the meantime, could you go next door to the drugstore to get us some pencils and coffee for the band, and doughnuts?'[25]

Norman felt that Curtis was challenging him, looking for his reaction to this seemingly innocuous request: "So, it's a twenty-dollar bill he gave me. He's probably tryin' to test me, see if I'm trustworthy. So, I went and got a bag of doughnuts and some coffee and the pencils after he asked me, so I say, 'I know how to drive.'" Curtis was impressed with the honesty, integrity, and energy of the stranger, and he offered Dugger a job as his personal assistant on the spot. Dugger noted: "He said, 'I'd like you to take care of my washin', take care of my horn, you know, put it on the stand, take it off the stand, we'll be goin' on some trips, you gotta drive the car.' So I said, 'Okay, fine.'"[26]

Curtis's new "valet" set up the saxophones before each performance. Dugger's rabid and reliable work ethic and organizational skills helped him quickly assume a new position as manager of the band. Norman Dugger was now doing everything from coordinating the band members before shows and practices to setting up the entire production onstage.

Aside from the fact that they were both Black, physically the two couldn't have been more different: the smooth-talking King Curtis, a towering figure of a man, and Norman Dugger, a thin man, short of stature and challenged by a significant stutter. The refined, confident, commanding, and often aggressive Curtis, working side by side with the waifish, affable, feet-on-the-ground chatterbox, Norman. Their relationship would transcend the standard sax player/valet relationship structure of the times and become a bond of friendship forged to last a lifetime.

Chapter 6

Small's Paradise and a Hit

One week after recording the *Soul Battle* jazz work, Prestige Records now directed Curtis to shift his focus again to support two blues albums for Roosevelt Sykes and Sunnyland Slim on the Bluesville label. There are very few musicians who would attempt to, much less succeed in, flipping back and forth between such disparate genres as jazz, R&B, and blues, but Curtis was adept at making these difficult stylistic transitions, many times doing so within a day or two of each other. This is why *every* recording artist, it seemed, wanted King Curtis to work with them in the studio. As he had so seamlessly transitioned between white and Black audiences during his early years in Fort Worth, Curtis had now evolved into the genre-chameleon of the recording studio.

Torching through the end of 1960, a veritable blur from recording date to nightclub stage, Curtis recorded on such labels as RCA Victor, Atlantic, King, Mercury, Fury, and others, working with the likes of Mickey and Sylvia, the Clovers, Andy Williams, the Shirelles (on their number 1 hit "Will You Love Me Tomorrow," the first number 1 hit song recorded by an "all-girl" band), and bluesman Arbee Stidham for the Bluesville label, and also supporting Ruth Brown, the Lionel Hampton All-Stars, and Connie Francis.

Late in the year, Curtis recorded *The Soul of King Curtis* for the tiny Mount Vernon Music label, an album that feels more like jazz. King Curtis discographer Roy Simonds places this session around the end of 1960 or in early 1961: "The only other clue to their vintage or origins is the fact that most MVM tracks were reissues from Herald/Ember [record labels] material of the 1959–1960 year; but whether that was the source of these tracks is unknown."[1] Author Rob Hughes lends his theory that "the track titles were made up by MVM (except for 'Perdido' misspelt as 'Perdito'), [since] I couldn't find any copyright entries for them. Maybe untitled jams from the Prestige label period."[2] In spite of Curtis's focus on continuing with jazz recordings, this album is an unremarkable jazz production, consisting of Curtis on sax paired with unknown guitar, piano, and drum support.

After backing Wilbert Harrison on a recording date, Curtis played on Bobby Lewis's hit "Tossin' and Turnin'" (where Curtis squeals using only his tenor sax mouthpiece), which was named the number 1 single on the *Billboard* Top 100 and R&B charts for 1961. Next, Curtis quickly recorded with the Coasters, followed by Hugo Montenegro, Little Anthony and the Imperials, and Nat King Cole. Very happy with their overall work with Curtis to date, Prestige Records decided to up the ante and this time asked Curtis and his band to change genres in order to be featured on a blues album for their Tru-Sound label.

Back in the studio, Curtis stayed true to his core band of Al Casey on guitar, Paul Griffin on piano, Jimmy Lewis on bass, and Belton Evans on drums to record the *Trouble in Mind* album. Much like his mentor Mickey Baker had done for him years ago, Curtis added young Mac Pierce on guitar, the son of a coatroom worker at one of the local clubs where Curtis performed. The album's liner notes by Joe Goldberg noted that Curtis had struck up a conversation with Pierce's mother: "She told me about her son and that one of his greatest ambitions was to sit with the band one night. I asked her to have him come over one night, and when he did, he just knocked me out. So when I wanted another guitar player for this record, I called him."[3] "Mac Pierce," however, was just an early stage name for this guitarist. His real name was Hugh McCracken, and he would later become one of the most sought-after guitar and harmonica session musicians throughout the '70s, '80s, and '90s.

Album cover for *Trouble in Mind. Tru-Sound Records.*

The *Trouble in Mind* album may be the most unexpected and compelling of King Curtis's early career. Along with his reliable expertise on saxophone, he not only plays a respectable guitar but also displays for the first time a solid singing voice. He added some seasoned background vocalists, three former Raelettes from Ray Charles's band, who billed themselves as the Cookies (Margaret Ross, Dorothy Jones, and Ethel McCrae) and scored top 10 R&B hits with "In Paradise," "Chains," and "Don't Say Nothin' Bad (About My Baby)," resulting in a notably enjoyable blues album with very soulful vocals as well as saxophone.

Regarding his decision to sing on this blues album, Curtis told Joe Goldberg that he had already added singing to his onstage repertoire.

Including his singing in the studio as well just made good economic sense: "Some of the clubs I was in, if a customer wanted you to sing, you sang or they would get somebody who could."[4] He opens with the title track, the melancholy blues standard "Trouble in Mind." He follows this with covers of Bessie Smith's "Nobody Wants You when You're Down and Out," Chuck Willis's "Don't Deceive Me," Amos Milburn's "Bad, Bad Whiskey," B. B. King's "Woke Up this Morning," and Jimmy Witherspoon's version of "Ain't Nobody's Business." He also contributes original compositions with "Jivin' Time" and "Deep Fry."

After this first Tru-Sound solo effort, Curtis worked on backing recordings with Ernestine Allen, the Isley Brothers, Ivory Joe Hunter, and LaVern Baker. Back in the Tru-Sound studio on July 11, 1961, King Curtis and his band cut much of the "B" side for his next album, *It's Party Time with King Curtis*. A vastly underrated album, it's Curtis at his brassy, sneering, Texas Tenor best, with two ballads thrown in for balance. From "Something Frantic," a title referencing the frenetic pace of the tune, to "Firefly" and "Keep Movin'," the album cooks with consistent up-tempo, Lone Star State saxophone. The second half of the album, ostensibly the "A" side, was cut six months later in early 1962.

Curtis continued to perform at Small's Paradise as the King Curtis All Stars with his dependable studio backing quartet of Paul Griffin on piano, Al Casey on guitar, Jimmy Lewis on bass, and Belton Evans on drums. About this time, a live performance was captured on a recording made privately by drummer Belton Evans. Decades later, in 2008, it was released as an album titled *King Curtis Live in New York*. In the back cover notes, Roy Simonds, author of the official King Curtis Discography, could barely contain his excitement at the release of the long-forgotten live session: "The album you have in your hands represents a minor miracle. In 1961, King Curtis was searching for a settled recording deal. The drummer of his group, Belton Evans, arranged to have one of the group's live sets recorded at Small's Paradise in Harlem … whether Belton's recording was intended for a promotional effort to secure a recording deal is unknown, but it may have been. Whatever its purpose, rarely would King Curtis again show the same spontaneity and authority as he does here."[5]

Although the recording quality leaves something to be desired, it gives crystal-clear insight into an average night out at Small's Paradise in Harlem with King Curtis—which was anything but average. Curtis grabs immediate command of his crowd, opening with his sax on "Jay Walk," then reels them in closer with Curtis singing "Trouble in Mind," followed by an instrumental in "African Waltz," then back to vocals with "What'd I Say," "I Have to Worry," and "The Twist." He closes the set by heating up with three jazz numbers, "Canadian Sunset," the rollicking "How High the Moon," and the energetic "K.C. Special" (also titled "Smooth Sailing"), where guitarist Al Casey takes the crowd into the stratosphere with a stunning solo. This is not just King Curtis the sax player; this is King Curtis the elegant entertainer. It's little wonder why people constantly badgered the Small's Paradise management with "Is King Curtis playing tonight?"

As the year came to a close, Curtis recorded with such luminaries as Ronnie Hawkins, the Falcons (with lead singer Wilson Pickett), and the Shirelles (on "Soldier Boy," another number 1 hit for the accomplished all-girl group), as well as recording a final solo album for Tru-Sound, *Old Gold*. Curtis gathered a new grouping of musicians for this album, utilizing his gambling compatriot "Brother" Jack McDuff on organ, Billy Butler (co-writer of Bill Doggett's huge hit, "Honky Tonk") and Eric Gale on guitars, Bob Bushnell on bass, Willie Rodriguez on bongos/congas, and for the first (but far from the last) time, Ray Lucas on drums. He also cut *Arthur Murray's Music for Dancing the Twist!* album for the RCA Victor label.

Drummer Ray Lucas would become a mainstay on King Curtis recordings and evolve into a consistent and visible contributor to the '60s and '70s rhythm and blues sound. He told author Jim Payne about the beginning of his musical education: "I was playing when I was in high school. I heard Gene Krupa, Buddy Rich, Big Sid Catlett, and the rhythm sections of Count Basie, especially with Sonny Payne on drums, Walter Page on bass, and Freddie Green on guitar. At that time you had to play everything: calypso, jazz, Spanish music, polka, bar mitzvahs—whatever. The way I look at it, that education was perfect, just as if I went to music school. There are some things you can learn that a school could never teach. So that was pretty much my education in music, and it never stops."[6]

King Curtis supported by Ray Lucas on drums.
Photo by Don Paulson / Michael Ochs Archives / Getty Images.

And like so many other musicians and music fans, his first impression of King Curtis was created by Curtis's significant Coasters work:

> I was still in high school when I heard 'Yakety Yak' by The Coasters, with King Curtis on sax. At that time I was playing bebop and jazz. I didn't care nothin' about rock and roll. I was born and raised in Harlem. All I knew was New York and bebop. If you didn't know Blue Mitchell, Miles Davis, Dexter Gordon, you weren't in my league.

But Curtis had a unique style of playing, and when I heard him on that Coasters record, I was knocked out.

Eric Gale, the guitar player, was the one who got me the audition with King Curtis. It was downstairs in the basement of Small's Paradise. It was King Curtis, me and [jazz drummer] Roy Haynes. He had Roy come in to check me out to see if I was all right. No piano, no bass, no organ, no guitar—just Curtis on sax and me on drums. The most important thing about being a drummer is listening. If he played the melody, I had to hear that and what the rhythm section would play. You've got to be able to do your own thing by yourself with just the melody. I had heard his band, so he could play any tune he wanted and I pretty much knew it.

Afterwards Roy looked at Curtis and said, 'That's a good kid. He's all right.' I was nineteen or twenty at the time. I played with Curtis from 1961 to 1966, and that was the best band I was ever in. When I came in the band it was Al Casey on guitar, Jimmy Lewis on bass, and Paul Griffin on piano. Now and then Curtis would augment it, but that was the basic band. Man, could he cover some ground. And that's when you're good—when you can make it sound bigger than you are. We recorded 'Soul Twist' in 1962, and that became a number-one R&B hit. It was a half-time shuffle with a backbeat. Later Chuck Rainey came into the band on bass. What a lot of bass players are doing now, he did forty years ago. Then Cornell Dupree came in on guitar and George Stubbs on piano.[7]

Buoyed by his increasing recording success, King Curtis still ached for another major record label contract. He was happy but not thrilled with his Prestige and Tru-Sound work; the peak of the *Billboard* Top 100 list he craved still eluded him. Hurtling down his chosen path, Curtis's aggressive pursuit of his next big record company deal would nearly cost him his first number 1 hit.

It was the fall of 1961 and King Curtis had been in New York City for nine years. He had quickly become the most sought-after saxophone session player in the city, much less the country. He was the backing horn player on an enormous number of hit songs and major albums, and he had become the leader of the house band at Harlem's Small's Paradise and was playing regularly at the Apollo Theatre. He had even experienced his own featured album deal with a major R&B recording label, Atlantic Records, as well as cutting multiple headlining albums with his band on the Prestige and

Tru-Sound labels. Yet, even with all the success he had achieved, something was missing: his own hit song.

And Bobby Robinson felt the very same way.

The founder of such record labels as Fire, Fury, and Enjoy and the owner of Bobby's Happy House record shop, a Harlem mainstay, Robinson had a real eye for talent and a special ability for getting the most out of his artists. It bothered Robinson to see and hear Curtis perform so well onstage yet never make it to any heights on the recording charts.

Robinson sought Curtis out at—where else?—Small's Paradise. Curtis had formed a new band, King Curtis and the Noble Knights, with Ernie Hayes on organ, George Stubbs on piano, Billy Butler on guitar, Jimmy Lewis on bass, and Ray Lucas on drums. After critically reviewing a few nights of the band's performances, Robinson was convinced he could get Curtis that elusive number 1 hit record. "He had a great band, a great sound, and people really flipped out over him in person," Robinson told *Melody Maker* writer Valerie Wilmer.[8] Robinson called Curtis over to the bar and had an animated discussion with the big man. Robinson was excited to speak with Curtis: "I said, 'I've discovered what's wrong. I can get you a hit record.' Feigning celebration, Curtis laughed loudly and responded cynically, 'That calls for a drink! Get Bobby Robinson a drink!'"[9]

Curtis had already had some less than satisfying experiences signing recording contracts with labels promising a number 1 hit record, and though he desperately wanted his own hit song, he was more than a little skeptical of Robinson's abilities to succeed. He considered rejecting Robinson but instead made him a counteroffer: "I'll make you a promise,' he said, 'we'll go in and cut a record and if we get a hit, I'll sign with you the next day."[10]

The following day, the aggressive Robinson responded to the challenge by assembling Curtis's band back at Small's to run through some of his ideas. His first thoughts, while innovative, immediately irked Curtis. Robinson wanted to improve the balance in the band and thought to feature the guitar player more often. Never one to back down from anybody, Curtis had numerous heated negotiations with Robinson regarding the producer's suggested change of stylistic direction. "I discovered that he [Curtis] had been honking that horn from beginning to end and that was what was wrong," observed

Robinson. "On everything he did, he blew and blew and blew. In person he was exciting, people could see him carrying on, but it got to the point where it was so exaggerated throughout all his music that there was no subtlety."[11]

Robinson knew that creating a hit record required a decidedly different formula compared to simply recording a song as a live performance. He had been impressed with some of the licks guitarist Billy Butler had displayed over the previous night's performances at Small's, although they were much too infrequent for his taste. He suggested to Curtis that instead of opening with standard honking saxophone fare, Butler open with a guitar solo, setting a different initial aura that would create a marked contrast to the commanding horn presence to follow.

Curtis's response was swift and unequivocal: "No man, I kick off my band always."[12] Robinson was adamant that this was the necessary missing piece to the elusive hit record puzzle that continued to confound Curtis. Robinson stood firm and, desperate for a hit, Curtis finally acquiesced. "He had never done this before, but he was anxious for a hit," Robinson said. He threw Curtis a bone: "You'll have your moment to shine, I'll give you a little solo down the line."[13]

Mollified somewhat by Robinson's promises and hopeful that this new direction would land him atop the *Billboard* charts, in November 1961 Curtis and Robinson started to arrange the tune "Soul Twist." Their focused effort jelled so quickly that they went into the recording studio that same day. Later that evening, the song was recorded and finished, and its release was set up, all in a single night, thanks to Robinson's hard-driving production machine.

Bobby Robinson had a well-established reputation for being a madman at promoting his artists, and he made sure that "Soul Twist" had as much exposure in the New York City area as it could achieve. His method was to use any means necessary, such as incessantly pounding the pavement down any street to any and all record shops in town to have them attract passing customers and get people hooked by playing the song on their outside speakers. He also stirred interest with the local radio stations.

Released on February 17, 1962, the advanced exposure that "Soul Twist" received from Robinson's ambitious marketing efforts caused the song to rocket to number 1 on the *Billboard* R&B chart, spending a total of nineteen weeks on the listing, as well as climbing to number 17 on the *Billboard* Top 100 (hanging around for a steady thirteen weeks).

A few days after the song achieved top status on the R&B chart, true to his word and buoyed by the initial optimism of his exciting collaboration with Robinson, King Curtis returned, pen in hand, to sign a recording contract with Bobby Robinson (and co-owner, brother Danny Robinson) and his Enjoy Records label.

The country was now in the midst of the Twist music and dance upheaval. Bobby Robinson had cleverly guided King Curtis into this feverish mix, capitalizing on the opportunity with "Soul Twist." Once Chubby Checker ("The Twist") and Joey Dee and the Starliters ("Peppermint Twist") had both soared to the top spots on the early 1962 recording charts across the US, "a flood of Twist records followed—'Dear Lady Twist' by Gary U. S. Bonds, 'Soul Twist' by King Curtis, 'Twistin' The Night Away' by Sam Cooke, 'Twistin' Matilda' by Jimmy Soul, 'Twistin' Postman' by the Marvelettes, 'Twist and Shout' by the Isley Brothers."[14]

In New York City, the Twist craze made an indelible mark by bringing the affluent white market stampeding back to Harlem. *Jet* magazine offered an overview of the hysteria about the new fad:

> Like Kennedy's Peace Corps has suddenly discovered Africa and South America, white café spenders have rediscovered Harlem again for the first time since World War II began. To them there's nothing like Tuesday nights when they get into their chauffeured cars and invade Big Wilt's Small's Paradise at 135th St. and 7th Ave., owned by lanky pro-basketball star Wilt Chamberlain, who bought the uptown landmark a year ago.
>
> The magnet that draws them in is the Twist—the dance fad that has both old and young wiggling and gyrating their hips.
>
> When first conceived as a gimmick last December to liven up an otherwise slow night, the Twist caught on with Harlemites like crazy. They passed the word to their downtown friends and the invasion was on in earnest.
>
> Paradise manager Pete McDougal had to put up a velvet rope to hold back the hordes that packed every inch of the 550-seat café from early evening to four a.m.—closing time. When bandleader

King Curtis swings into "Twisting Soul," the dance floor becomes a mass of writhing bodies. It's a case of every man for himself, and no two people can be found executing the same movement.

Authors John Johnson Jr., Joel Selvin, and Dick Cami have also noted that soon many different Twist dances emerged from the phenomenon:

Almost as soon as the Twist became established, variations appeared. The Bowler's Twist used a pendulum arm swing. The Oliver Twist employed a side-to-side arm motion. The Pulley involved imagining using a weight-lifting machine. In the Peppermint Twist, the body moves to the left, while the hands move to the right. The Fight features shadow boxing. In the Back Scratcher, the dancer pretends to scratch his back against an invisible pillar. The Organ Grinder's Twist combines the Pulley with the Peppermint Twist, with a circular flourish by the hands. On the Jockey's Twist, the dancer pretends he has a whip in his hand. The Lasso ... the Seventh Inning Stretch ... the Oversway ... the Fly (the latter variation actually was the subject of a Chubby Checker single the month before his version of "The Twist" came back).[15]

At the epicenter of this Twist hysteria, there was King Curtis and Small's Paradise. *Jet* magazine observed the "hottest record at teenage dance parties is bandleader King Curtis's 'Soul Twist.'"[16] Johnson Jr., et al. noted:

Saxophonist King Curtis was a one-man Twist Army. Not only did he lead the house band at Harlem's Twist headquarters, Small's Paradise, and have a hit instrumental called "Soul Twist" (the first chart record to use the word "soul" in the title), but he was all over other people's Twist records. The Arthur Murray "The Twist!" album by RCA Victor was performed by the King Curtis Combo. Curtis had laid down the requisite raspy solos on society bandleader Lester Lanin's Twist album on Columbia [correction: Epic Records, a subsidiary of Columbia] and cut more Twist albums of his own such as *Doing the Dixie Twist* [Tru-Sound] or *The Shirelles & King Curtis Give a Twist Party* [Scepter Records] for different labels around town.[17]

When King Curtis and his band were at Small's Paradise, particularly during this provocative time period, there was always fun and laughter, with anyone and everyone gorging on the Twist atmosphere throughout every evening, as *Jet* magazine snorted: "When 290-pound pro football player Gene (Big Daddy) Lipscomb did the Twist at Small's Paradise, comedian Redd Foxx turned to bandleader King Curtis and said: 'Look at that backfield in motion.'"[18]

Early in 1962, Curtis finished recording his *It's Party Time* album for Tru-Sound and then quickly played on studio recordings by Ben E. King, Panama Francis, the Ravens, and George Hudson. Next he recorded the album *Soul Twist with King Curtis* for Bobby Robinson's Enjoy label, under the band name King Curtis and the Noble Knights but using his standard backing band. He also recorded another album for Tru-Sound on February 15, 1962, *Doing the Dixie Twist*.

At the same moment, Ray Sharpe, a classmate from I. M. Terrell High School (younger by two years) who was now a successful guitarist, came to New York City. Curtis made sure he rolled out the red carpet for his Fort Worth friend, showing up in a huge automobile to squire his buddy around town. While clearly saxophone was Curtis's preferred instrument, he had not

Practicing guitar overlooking Central Park. *Courtesy of Modeen Brown.*

forgotten the early guitar lessons Sharpe had given him in Fort Worth. Sharpe remembered: "Guitar was just a novelty thing to him at the time, he just liked the instrument and wanted to know how to play it, and to some degree he did because when I went to New York to record there in 1961, I met him there and he kinda took me and showed me around to see a little bit, and I sat in on a few gigs with him, and I went to a few places where he performed, and he was doin' real good then."[19]

Curtis's band was now well entrenched in the Prestige/Tru-Sound recording house as their backing band in the studio. It was not at all uncommon for the label to send their artists over to Small's Paradise for a little live practice with Curtis and his band before their featured soloist would then sit down to record songs in the studio the following day.

Bluesman Eddie Kirkland had Curtis and his band backing him on a few recording sessions in 1961 and 1962 for the Tru-Sound label. And like so many other artists, he was overwhelmed by the immediacy of Curtis's support for him onstage and in the studio. In a Norman Darwen interview, he said:

> King Curtis, I give him a lot of respect. He was one hell of a man inside his heart and he was one hell of a musician of top of that. One thing I liked about Curtis, … in 1961 when I was told to go to New York, Harlem, a club on 35th Street. That club had King Curtis's band, Redd Foxx was the comedian downstairs doing a show, Etta James was upstairs playing a dance. So I was sent over by Prestige to do some numbers with Curtis that night because that was going to be my band backing me on the album, on the record. I just had got a new contract with Prestige, my first important contract I'd figured for myself. So I went, showed up, met King Curtis when they took their intermission and came off. He treated me like I wasn't a stranger, like he'd been knowing me for years and years. He told me, said, 'Just get up there and play yourself, we're behind you. Let's get up there and do it.' I like him for that.[20]

Kirkland recalled the thrill of the moment and how he made the most of his opportunity:

> Then I got up and I think I did about two numbers, went to get down. He wouldn't let me get down, said, 'You got to play some more.'

So I played about six songs, the crowd went crazy, man. He come and told me, said, 'You know, you're one hell of a blues singer. Someday, man, you're going to be trouble for some of these people that are out here singing the blues, once you get out there. Man, we're going to do everything to make you sound good on that record.' Oh man, he was so great; he wasn't like a lot of guys that made a success and they acting all up in the air. He was just like a home country boy, a home boy, you know what I mean? He was a wonderful guy, and we went in that studio that day, he got them musicians on the ball, man. That's just how good a musician he was and the group he had with him.[21]

Curtis always had great appreciation and respect for the early assistance he received from Doc Pomus and Mickey Baker. Now that his career was in full swing and he had become an easily recognized star, he paid this early debt forward by working very hard to help other musicians succeed, whether it was Hugh McCracken, Eddie Kirkland, or any other young artist trying to gain a foothold in the music industry.

Chapter 7

Capitol and Sam

After assisting on recordings by Clyde McPhatter, the Shirelles, Eddie Kirkland, and Chuck Jackson, Curtis was asked to come to the Capitol Records studio to back George Hudson and Gil Hamilton. While these initial Capitol recording dates did not reap much critical success, producer Bert Berns got a front-row eyeful of the talented Texas Tenor and his command of the recording studio. When King Curtis was playing, there was no messing around. Bert Berns liked what he saw.

Curtis returned to the Atlantic Records studios to back Solomon Burke and then went over to Scepter Records to record a duet album with the Shirelles. The album cover of *The Shirelles and King Curtis Give a Twist Party* shows Curtis gyrating amid the gleeful singers and gives an indication of the high jinks and laughter that usually followed whenever King Curtis was around. King Curtis was the nimble marathon runner of the New York recording studios, never tiring and always available, always professional, and always having a great time.

Bert Berns of Capitol Records had seen enough. He quickly offered King Curtis the second chance the saxophonist had been seeking to become a featured artist at a major record label. Instead of dwelling on his earlier

Album cover for *The Shirelles and King Curtis
Give a Twist Party. Scepter Records.*

Atlantic foray into headlining-artist experience and feeling soured, Curtis
embraced his good fortune and jumped at the opportunity to sign with another
rising player in the recording industry. He quickly grabbed his round table of
Noble Knights (Ernie Hayes, Billy Butler, Jimmy Lewis, and Ray Lucas) and
added George Stubbs on piano and Joe Richardson on guitar. The updated
band hit the Capitol Records studio in New York City on May 22, 1962, to
record two feature tracks, "Turn 'Em On" and "Beach Party." The latter would
be a hit, climbing to number 60 on the *Billboard* Hot 100 pop chart.

So immediate was Curtis's initial impact at Capitol Records that
King Curtis and the Noble Knights would win *Billboard's* "Most Promising

Instrumental Group of 1962" award after recording a mere two songs at his new label.

Curtis then threw himself into the Capitol studio to record his first full length album, *Country Soul*. It was designed strategically by the record company to counter its competitor, Atlantic Records, and follow on the coat-tails of Ray Charles's seminal ABC-Paramount album effort, *Modern Sounds in Country and Western Music*. However, this uneven King Curtis collection of a few soul tunes coupled with several covers of country songs simply misses the mark.

Among the diverse songs on the album, "Brown Eyes" is an up-tempo, original twist song, and Hank Snow's "I'm Movin' On," is a jazzy country instrumental. Curtis covers country songs in "Tumbling Tumbleweeds," a passable instrumental, and "Walkin' the Floor Over You." He also performs an unusual interpretation of Hank Williams's "Your Cheatin' Heart," where his sax is nowhere to be heard. Backed by monotonous background singers, Curtis gamely tries to carry the song with his voice, but any momentum his singing generates is quickly squashed by the entrances of the backing vocals. Instead of his singing voice, the song may have been better served with Curtis on horn, his trademark when successfully replicating the vocals on covers of hit songs. Curtis also covers Roy Acuff's "Night Train to Memphis," solid enough as Curtis returns to his horn. The remainder of the songs graduate to a more consistent country western style, with Curtis leading off on guitar as well as sax. He attempts to give an up-tempo swing interpretation to the remaining country and western tunes, while settling into playing his horn (augmented only a few times with his voice). All in all, it's a strange and inconsistent album in its experimental attempt to mix a little soul and jazz with country—a recipe that may look interesting on the menu but leaves one hungry for more and eventually disappoints.

The liner notes on the back of the album are just as peculiar (not unlike the inconsistent direction of the record). Written by one of Curtis's friends, NBA basketball star and co-owner of Small's Paradise Wilt "The Stilt" Chamberlain, the notes glow with respect and adoration for the saxophone player from Texas. Chamberlain's words give great compliment to Curtis's talents, not just on his sax playing but also giving him credit for the jazz guitar, vocals, piano, and drums (which were, quite obviously, played by other musicians). Then Chamberlain goes into a deep discussion on what "soul" is, and why King Curtis is very much a part of the soul movement. While Chamberlain's words hit the mark with his sincere respect for Curtis as a jazz and soul artist, he only mentions country music briefly. Clearly this is a desperate effort to use the words of a major sports figure to help promote the album while also attempting to render more coherent its combination of soul and country. What with the minimal focus on the album's country-specific material, Chamberlain's comments seem misplaced, making one wonder why Capitol chose to have Chamberlain, an avowed jazz fanatic, write liner notes for a production that was primarily a country and western platform.

Maybe Curtis and his horn were never meant for mainstream country music, despite Earl Scruggs's earlier enthusiasm for pairing saxophone with banjo. Or, more probable still, it may have been a poor attempt at appeasing too broad a segment of music listeners, trying to combine too many genres that clearly don't mix well on the same vinyl. Despite Curtis's reputation as a stylistic chameleon, he clearly fumbled the record's combination of soul and country. This may also have been the first early sign of some creative and philosophic differences that would later fester and grow between Curtis and his producers at Capitol Records.

Wilt Chamberlain had first seen King Curtis three years prior to the production of the album. Curtis was performing at Small's Paradise in Harlem, and Chamberlain was so enamored with the venue he ended up purchasing a minority share in the club. Given Curtis's well-entrenched role in leading the house band at Small's and Chamberlain's overt fondness for jazz, it's no wonder the two became fast friends. Couple this with the weakness both men had for dice, and it is easy to believe that the two spent many a late evening (and early morning) in Chamberlain's back office, long after the club had closed, "rolling bones" with everyone from sports icons to movie stars to music legends.

Back home in Fort Worth, Texas, Aaron and Robbie Watkins continued to keep in touch with Curtis. Their club, the Paradise, was still as successful as ever, and Fort Worth music had never been more popular. The emperor and empress of the local Black music scene now had a new protégé under their wing: guitarist and recent I. M. Terrell High School graduate Cornell Dupree.

Like King Curtis, Dupree was in his early teens when he realized that he wanted to pursue music as his vocation. When asked how his specific segregated Texas high school continued to churn out such tremendous young musical talent, Dupree said to me: "I don't know if I have an answer to that. It is obviously within the person of what they perceive for themselves and what they are going to attempt to do or become."[1] There is no question, however, that the supportive influence of school music teacher Gilbert Baxter gave many young and emerging musicians not only the technical information to succeed but the necessary emotional drive, as well: "When I was a junior in high school, I played the saxophone. That is where I met Mr. Baxter—he taught me. I then went with the guitar and fell in love with that and begged my mother to buy me one. Again, I guess it is what you want to become within yourself."[2]

Certainly, Dupree had followed closely the activities of his older classmate King Curtis, whose career was in full swing in New York City. When passing through Fort Worth on tour from time to time, Curtis always dropped by to visit his mentors, the Watkins family. Home for his adoptive father's funeral (who had passed away on April 15, 1962), he happened to stop by the Paradise Club to visit. There, he ran into their new young guitar prodigy, Cornell Dupree.

This first meeting left such an indelible impression on Dupree that he decided he wanted to not only follow King Curtis's professional trail but also be a member of his band. Robbie Watkins later called Curtis in New York on behalf of Dupree from her Fort Worth kitchen and suddenly pointed the telephone towards the startled young musician, who picked up his guitar and auditioned for Curtis on the spot. Curtis hired Dupree and sent his new guitar player a one-way plane ticket to New York City. "In fact, I stayed with him when I first got there," said Dupree. "I stayed with him about four months— the Whitehall Hotel on Broadway and 100th Street. He kind of took me in and showed me the ropes—schooled me. I was scared to death and didn't know how to act. If it hadn't been for him, I would still be running around here [Fort Worth] at the clubs. He was doing a few sessions—not a lot. He was doing the clubs, traveling … we just worked certain places often, like the Apollo Theatre."[3]

Not unlike the strategic plan of attack Mickey Baker had devised years before for a certain young saxophone player from Mansfield, Texas, Curtis quickly got the young Fort Worth guitarist into the New York recording studios, having Dupree support five tracks for King Curtis and the Noble Knights at Capitol Records on October 25, 1962. Dupree was completely impressed; not only did Curtis "school" his new protégé on the finer aspects of music but he also educated him on becoming business-savvy and street-smart: "He was a great musician and a good businessman. You don't often find that in musicians. He could deal with each side of it well."[4]

While championing his new protégé and continuing to cultivate his own career, Curtis now set his sights on amassing the most talented collection of musicians available to form a new live band. Curtis wanted a different group with him onstage versus in the studio. With fellow Texan Cornell Dupree now ensconced at lead guitar and Ray Lucas solidifying the critical drummer position, Curtis needed a bass player.

The spring of 1962 had brought bass player Chuck Rainey to New York City. Born in Cleveland, Ohio, and raised an hour away in Youngstown, Rainey had been playing in Cleveland and had set his sights on relocating to New York to further his career. He told me:

> I was just one of the bass players in New York. Now, I was in a band—it was a pretty good band. It was called Lester Young and the California Playboys … Lester Young was the guitar player, and that wasn't his real name. His name was John Rubin.
>
> We were the California Playboys and never been to California, of course, but we were playing a club on 25th Street. I remember getting this introduction and going this way, all of a sudden, King Curtis showed up on the gig, and he came past the bandstand, and he was popping his finger with the groove and he said loud enough for every-body in the band to hear, 'Go ahead, Chuck Rainey, play Chuck Rainey, go ahead, Chuck.'
>
> Well, I didn't think anything more about it, but the bandleader, who was Lester, he said, 'Yeah, that man, you know, he's comin' by here,' because Curtis would hang out every now and then and usually just for five minutes. 'Cuz, he was well known everywhere, and this

time, he stayed for about twenty minutes. And so, the bandleader told me on a break, he said, 'You know King Curtis, he wants you to play in his band.' And I said, 'Why do you say that?' Well, we had a good band. We really had a good band, and he said, 'Curtis wants you to play in his band.' I said, 'Well, no, not King Curtis.' Jimmy Lewis was his bass player, and Jimmy Lewis was *bad*. I mean, he was a great bass player. And, I couldn't see King Curtis wantin' me to play with Jimmy Lewis in the band, and so I said, 'Well, he ain't saying nothing to me.' And he said, 'Well, he will.'

And, so the next day, I talked to Lester—came by my flat, and he said, 'Curtis wants you to play in his band, and he asked me,' which is one thing I really appreciate with King Curtis. He was a business-man and was real good. Curtis came to Lester, and he said he wanted to trade bass players, and he wanted me to play. He wanted to hire me, and rather than just go behind his back, he thought he'd ask him. He [Curtis] came by my flat and told me, you know, what he had talked to Lester about, and he wanted me to play, and we discussed money, and as a matter of fact, I worked for him that very same night ... I was late, by the way. And it was at Small's Paradise.[5]

The critical pieces of Curtis's new live band were in place: Cornell Dupree, Chuck Rainey, and Ray Lucas. King Curtis and the Noble Knights were now ready to hold court.

After his success at Enjoy and his initial Capitol work, Curtis was quickly tagged to go on tour with his friend Sam Cooke. The two had struck up a deep friendship during previous collaborations at the Apollo Theatre and in Alan Freed productions in the late 1950s, with Cooke soon paying homage to his good buddy in his swingy hit, "Having a Party," where Cooke is heard requesting the disc jockey on the radio to "play that song called 'Soul Twist'" in reference to Curtis's number 1 hit record for Bobby Robinson's Enjoy label. To kick off the tour, Cooke's record producers, Hugo Peretti and Luigi Creatore, schemed to target the Harlem Square Club in Miami, Florida, to be the locale for a new live album, taking advantage of Sam and Curtis touring together.

Charlie Gillett, a historian whose work has focused on Atlantic Records, queried Curtis on not only his relationship with Cooke but his good fortune in being able to dictate which artists he toured with on the road. "I used to travel with Sam a lot," answered Curtis. "I only ever travel with those I like, I don't

Philadelphia deejay Jocko Henderson backstage with Sam Cooke and King Curtis. *R. H. Andreas / Bear Family Records Archives.*

travel, I never work with them I don't."[6] The surprised Gillett wondered how Curtis could afford such a pick-and-choose attitude when he must have had to tour with less than favored artists occasionally, simply to make a living. Curtis responded: "By the time I got around to any of them wanting me, I could choose, 'cuz by the time any of them wanted me, I had my choice of working with any of them. But before it was hard. Before that it was nobody!

Either it was everybody or nobody, you know when I was working in that place for seventy dollars a week, you know."[7]

When compared to his other live recordings, listeners of *Live at the Harlem Square Club, 1963* are treated to a vastly different Sam Cooke this time. Where previous live efforts highlight the serenity of Cooke's refined, gospel vocals, this January 12, 1963, concert brings a raw and edgy Cooke to center stage, his voice coarse with emotion and passionate tension. *This* is the Sam Cooke that made women swoon, that riled men with his earthy energy, crossing over from his gospel roots to rock and roll and rhythm and blues.

After the crowd is brought to a simmer just below the surface by King Curtis's opening solos with the backing band, Curtis came to center stage and the big man's exuberant personality can hardly be contained as he announces to the crowd, "And now we get to the feature part of our show." He then roars, "So let's *all* get your hands together and let's hear it for Mr. Soul—let's hear it for Sam Cooke!"[8]

The band thumps a few loud chords of introduction and the crowd roars as Cooke leaps to the microphone. He yells, "How you all doing out there?" Not pleased with the crowd's initial timid response, a more insistent, aggressive Cooke raises his voice and pointedly repeats, "I said, *how you all doing out there*?!!?" King Curtis has the crowd frothing, but Cooke intends to turn up the heat, getting the crowd to a full boil of anticipation. He is clearly in charge of the kitchen and will whip this crowd into a frenzy. Cooke quickly launches into a rough-edged and raspy "(Don't Fight It) Feel It."

This Sam Cooke was not the ethereal poster child famous for courageously vaulting the broad expanse between gospel music and rock and roll. That persona of the sophisticated, resplendent ambassador for crossover gospel artists had been left at the front door of the Harlem Square Club. The down-and-dirty Sam Cooke that entered the club that night was hoarse with raw emotional passion for his music and his audience.

The band was in fine form and meshed perfectly with Cooke's vocal theatrics. Curtis followed Sam perfectly. On "Twistin' the Night Away," Curtis and Cooke exchanged raucous interplay, first Cooke, then Curtis answering with roiling solos to Cooke's energetic choruses. They followed this up with more bantering interplay on "Somebody Have Mercy." Listening to the album,

Sam Cooke onstage with King Curtis. *R. H. Andreas /
Bear Family Records Archives.*

you can feel how much fun the two were having onstage together and how
well it translated to the crowd.

While the album was originally to be titled *One Night Stand*, it is interesting that RCA Victor Records shelved the album, thinking it too raw and
edgy for the image they had in mind for Sam Cooke—to the point that the
album wasn't released until June 1985.

Stopping by to take in the show, a young local singer named Sam Moore
walked backstage to greet Cooke. Moore was the lead singer of the duo
Sam and Dave, joining up with David Prater in 1961 in Sam's hometown

of Miami, Florida. The pair soon captured the imagination (and the ears) of the local Miami music scene and headed to Memphis, where they would quickly rock the soul music world with such successful Stax Records songs as "Hold On! I'm Comin'," "When Something Is Wrong with My Baby," and "Soul Man," among other hits. Sam and Dave would eventually be inducted into the Rock and Roll Hall of Fame in 1992.

Sam and Dave would quickly develop a reputation for onstage histrionics and effervescent live vocals that would scare the daylights out of any other performer unlucky enough to share the same concert bill, including the headlining act. Add to this illustrious list of "unfortunate" concert lead acts one Otis Redding. In 1967 the Stax/Volt Review went on tour in Europe, drilling soul music into the European consciousness. As the featured artist on the concert bill, Redding would follow Sam and Dave for the final act each night. Each date, Sam and Dave's warm-up performance not only set the table for Redding, it pushed the crowds to near riot, prodding Redding to the point of collapse trying to keep up with their electric performances.

The first tour Redding ever made with Sam and Dave had started much the same way. "The name of the game was upsetting the show," said Redding manager Alan Walden, who was booking both acts. "Otis did thirty-seven days with them that first tour, the first seven days at the Apollo. I arrived at the Apollo to find him sucking lemon and eating honey backstage; he was as hoarse as he could be and more nervous than I'd ever seen him. 'These motherfuckers are killing me,' he said. 'They're killing me. I'm going as fast as I can, but they're still killing me. Goddam!'"[9]

Backstage at the Harlem Square Club for that live Sam Cooke recording in early 1963, Sam Moore would chat with King Curtis for the first time. Though both were familiar with each other as well as their work and special talents, neither had any idea that they would form a deep and emotional bond eight years later when Curtis would champion Moore's first solo effort for Atlantic Records, an effort that would remain shrouded in mystery and misinformation for well over thirty years. "I met King Curtis when he was with Sam Cooke," Moore told me, "I was still living at home in Miami and I knew Sam when he was young, so I went to the show. I was introduced to King, and we had a long talk. We shared a lot of respect with one another. He liked some of the things that Sam and Dave was doing, and I thought that he should have been put in the class as a saxophonist with the Cannonball Adderley league and the Bird [Charlie Parker]—people like that. This man could play a lot of horn, man. He had a lot of emotional feelings coming out that big body of his. We talked, and when he and I hooked up to do the album [in 1971], this guy really was a genius."[10]

Aside from the fun that Curtis and Sam Cooke had onstage during the tour, there was always time for Curtis's real passion on the road: gambling. Sam's brother Charles fondly told author Peter Guralnick of being on the tour with King Curtis: "King Curtis and I, you understand, we love to gamble. King Curtis had a lot of money and I had a lot of money—because I had *Sam's* money—and anytime he's offstage, like for intermission, we'd get to gambling. Sam knew I could gamble. And boy, I used to win a lot of money off of old King Curtis; I used to beat him out of his money!"[11]

New King Curtis guitarist Cornell Dupree was also on the tour. "A lot of times," he told Guralnick, "we'd be driving [to the next town after the show], get to the hotel, and instead of going to bed, they'd get on the floor and start shooting craps. I can remember one incident when Curtis had won a lot of money and handed the money to me [to] hold, and I nodded off to sleep, and Charlie was sneaking the money out of my hand while I was sleeping and shooting that with Curtis!"[12]

Allegedly, Charles bested Curtis so severely one night that Curtis had to borrow money just to pay his band. When Sam Cooke heard of this, he immediately demanded that his brother give his winnings back to the game's losers. Sam didn't want anyone to have to suffer any financial burdens on *his* tour. Incredulous, the protesting Charles acquiesced to the point of actually overpaying a number of his fellow gamblers with his reimbursements.

Gambling was Curtis's one main vice. From playing dice minutes before an Apollo Theatre opening (once Tyree Glenn Jr. thought Curtis would miss the entrance, as he was nearly naked just before curtain call) to playing with Sam Cooke's brother while on tour, if there was a dice game nearby, you could be assured King Curtis would be in the middle of it. Despite his newfound success and breakneck work schedule, Curtis always found time to have fun and never backed down from any challenge. Anytime Curtis played at the

Apollo or other Harlem haunts, he invariably made time to "roll ivories" with his main gambling compatriots. Curtis was not only extremely competitive, he also happened to be either extraordinarily talented or very lucky at shooting dice and would win often.

One member of the backing band, performing with Curtis often at Apollo Theatre concerts, was guitarist Curly Palmer. Thomas "Curly" Palmer, the music director for the Coasters since 1964, also happened to be a charter member of Curtis's elite gambling entourage, along with Hammond B-3 organist "Brother" Jack McDuff and trumpet player Danny Moore. These four could always be found playing dice from right after a performance until the wee hours of the morning (and much later). Palmer had initially met King Curtis during a Coasters recording session. He said to me:

> They had a session in New York, and they wanted a saxophone player, so he did a session with us one time for King Records. I thought he was a phenomenal player, you know what I mean? Because he definitely had a different sound—he had a different sound from most of the other session players at the time. When I heard him with what they call the Yakety Sax sound—you know, this guy's great! I played with him at the Apollo Theatre—we did a record, *Apollo Saturday Night*—the show was recorded by Atlantic. And I played off and on with King Curtis in one-night stands around New York. He had another guitar player that played with him named Billy Butler. And Billy Butler also played with Bill Doggett, and so Billy Butler was left to go on his own, but he was doing so much studio work he didn't want to go on the road. So theoretically, when King had these one-night stands, you know, and he would need somebody ... he would give me a call.[13]

But playing onstage with King Curtis was only half the fun; the real entertainment was always backstage:

> And getting back to the Apollo Theatre, that's why the big craps game would come off. He was a phenomenal craps shooter, man. There was this time, with King Curtis, Danny Moore, who was married [engaged] to Ruth Brown, Jack McDuff the organ player, couple of known local guys; and myself. You'd have a big shindig at the Apollo, sometimes it would get so involved they would lock up the theater. We was shootin' craps and couldn't get out 'til the next day. Sometimes, the craps games

got kinda serious, you know? I remember one time when Jack McDuff had just come back from Sweden. And when he came up to the Apollo about 2:30 in the afternoon, and he had this big money sack, you know? And he was swingin' it around like it was a baton. He said he came to play craps. King Curtis was the kinda guy, he didn't back down from a challenge, you know? So he [Curtis] said, "What do you want to do with that money?" McDuff said, "I wanna try to beat you with it." And so, *that* started it.[14]

Although a widely respected dice thrower, Curtis was not immune to the occasional defeat. Palmer continued: "I think the last time that we played at the Apollo, I got lucky, I guess I must have won a bunch, and that started the rivalry between Curtis and myself. It was, I would say, somewhere around three thousand dollars to four thousand dollars, something like that."[15]

Curtis had been bested, and that didn't set well with the übercompetitive gambler. Palmer was clearly under his skin, so much so that he wanted his friend to play again as soon as possible to win back his losses: "So the next day, I pick up another couple of thousand dollars and I went back up to Small's. And I bought him some champagne, so he says, 'Come back around, the place is slow.' We went up to his house, we played, head-up, just the two of us, from four o'clock in the morning 'til three o'clock in the afternoon."[16]

The lucky Palmer was in a groove. He had beaten Curtis yet again, so badly that Curtis, after losing all his money, also lost personal jewelry and signed over multiple IOU's: "So I took his IOU's—I broke him that time. I took his IOU's, he gave me his rings and stuff … after I broke him, I said, 'You owe me quite a bit, and you gotta pay up because I can't keep givin' you IOU's and holdin' your property.' I'm holdin' rings and watches he used as collateral. And he said, 'Well, let's go to the bank and straighten it out.' So we go downstairs, caught a cab, and went to the bank. He took all his stuff back, paid me my IOU's."[17]

After playing all night and into the next day, the happy Palmer, delighted by his rare success, was now exhausted. Knowing King Curtis as well as he did, however, Palmer realized that from Curtis's perspective the game was far from over. Fearful that Curtis would not drop the situation, Palmer hatched a plan:

> While he (Curtis) was in the bank, I had told the cab driver, I said, "Listen, if he comes outta the bank and he gives me my money, I'm not gonna get outta the cab when we get back to One Hundred-Sixth Street." I said, "When he gets out, I want you to lock the door; I'm goin' home," 'cuz I had me about four thousand or five thousand dollars. So when we got back, Curtis got outta the cab first 'cuz he's ready to go. As soon as he got outta the door, I said, "Lock the door." The cab driver locked the door. He [King] said, "You're not comin'?" I said, "No man, I'm tired—I'm tired, I got to go."[18]

Enraged, Curtis couldn't believe he had fallen for Palmer's trap, and he was even more incensed that Palmer wouldn't allow another opportunity to recoup any of his major losses. Like flipping a light switch, he instantly exploded. Palmer was taken aback by Curtis's hair-trigger reaction: "Curtis picked up a garbage can out of the street and threw it at the cab. I yelled to the driver, 'C'mon, man let's go!!' See, I had already paid the guy to go, to drive off. I gave him a fifty-dollar bill because I wanted to get outta there and I knew if I kept playin' with him, he was gonna eventually win his money back because that's the way the game is played."[19]

To this day, Palmer has never forgotten his rare victory over his friend, the seasoned gambler King Curtis. And he also hasn't forgotten how quickly and completely enraged Curtis became in response to losing so badly and not being allowed to win back any of his losses. It would not be the last time that Curtis would let his temper get the best of him.

Chapter 8

New Label,
New Love and Loss

uoyed by his tour with Sam Cooke, and despite achieving only minor chart success, at best, with his initial Capitol recordings, Curtis charged back into the studio to record his second Capitol album, *Soul Serenade*. He had written the title track by collaborating with the Shirelles' producer, Luther Dixon. The catchy, soulful tune featured Curtis using a curious instrument, the saxello, which is a B-flat soprano saxophone with a distinctive shape. Its partially bent bell looks like a cross between a bass clarinet and a straight soprano sax, and it has a slightly bent neck as well. The sweetly melodic tune would become Curtis's signature song, sitting on the *Billboard* Hot 100 pop chart for twelve weeks and achieving a top ranking of 51. When Curtis later recorded the song for Atlantic Records using a tenor sax, "Soul Serenade" received the 1968 BMI (Broadcast Music, Inc.) Rhythm and Blues Achievement Award as one of the most played songs in the BMI repertoire between July 1, 1967, and June 30, 1968. The song would later be covered by Gloria Lynne (1965), Maxine Brown (1967), Willie Mitchell (1968), Lou Rawls (1968), and even Aretha Franklin (1967). Among the various recent artists that have recorded "Soul Serenade" are saxophonist David Sanborn (1992), the Allman Brothers (paired with their song "You Don't Love Me" in 1971), and the Derek Trucks Band (2003).

But all was not serene for Curtis at Capitol Records, some early success on the *Billboard* charts notwithstanding. Having a major label recording contract had translated, in this instance, to major discord between the producers and their star in the studio. Capitol was uninterested in recording "Soul Serenade," possibly trying to keep with an up-tempo platform that left no room for a dulcet melody. Curtis was so sure it was a hit that he actually paid for the cost of recording it. While "Soul Serenade" was a critical and commercial success, Curtis later told Charlie Gillett that the process of initially recording the song had left him with some creative claustrophobia:

> I was signed to Capitol when I recorded that, "Soul Serenade." I was signed to Capitol, but I had this hit, unfortunately, "Soul Twist." Then I had "Beach Party" and a few records from there. They didn't want "me"; they kept wanting me to do this type of bag. They'd given me a guarantee, so least of all they didn't want to know about what *I* wanted to do. They just wanted me to do what they wanted me to do. So, I wanted to do "Soul Serenade." So I went into a studio and cut "Soul Serenade" myself, I laid out my own money. Matter of fact, up there [on the shelf], see, up there, in that thing [tape recorder] I could pull you out probably some renditions of "Soul Serenade" that I've still got there that nobody's ever heard, 'cuz I cut it three times.[1]

November 16, 1963, found Curtis playing saxophone on an Atlantic Records live album, *Apollo Saturday Night*, which was recorded at the Apollo Theatre featuring the Falcons, Otis Redding, Doris Troy, Rufus Thomas, and Ben E. King. King Curtis drummer Ray Lucas always loved playing the Apollo:

> The Apollo Theatre will always be my Carnegie Hall. When I think of the people who stood on that stage—Louis Armstrong, Duke Ellington, Big Joe Turner, Ella Fitzgerald, Art Blakey—that's where the best played, as far as contemporary rhythm and blues and jazz was concerned. I got out of high school but didn't go to college and I was on the same stage as them. That was special. During the week it was five shows a day. Saturday and Sunday, it was six shows. I was making $129 a week. After we got through at the Apollo, sometimes we

had to go play a dance at the Audubon Ballroom [in Washington Heights]. We also traveled a lot, all up and down the East Coast. We went on the road with the Supremes, Patti LaBelle, the Coasters. One time we drove from New York to Columbia, South Carolina, for a one-nighter. When you're young you can do anything. I didn't care. As long as I was playing.[2]

Curtis continually tinkered with his bands, often using vastly different musicians to form a new grouping, depending on the venue. The aggregate that played in his house band at Small's Paradise, for example, was frequently quite different from his compilation of studio musicians or any of his touring bands when on the road. Ray Lucas had never forgotten the energy there would be at Small's any time King Curtis and his band played the house:

When we played there, the people that came in, they never left. They were moved. When we came on that stand, we took care of business. Even the most non-musical person couldn't leave that table without shaking back and forth a little bit. I thought that was heaven. It couldn't get any better than that. We always had a good audience. [Comedian] Redd Foxx would come in. He was the funniest dude. He'd look at me and say, "Look, there's God on the drums!"
        Every now and then we'd do something like a Clifford Brown tune, and I'd have to take a solo like Max Roach, in that style. Curtis knew I liked Basie, so sometimes we'd do "One O'clock Jump" or "Jumpin' at the Woodside." You had to play different styles of music in the types of clubs we were working in. You worked in the club to please the boss and the audience.[3]

Keyboard player Jimmy Smith, the self-professed "longest tenured, least known" of these select live musicians, recalled to me: "Curtis didn't really have a traveling band, and I was working for Chuck Henley's band. You know, I came to New York with, like, a Wurlitzer on my shoulder on a Greyhound bus from South Carolina."[4] Smith then joined a band that had a cocky sax player. Smith smiled:

The leader was a sax player, and his idol was King Curtis. And, he was one of the guys who used to always challenge Curtis all the time. And he was one of those guys, along with a few other guys, and Curtis would laugh at them and blow them off the stage. Curtis hired my entire band to make a couple trips with him. Basically, we went to Toronto, Canada, a couple, a few times, and during the course of this, we backed him up for a while and then afterwards he spoke to me many, many times. He was trying to convince me to leave that band and come with him, 'cuz evidently, in that band I was the only one he was interested in using. He kept calling me, like, every week giving me offers, and I would say, "No, no, no, no." At the time I was working during the day, and finally he made me a proposal. He offered me a salary that was above both salaries combined![5]

Smith couldn't believe his good fortune, coming to New York and suddenly becoming a mainstay of King Curtis's live band, an accomplishment that was far from trivial. Smith reminisced: "He was a very good musician. He always got really good musicians—most of the time. Every now and then, he got somebody that wasn't really up to par for the band, and that was noticeable almost immediately. There was, like, nobody [that] stayed in the band that long that wasn't good. He knew exactly what he wanted from each instrument, and he would tell you what he wanted. He was a pretty decent guitar player. He was a pretty decent singer, but an excellent saxophone player."[6]

When asked to define the challenges of working with King Curtis as his new bandleader, however, Smith had an interesting one-word response:

Tough. He would come up and say, "Well, we gonna do a rehearsal tomorrow at twelve o'clock," or something like that. So, they would do the rehearsal, and during the rehearsal he would say, "Oh, by the way, we're going to Italy tomorrow for three weeks." And I'm saying, "Hey, you know, wow, you need some other kind of notice for this stuff," but this is the stuff he would regularly do. I mean he would just jump up and say you gotta gig, and you're going away for a month or a month and a half or something like that, and you're going somewhere halfway around the world, and it's like no prior notice to it.[7]

Smith also noticed that Curtis was not afraid to use his physical stature to maintain authority and focus during rehearsal, which many times was quite effective.

And in a way, he kind of disrespected people, but it was all in a playful manner. But, because he was kinda big and because he was kinda strong, he would badger people. He was definitely a bully, and he would grab somebody and try to physically hurt them, you know, from the back. He'd grab you around the shoulders, not on your neck, but between your neck and shoulders, you know? He'd kind of grab, a squeezing motion with his hand, and he would do this to people. We had a drummer who was very sensitive to that. And he used to mess with him all the time with that. And he did it once to me and I just, it didn't bother me at all. That bothered him that it didn't bother me, but it did. I just pretended I didn't feel it.[8]

Aside from his intimidating methodology, with King Curtis in charge of his studio band, the Noble Knights, and the band fully entrenched at Small's Paradise, Smith felt a dynamic cohesiveness and electricity that permeated the band like nothing he had ever experienced. And everyone in New York City, it seemed, knew it. Smith stated matter-of-factly:

No one could compete with us. No one could compete with us as a band. Even [though] there were, like, really great groups in there—but what we did no one could compete with it, and what we did was, we locked as a group. I mean there were groups in there like the Ohio Players. Everybody went through there. But, when we were there, there would be, like, four cars deep in the street. I mean it was unprecedented when we worked there—when the band would be playing and we would be grooving—and when Curtis stepped on the stage, we went into another gear. It was an automatic thing. It was nothing practiced. It was like an automatic thing of guys working together, playing together, and listening to each other, which is something that doesn't happen now. It doesn't happen. Everybody's in their own world when they're playing.

Anyway, then we went into another gear ... and then another gear ... and another gear ... until it was like a static, like a whole trance thing with the audience. And this is something you don't get today. You do not get it. You know, it's like a rare occasion that people play together.[9]

The date December 11, 1964, became another dagger in Curtis's heart. His dear friend Sam Cooke had been shot dead. There were several conflicting, often unsubstantiated versions of the events leading up to Cooke's death, but the undisputable truth was this: Sam Cooke had been shot by Bertha Franklin, the night manager at the seedy Hacienda Motel in Los Angeles, California, and had died from a single bullet wound.

Album cover for *King Curtis Plays the Hits Made Famous by Sam Cooke. Capitol Records.*

Curtis was deeply troubled by the circumstances of Cooke's death, vocalizing his heavy sorrow and personal loss the only way he knew how: through his saxophone. He demanded to go immediately into the recording studio and recorded his next album for Capitol Records, *King Curtis Plays the Hits Made Famous by Sam Cooke.* The album cover says enough all by itself: Curtis sitting at the window seat of his second-floor Manhattan apartment, horn lying in his lap, wistfully gazing outside at Central Park. He badly misses his friend.

While many critics maintain the Supremes' album, *The Supremes: We Remember Sam Cooke,* as the gold standard for Sam Cooke tributes,

King Curtis's emotional nod to his fallen friend should also be considered as one of the definitive Sam Cooke eulogies. Mixing Cooke party songs such as "Twistin' the Night Away," "Having a Party," and "Shake," with successful ballads like "A Change Is Gonna Come," "You Send Me," and "Send Me Some Lovin'," with tenor sax and saxello, the album is by far Curtis's finest Capitol effort. Critic Bruce Eder heartily agrees:

> This is about the only Sam Cooke tribute record—other than individual songs cut by Otis Redding—that one could imagine Cooke himself not only would have approved of fully, but might have enjoyed himself, had it been recorded under other circumstances. One could even visualize him dancing to the versions of "Shake," which does have a few echoes of "Night Train" in it, or "Twistin' the Night Away" or "Good Times." Curtis had known and worked with Cooke, and the singer's shooting death late in 1964 affected the saxophonist deeply, as it did millions of people. This album was the result, a dozen covers that blow away most any other Sam Cooke tribute album (including the still highly collectible *The Supremes: We Remember Sam Cooke*).[10]

Capitol Records producer Dave Cavanaugh augments the album with his heartfelt liner notes, opining: "If he had never known Sam Cooke, King Curtis would still have felt very strongly about making this album. For Cooke and his songs have left a permanent impression on every soul musician. But King did know Sam—personally and professionally—and made several tours with him. So now you'll understand the extra breath of heart King blows into each of these masterpieces."[11] Cavanaugh closes by saying what anyone who has listened to this album would say: "If you already know King's work, you'll quickly agree he's at his best here. If this is your first session with King, you've picked a memorable one. It's so memorable that King's only regret is that Sam couldn't hear it himself as a testimony, instead of a tribute, to his greatness."[12]

As successful and critically acclaimed as this album would become, however, this was to be Curtis's last endeavor for Capitol Records. It was time to move on, time to look for new challenges and new direction. This was not about the money; nor was it about the mixed success he had shared with

Capitol. As he later explained to author Charlie Gillett, his exasperation with the major record label was artistic:

> They had 9-to-5 engineers in there who went specifically by what they had learned technically from a technical institute, that had no knowledge of recording a Fender bass or recording the drums to make them sound live. The guys just wouldn't cooperate. I know when producers have gotten into almost physical fights with the guys, like at Capitol. They'd say, yeah, and just wouldn't experiment. They would say this is how it is … most of those big companies don't know nothing about [the music]. They got a guy sitting there with his grey suit on, with his dog tie; he knows nothing about people and their music. He's not really concerned unless he can get concerned between 9 'til 5. Then he goes into his own little world.[13]

While the step up to Capitol had significantly increased Curtis's visibility in the world of rock and roll, jazz, and soul and had done reasonably well commercially, in his view it had come at a high cost. Curtis longed for the return of his creative freedom and the ability to be the one in control, to define himself. Having to shell out his own money to record his hit "Soul Serenade" because the Capitol producers were not interested was but one example of his frustrations with the label. With his three-year contract with Capitol Records expiring, Curtis would have the ability to take back control, review his career's direction, and decide where and how to take the next steps forward.

If Curtis had any doubts about leaving Capitol, his weighty decision was quickly validated as he landed a new major record label deal, found the love of his life, and took a seemingly minor detour that would march him straight into rock and roll history.

While traversing from record label to record label in the early 1960s, Curtis had never lost touch with his friend Jerry Wexler. Even though Curtis's initial Atlantic solo album in 1959 had not done well, the two continued to see each other often in the recording studio as well as socially around town at various musical haunts. Curtis also had a string of hit songs under his belt and was a much more successful and established artist this time around.

Wexler, as he had with so many other artists before and since, pounced on the available sax man by signing Curtis and his band to an Atlantic Records contract in 1965. This second stint at Atlantic was characterized by a much better match between the contemporary culture of the recording company and the matured Texas Tenor. Curtis became cemented as a permanent fixture at Atlantic Records. King Curtis was finally home.

Curtis was freed from the shackles of previous record companies that had tried to control him and mold him into their view of Sam "The Man" Taylor: just recording songs, not creating them, never allowing for more individual personal expression. Ahmet Ertegun and Jerry Wexler would grant Curtis the freedom to explore and expand his creativity and to ascend to his rightful throne as king of the saxophone, where he would stay for the remainder of the decade.

Curtis jumped back into the Atlantic studio on July 22, 1965, cutting the first song for his first "next-time-around" Atlantic album, *That Lovin' Feeling*. The song, "Spanish Harlem," would later spend five weeks on the *Billboard* pop chart, peaking at number 89. He would record the remainder of the album over the next few months.

Atlantic Records was not just any record label to Curtis: they became family. Curtis would also meet and befriend the magnificent group of studio engineers at Atlantic, among them Tom Dowd, Arif Mardin, and Joel Dorn. Mardin, who had first been hired as Ahmet Ertegun's assistant at Atlantic in January 1963, told me his appreciation for the level of talent he saw in Curtis: "I met King Curtis, you know, in the corridors and we would be doing stuff together, experiment in the studio, and he would play—in fact, I have some CDs of him playing three instruments on one of my pieces: bass guitar, baritone and tenor sax. He played them all. And Curtis was a friend. He took me by the hand, and he helped me. So that was a friendship and a musical relationship at the same time."[14]

Curtis also continued his extended term as leader of the house band at Small's Paradise. On a particular Harlem evening at Small's in 1965, a young female acquaintance of Curtis's named Modeen Broughton (who later became Modeen Brown) had an idea. As she later told me:

I went there to introduce him to my girlfriend. We went to his performance, and we were sitting down front—he came offstage and came over to talk with us and then went back on to do the other part of his show and asked if I would have breakfast with him after. Of course, I said, "No, but my friend will have breakfast with you." Her name was Karen Falter. He said again, "Can I take both of you to breakfast?" One thing led to another, and we went to breakfast and, I want to say it was the Braxfree; everybody hung out after hours in New York.[15]

Beauty contest winner, Modeen Broughton. *Courtesy of Modeen Brown.*

Brown, a stunning model and a single mother of five, had struck out to New York City from her home in Sarasota, Florida, to make her mark while leaving her children in the care of her ex-mother-in-law back in Southwest Florida: "I had five children when I met Curtis. I had purchased a house in Sarasota and put my children there with their father's mother. She lived there, and it was like a second home for me—I commuted back and forth."[16]

Having legally separated from his wife, Ethelyn, earlier in 1964, Curtis was ready to move on to a new relationship. And Brown had no interest in him:

> I keep getting on the other side and putting her [Karen] next to Curtis. Curtis keeps talking to me. He was playing Philadelphia the next day and said, "Why don't you come to Philadelphia to my concert tomorrow? I'll have my driver pick you up, and I'm not staying over." I said, "No." and he said, "Yes." I said no to going to Philadelphia, and he was on the phone bright and early the next morning and said, "I'm not staying over; I am just going down and coming back." His driver, Norman [Dugger], will drive us down, and we'll come back.
>
> We start talking, and finally I decided that I would ride with him to Philadelphia to hear him play the theater there. It is an old theater in Philadelphia [the Uptown] where everybody used to play—so we drove down for that—and we drove back, and the rest is history. Funny how I wind up with him instead.[17]

Modeen laughed at the surprising immediacy of the connection between the two, particularly because they had met under the auspices of setting up her friend with Curtis, and she had had no designs on him. She didn't fall for him right away: "It was one of those things [where] I had no eyes for him. I wanted to be his friend, and I wanted to introduce him to my friend, who is a lovely girl; she was a nurse, and we lived in the same building and we had dinner and breakfast together. I just had come out of a relationship with someone and just wasn't ready for meeting anybody. Somehow he [Curtis] was the pushy type."[18]

And that "someone" who had been in a previous relationship with Modeen? None other than Lloyd Price, who launched a major hit with the recording of his number 1 song "Lawdy Miss Clawdy" in 1952. The tune stayed atop the R&B song list for seven weeks. Price regretted the end of

Out on the town: Modeen, Curtis, Karen Falter, and Erma and
Cornell Dupree. *Courtesy of Modeen Brown.*

his relationship with Modeen and would jokingly let Curtis know it every
time he saw him around town. Laughing as she recalled these incidents,
Modeen said, "Every time he saw Curtis, he would yell, 'There goes the
guy that stole my girl!'"[19]

From that moment on, Curtis and Modeen were inseparable compan-
ions. Curtis never wanted to be away from Modeen for long, and the pair
quickly moved in together. For the rest of their life together, they would
never be separated for more than a day or two (short of the rare lengthy international tour). If Curtis's travels would last more than that, Modeen would
either accompany him the entire tour or meet up with him a day or so later:
"I traveled with him a lot. Curtis loved company, and if he was going someplace for over three or four days and if I didn't go with him, I came right
behind him. We spent a lot of time together and it wasn't that I always went
to his shows, but I was there to have dinner with him and if I wanted to go to

the show, fine, if not I didn't have to. If he was going to be anywhere for ten days, I was there for half."[20]

Although working far away in New York, Modeen did not regret the challenges her arrangement created for her children back in Sarasota:

> They lived well for children that had one parent. Their father lived in Sarasota, but because they lived with his mother, he didn't really feel the responsibility of really doing for them the way I did, and his mother didn't make him. I remember saying to my ex-husband that "I would never ask [you] for anything for my kids again," and I was off to New York. I purchased a home for them and sent them all through college; my kids didn't have any scholarships or loans. I started my business [coordinating charity events], and they do work for me. I paid them enough for the summer to pay their tuition.[21]

And her secret to maintaining any consistent level of discipline and structure with her five children while being a very distant fifteen hundred miles away? Laughing loudly, Modeen sheepishly responded: "I think they were afraid that I would *kill* them. My favorite thing I would say to my kids used to be, 'I'm two hours and thirty-five minutes off of your behind.' I would threaten them a lot that I was going to kill them."[22]

What did Curtis make of this impressive woman's many offspring? "He loved children," said Modeen, smiling. "Then it became at a point when my first daughter went away to college, and she would not call me for money. She would catch Curtis, because Curtis would give her anything. I would say, 'You are on an allowance; you spent it and that's it.' He would do it without me even knowing. He was good to old people and to young people. My kids loved him and still talk about him."[23] Noticeably proud of all her children, Modeen rightfully boasted:

> I have five kids and all five have graduate degrees and masters'. One is a doctor, and they are all doing well. They knew that when they came out of college, they had to have it together—that is the way I was raised. My mother died when I was two years old, and her sister and her husband raised me. That is the only mother and father that I knew. I got married young and I didn't go to college. ... I decided that I wanted to go to New York, and I asked my mother if she would

keep my kids and she said, 'No, I raised you and I'm finished.' When my kids came along it was like, 'Okay you're going to college whether you want to or not. You are going if you plan to live (because I didn't have a college degree and I was just blessed, but I stepped in the right places), but you are going to college if I have to drag you there.' It was easier to go to college than listen to me.[24]

On the surface, the two lovers could not have been more dissimilar. Curtis was the night owl of the pair, always finishing club dates between ten p.m. and two a.m. and wanting to immediately go out and have some fun afterward. Modeen, on the other hand, needed her sleep. Her plan was to get home from work as soon as possible and get to bed as fast as she could, waking up by ten or eleven p.m. (whenever Curtis came home or would call) to be ready to hit the town with her man.

The band's early reaction to the new woman in Curtis's life, however, was initially mixed. "I know myself and everyone who was close to Curtis

It was obvious to all: Curtis only had eyes for Modeen.
Courtesy of Modeen Brown.

was jealous of Modeen and really didn't like her at first until we realized that he was in love with her," said guitarist Cornell Dupree. "She is here to stay."[25] In fact, Modeen and Cornell's wife, Erma, would become fast friends, spending hours together, even when their men were in town. "Curtis was closer with Cornell than anybody in his group socially, because I was close to Cornell's wife," recalled Modeen. "The four of us, even if the men were not working, it was like we would have dinner or we would go out, and Erma and I would chat and Curtis and Cornell would be in the room writing new things. They always had something going on. I don't remember Curtis ever being without Dupree as a musician."[26]

Cornell Dupree smiled when he recalled the humorous conclusion of one particular night out gambling with Curtis when they got separated from the women: "I remember some scene when we went to [Mickey] Baker's and we separated there. Me and Curtis went gambling. Curtis lost the car, and we were walking back to the hotel and they [Modeen and Erma] passed us right by in a taxi."[27] Needless to say, the ladies didn't even think to stop and pity, much less assist, their disheartened men. They just drove right on by, gleefully laughing, taunting and waving out the taxi windows as they passed the humiliated gamblers into the night.

Modeen would not only play an integral part in Curtis's love life, she also became a critical piece to his professional one. She became the official bookkeeper for all the King Curtis bands, from studio to live versions, overseeing the finances for Curtis and paying the band members, allocating expenses, and so forth. Modeen would also oversee paying Curtis himself, something the two would joke about for years to come:

> I would give Curtis five thousand dollars at a time and put the rest away because he loved to gamble. And he knew, if he lost five thousand dollars, that was it, there was no more money. Yes, he loved to gamble—that was one of his things; he was hard to control. He used to complain to me about this often, between laughs, claiming he was "the hardest working man," the "brokest man in the world," because I took all of his money. "She takes all of my money—she gives me an allowance, and I walk around and I have no money"—it was like a joke. He was out of control with the gambling part because he loved to gamble. One thing that I admired about him was that he never touched

savings [and] he would never bother with stocks. What I used to do with him when he signed a contract and I got the check: I would put X amount of dollars over to pay the band and pay the bills, and then I would put the other in the stock market where it was out of sight. He wouldn't touch it if it wasn't there, but if it was in the checking account it was like play money, no value for it.[28]

The year 1965 also brought Curtis together with comedian Soupy Sales when both performed on April 17 at the Paramount Theatre in New York. The show also featured the Hullabaloos, the Detergents, Shirley Ellis, the Hollies, Little Richard, Joe Stampley and the Uniques, the Vibrations, Dee Dee Warwick, and Sandie Shaw. Previously, the two had worked together in the studio to cut Soupy's novelty single, "The Mouse," earlier in March of that year for ABC-Paramount Records, so the two were very familiar with each other. Backstage at the Paramount, Curtis and Soupy continually cut up, bantering back and forth all night long to the continual amusement of the other performers.

Bobby Elliott, the drummer for the band the Hollies, famous for hits such as "He Ain't Heavy, He's My Brother," "Bus Stop," and "The Air that I Breathe," told me he remembered the date well:

We had arrived at the Paramount a few hours late. There was a problem with the US Immigration, and the Hollies' visas were late in being issued. Graham Nash and I began exploring the backstage area. At the bottom of some concrete steps that led to the bowels of the theater, we found a door, which we slowly dragged open. It was very dark, but through the pot-laden atmosphere and the twinkling eyes, a lone voice [Curtis] drawled, "Hey, where's Ringo?," followed by much mirthful laughter.

It was the sixteen-piece King Curtis Orchestra assembled on the stage, which was about to be raised. They'd heard our Northern English accents, and the Beatles were massive. Showtime! The band kicks up and the stage began to raise, transporting the screaming horns and rhythm section up to stage level where they would join King Curtis and the dancers for the opening number.

The Soupy Sales Easter Show ran for about ten days over the holiday period. At nine a.m. every day a film would be screened—I think it was *The Unsinkable Molly Brown*. Then the live show would run, then the film again, right through to about ten p.m.

Our dressing room was upstairs next door to King Curtis's room. I used to pop in and chat to his valet and KC's son, Curtis. I remember seeing dozens of pairs of highly shined shoes around the place and racks of cool-looking suits. KC was always friendly, and we'd chat about music and his band and record companies. He had a pronounced lisp when he spoke, which probably enabled him to get that unique sound out of his horn. On the final day, as we were saying goodbye, I asked him to sign the photo in my theater program, which I still have today. He wrote, "To my friend Bob."[29]

Regardless of whatever major musical event Curtis played, he always left a distinctly positive impression on every performer in attendance. His talent, kindness, and support of his fellow artists were always unforgettable.

Chapter 9

The Beatles and Hendrix

Forty-six-year-old Sid Bernstein had an itch that just had to be scratched. After previously spending four years as a successful booking agent under Lee and Billy Shaw at the Shaw and Associates Agency in New York, in 1959 Bernstein became a concert promoter. He wanted to attract a band, pay for the venue, control the logistics, and promote the heck out of the event, all the while possibly turning a profit. Experts in this field could do quite well, but the risks, both financial and professional, were frightening. The economic reward and social stature that he could generate, however, was only half the motivation for Bernstein. He also longed to direct musical experiences for the public, to have a hand in the quality and quantity of the entertainment he could provide for the populace of New York City.[1]

After his first effort at promoting proved a success—a Miles Davis concert (with Ruth Brown as the opening act) for the Apollo Theatre in 1959—Bernstein was quickly on the fast track to organizing some of the most memorable concerts in New York City. By late March 1963, the now seasoned promoter had his interest piqued by four mop-topped young men from Liverpool, England. He noted that the lads had set the entire continent of Europe on fire with their music, humor, shaggy good looks, and light-hearted personalities. From London to Munich to Copenhagen, the youth of Europe were consumed by this musical infestation, and Bernstein had the vision to bring them to America. So, Sid Bernstein picked up the phone and dialed the manager for the Beatles, Brian Epstein.

The Beatles were just beginning to get some infrequent air play in the States, and Bernstein thought the time was ripe to bring the boys to the United States. After coming to terms with their manager, the Beatles were booked for February 12, 1964, to perform in New York City.

On January 27, 1964, two weeks before the Beatles first appeared on television's *The Ed Sullivan Show*, tickets for the concert went on sale at the Carnegie Hall ticket office and all 2,830 seats sold out in a record forty minutes, with hundreds turned away at the door. The ticket manager told Bernstein they could have sold the tickets for four times the price, which was $5.50. Sid Bernstein's uncanny intuition to bring the international group from England had paid off, but he was far from done.

Rather than resting on his laurels, Bernstein dreamed bigger. By the time 1965 rolled around, though, even those who knew him well thought Sid Bernstein, now the "Golden Boy" of the New York concert scene, had finally lost his marbles. He called Beatles manager Brian Epstein again with a new idea. Sid Bernstein now wanted to book the Beatles at the home of the New York Mets professional baseball team, the fifty-five-thousand-seat Shea Stadium.

Epstein was completely bewildered by the mountainous scale of the proposed event and initially refused. He eventually had to give in to Bernstein's guarantee of $100,000 for the group, with $50,000 up front, a preposterous sum of money at the time.

Bernstein now turned his attention to the concert bill, looking to source reliable and professional warm-up bands to kick off the concert. This was not just any concert event, and he felt the opening acts were critical to setting the right tone for the evening. His first stop was a visit to his previous employers, Shaw and Associates. As he told me: "The Shaws presented King Curtis to me to see if I wanted to use the Kingpins to open for the Beatles. Curtis was so easygoing and such a lovely man, I thought the Kingpins was a great idea."[2] The Shaws had been saddened by the earlier departure of one of their best employees, but there was no animosity, and they were happy for Bernstein and his incredible success. They also realized that opening for the Beatles would be tremendous exposure for their star saxophone player and his band.

There were still significant concerns. For one thing, no one had ever hosted a live concert of this magnitude, anywhere. Bernstein needed to worry about the facilities and personnel to support a fifty-five-thousand-fan crowd: the stage, the insurance, and foremost in Brian Epstein's mind, the security for the Beatles and all their fans in the stands.

It was planned that triple barricades would be erected between the stands and the baseball field where the Beatles would perform on a stage erected over second base. Along with the obligatory security personnel and ushers, off-duty New York City policemen would act as the second wave behind the initial buffer line of standard stadium security ringing the field. Additionally, Bernstein would hire forty black-belt karate experts, ostensibly to perform before the concert, but also conveniently to serve as the final barrier of security that any hysterical fan would have to negotiate when rushing to get to the Fab Four onstage. Sid Bernstein had taken every precaution available to insure against any misguidedly overenthusiastic fan having even a small chance to reach the Beatles.

The day of the concert, Bernstein was understandably nervous and reviewed every topic over and over with a fine-tooth comb, detail upon detail. Evaluating the final inspection with one of Brian Epstein's assistants, the staffer observed that there was no piano on the stage. "I looked at the assistant," Bernstein recalled, "and countered, 'The Beatles don't need a piano' to which the assistant replied, 'No, but King Curtis does!'"[3]

Stunned, Bernstein had to catch his breath; he was mortified. He immediately sought out King Curtis and began to apologize profusely. This was exactly what he had feared—that while trying to remember every single detail necessary for a safe and successful concert, he would let something slip through the cracks. Curtis replied, "'Don't you dare apologize. Forget about it. No one will even notice that there is no piano!'"[4] Bernstein was forever grateful to Curtis for his understanding and patience in an extremely difficult situation.

On August 15, 1965, the night of the Shea stadium concert and the opening date for their national tour, the Beatles were sequestered off-site for security purposes, and they never saw (much less heard) the opening acts. After tuning up, King Curtis performed the national anthem. A performance by the Discotheque Dancers followed, and then it was time for King Curtis and his band.

Prominent New York deejay Cousin Brucie introduced the assistant music director at 1010 WINS radio station in New York, who was also a popular deejay for WBIC in Long Island, Scott Ross. As Ross stepped to the microphone, he was shocked at the frenzy in the crowd and could be overheard chuckling: "Young lady over there jumped up and ripped her girdle, unbelievable." Realizing his microphone was on, Ross regained his composure and said to the crowd, "Alright, we're going to be here for quite some time, and I want to bring on a group. Fantastic. You remember their records of 'Soul Twist' and 'Soul Serenade.' Here now is King Curtis!"[5]

The band launches into a feverish cover of Ray Charles's "What'd I Say." They follow with "The Branch" and finish their set with Curtis's number 1 hit, "Soul Twist." It appeared that Sid Bernstein's omission of a piano for the band was a non-factor. Lead guitarist Cornell Dupree remembered vividly: "It was incredible to see all these kids fainting and falling over the banisters. It was really mad. We pushed out and rushed to the stage and did our thing. I don't even know if they heard us."[6] And the hysteria was not left only to those who attended Shea Stadium that night, for Dupree observed the rest of the national tour met with equal pandemonium: "In some cases, especially when the Beatles would try to exit, they would have to get cops to get the people out of the way. They were beating on the cars; I've never seen anything like it, before or after."[7] Bass player Chuck Rainey was just as confounded, not only by the hysterical crowds, but by the Beatles, as well:

Well, it was definitely incredible. Now, I had been in Jackie Wilson's band. Jackie Wilson, also, too, drew a very large audience for those kinds of things. As a matter of fact, when I was with Jackie, it was—those were very large audiences. It held twenty-five hundred, three thousand people. It was very, very successful. Going to Shea

Stadium—it was quite an experience. I can say that for the first time, for me in particular—and I had been around a bit and worked a whole lot of dances and stuff—but this was incredible in that the place was so big, and one interesting thing about that was: it was a gig, and we, the band members, we had no idea at all who the Beatles were. We had no idea of their music, and we had no idea of their popularity. We didn't know who they were, just a white band from Europe called the Beatles, and they were cute and all the stuff like that, so we did not listen to the music. We were unaware of the music. All we knew was that we had a gig, and it was a gig that was going on the road for about two weeks.[8]

To maximize the security of their entrance, Sid Bernstein had arranged for the Beatles to hop into helicopters off-site and head for Shea Stadium. They would land on the roof of the World's Fair Building in Queens, disembark, and then jump into armored cars for the drive onto the Shea Stadium field. After entering the infield, the trucks slowed to a crawl, then to a stop, just in front of the stage. The crowd went berserk. As the four young lads leapt out and jogged to the stage, waving to the convulsing crowd, fifty-five thousand people erupted in unison, filling the New York City sky with screams and flashbulbs, many people fainting on the spot. Everyone has seen the videos of hysterical girls climbing the chain-link fence behind home plate trying to get closer to the singers, sobbing uncontrollably.

The rest of the two-week, ten-city tour was equal parts delirium, bewilderment, and excitement, coupled with a modicum of fear. Everyone loved it. Chuck Rainey remembered:

I think we did nine or ten concerts on that particular tour. Flying into an airport where there were just thousands of screaming girls, and up in Wisconsin or Montana, wherever that gig was, they broke down a barrier and rushed to the plane before we got off the plane. That was very, very dangerous. You know, I've had my shirt—my shirt was torn at least five, six times when they pulled at it, you know, but just being associated with that particular tour made us all very important to the eye, which makes you feel good, more so than usual, you know, with other gigs. But the Beatles tour of '65 was—I mean, I really enjoyed it.[9]

Drummer Ray Lucas also found the entire Shea Stadium / 1965 Beatles tour experience completely unforgettable:

> It started at Shea Stadium. We played some of Curtis's tunes and backed up some other acts from the States that were opening up the show [Brenda Holloway, Cannibal and the Headhunters, and Sounds Incorporated]. We really didn't have to be there. We just added more excitement to the fact that they were coming. Ringo and I had never met, but we had the exact same drum kit, Ludwigs, oyster-gray pearl. He's lookin' at me and I'm lookin' at him. ... [laughs]. We spoke a few times. On the first two or three days we all rode on the same plane. After that they had their own plane and we had ours.[10]

Short of the piano he omitted from the stage at Shea Stadium, Sid Bernstein had thought of everything. Even the Beatles' tour jet had been specifically outfitted with all sorts of food and drink for the tour members' enjoyment. While on the plane, King Curtis and Brian Epstein shot craps at a gambling table especially installed. To no one's surprise, it's been reported that Curtis won a tremendous amount of money from Epstein over the entire length of the tour.[11]

Ray Lucas continued:

> When they [the Beatles] checked into a hotel they had three floors. They were in the middle and they had security above and below. And every day it was a mob. I'd never seen anything like that. People just wanted to be around the Beatles. They were magic. At the Cow Palace, there were fifty-five-thousand people in front of the stage. They were sold out everywhere, all the biggest places. The crowd was always screaming. You couldn't even hear their singing! After that tour was over, we had to sign a waiver. We couldn't associate ourselves with the Beatles at all. We couldn't even have a marquee outside a club that said, 'Just back from a tour with the Beatles.[12]

The last stop on the tour was the Cow Palace in San Francisco. The opening acts performed, then decided to stick around as they had not had an opportunity to really see the Beatles run onto the stage and perform. Chuck Rainey, the accomplished bass player who had played with Jackie Wilson and was now a mainstay in one of the most popular studio and live bands in the R&B industry with King Curtis, was struck, as were his band-mates and all the performers, by the level of talent and synergy shared by the English youngsters onstage:

> At the Cow Palace something happened—where our dressing room was so far away from the stage that after we played in that immediate area, we just put up our instruments. And rather than go back to the dressing rooms, because we were looking at all these screaming girls and all these people, and we wanted them to just look at [the show], and so we stayed around and listened to the Beatles. We had never heard them play before. And listening to the music, I was just blown away, and how four people had such good harmony. And played so well together."[13]

Rainey's respect for the lad's collective talent, however, was tempered by the significant differences in their personalities: "We had enjoyed ourselves immensely with John and with George, who were very, very compassion-ate and very, very warm toward us, whereas Ringo and Paul were just ... just very, very snobbish. Didn't speak to anybody. Stayed in their part of the plane, whereas George and John came back and played cards. We talked. Every hotel we went to, the Beatles had one floor to themselves, and John and George were always on our floor, talking to us, having fun."[14]

By opening for the Beatles at Shea Stadium, King Curtis's band would become a part of rock and roll legend. Because of Sid Bernstein's courageous vision and ability to pull off the event as seamlessly as he did, concert promoters the world over now took notice of what were previously thought to be uncontrollable, impossibly large concert venues, to maximize the gross revenue provided by these new outdoor locales. Nowadays fans do not think twice about attending a concert at a major sports stadium. The repercussions of this single successful event in music history are still being enjoyed today, thanks to Sid Bernstein, the godfather of the outdoor stadium concert.

After the Beatles tour, Curtis looked to shake up the band a bit, so he renamed it King Curtis and the Kingpins and started looking for a second guitar player. A certain young left-handed guitar player from Seattle, Wash-ington, would soon look to become the newest member of the band.[15]

Jimi Hendrix playing at a party in Curtis and Modeen's apartment,
1966. *Courtesy of Modeen Brown.*

In Sharon Lawrence's biography, Jimi Hendrix is quoted as saying:
"I had to be quick to pick up what King wanted, and I think I did a pretty
good job. Cornell Dupree, a very pure player, was on lead guitar. Bernard
'Pretty' Purdie and Ray Lucas alternated as drummers. Chuck Rainey played
bass, *great* bass. They were the classiest musicians I had ever played with.
I did some recording with them, too."[16]

After Hendrix's audition in early 1966, King Curtis instantly hired
him. Curtis, while always championing opportunities for young musicians
(as his friends Doc Pomus and Mickey Baker had extended to him earlier),
nevertheless gave sparse praise to young artists, especially early in the
acquaintance. New musicians had to earn their place, just as he had with
the local New York City nightclub market:—it's what you did with that
opportunity that defined you and then earned the appropriate plaudits and
respect. In this instance, Curtis was completely impressed with Hendrix's
talents. As Curtis had also played guitar on several albums, he already had

Hendrix, in uniform, tuning up before a King Curtis and the Kingpins performance. *Courtesy of Modeen Brown.*

a deep understanding and appreciation for Hendrix, who could do things on his guitar that Curtis could not believe. "I remember his words," recalled Modeen, "He said, 'Jimi Hendrix has to be the most talented artist I've ever met. We go into the studio, and I can tell him that I want to record something, and I play it once, and Jimi Hendrix plays it note for note.' He really admired Jimi Hendrix."[17]

Jimi Hendrix thought that his association with King Curtis and the Kingpins would surely provide the critical visibility necessary for him to land his coveted goal of a solo recording contract. He had the appropriate self-confidence to become a star. "Not bragging," he said of his high hopes back then, "but I was greatly improved from the way I was playin' in 1963. Some nights, I swear to you, I just sizzled!"[18]

In addition to Hendrix's uncanny, King Curtis–like ability to instantly pick up and accompany any song onstage or in the studio without rehearsal, he possessed charisma. Fellow Kingpin Cornell Dupree also remembered playing with Hendrix and his magnetic stage presence, oblivious to any issues it ever created with his fellow musicians. "He played [with the Kingpins] … it might have been about five or six months. We traveled quite a bit. I remember once we opened for Chuck Berry and Jimi stole the show. Chuck didn't like that very well, because Jimi was doing his thing. He had that certain something about him."[19]

Drummer Ray Lucas also found Jimi Hendrix intriguing: "Jimi Hendrix, man, you're talking about one of the nicest guys. He was so kind and courteous. He played with his teeth and all that, but he could play. Jimi would play Curtis's tunes and then do some of his own. He would sing more or less down-home blues, rather than the psychedelic things he got into later. We were doing mainly contemporary tunes. He stayed with us for about six months, and then he went on his own."[20]

When the band would get together at Small's Paradise to rehearse before a tour, Lucas was spellbound by Hendrix's talent:

On a lot of songs that Jimi didn't know, the bass player had to whisper the chords to him. But I never, in all my fucking life, saw anybody pick up songs as fast as Jimi did that night. Jimi and I used to play together in the studio, just me and him. He'd try all kinds of different things. He'd plug into the Leslie speaker from the organ. I'd play a backbeat or a shuffle or whatever. This went on for maybe two or three weeks. It was a studio on Fifty-Fourth Street. That's how he built his recordings. I never heard any of the final versions. One day a little later I ran into Jimi on the street downtown. He said, 'Hey, Ray, what are you doing?' He said, 'Man, I got my passport and my papers from the State Department. I've been trying to do my thing here, but it's not working out that great. I just got an offer from England. If you want to do it, I can get the finances together. Do you want to come with me?' Of all the drummers he knew, he asked me. I told him I couldn't do it, and in less than two years he was the biggest thing out there.[21]

Drummer Bernard Purdie also was spellbound by Hendrix's talent: "On a lot of songs that Jimi didn't know, the bass player had to whisper the chords to him. But I never, in all my life, saw anybody pick up songs as fast as Jimi did that night. In a couple of days he knew everything, so he didn't have any problem."[22]

There was a May 5, 1966, Atlantic Records celebration party for Percy Sledge's number 1 hit, "When a Man Loves a Woman," at the Prelude Club in New York. The song, released a month earlier in April, achieved number 1 status on both the *Billboard* Top 100 and R&B charts. Atlantic had King Curtis and his band (including Jimi Hendrix) backing Esther Phillips, among others, during the event. Steven Roby and Brad Schreiber's Hendrix biography noted that Sledge was also completely impressed by Jimi Hendrix: "After the show, I approached Curtis. I told him, 'I'd really like to steal your guitar player.' Curtis said he hoped to hang onto Jimi for at least another year or so, but after that, nobody would be able to hold him down. He's sure to be a superstar."[23]

Jimi Hendrix, for all his limitless talents, was also a bit odd. Modeen and everyone else in the band were keenly aware that their newest addition was a little off-center. Modeen smiled and said: "Jimi Hendrix was weird, because I wrote the checks for all the musicians after work. Jimi would play and he would disappear after they played, and he would come back for the next gig and that is when I would give him his check. Most guys were waiting

Esther Phillips backed by King Curtis, Cornell Dupree,
and Jimi Hendrix. *Courtesy of PoPsie Photos.*

for their money; Jimi would play, get off the stage, and he would go on."[24]
Cornell Dupree observed:

> When I knew him, Jimi was a pretty quiet guy. He never really had
> too much to say unless something was drastically wrong—unless you
> stepped on his foot or harmed him. He would go off by himself or just
> disappear. You'd never see him 'til it was time to go to work.
>
> He would always find someplace to go—be it in a strange city.
> We would get there, and we didn't know anything about anybody.
> He would always find a party or something to do, no matter what time
> and where it was. He was kind of a 'hound' [one who chases women]
> you might say.
>
> We might be going for three or four [performances] a day.
> He would have a couple of clean shirts and his toothbrush when we go
> on the road and that is all he took, along with his guitar.[25]

Hendrix would also record a number of songs with King Curtis
and the Kingpins, most notably on several Ray Sharpe tunes, such as

"Help Me," a song very similar in structure to "Gloria" by Van Morrison's band, Them.

Accounts vary of Hendrix's abrupt departure from the Kingpins a few months later, in the summer of 1966. Some versions claim that Curtis fired him because he refused to adhere to the band dress code—or, more accurately, the band uniform—and wear cuff links. Keyboardist Jimmy Smith, who was not in the band at the time, stated: "I forgot who told me that on the last night ... they were doing a gig somewhere and Jimi came in late, walked into the crowd with his tuxedo rolled over the guitar or something like that. He was all shabby-looking and coming through the audience with his guitar in one hand and clothes in the other hand. He got halfway up there, and the guys were laughing at him. And he just stopped and turned around and walked back out, and that was his last night with the band."[26]

Bass player Chuck Rainey had this perspective on the future rock and roll star's early exodus from the band: "Jimi left us shortly after that show, but it wasn't over money. Curtis always paid on time, right after a gig. Like me, he must have got tired of playing the same songs over and over again, like 'Misty' and 'When a Man Loves a Woman.' I still get sick to my stomach every time I hear those songs."[27]

Years later, when queried by interviewer George Massey on the rumor that Hendrix was fired due to a uniform violation, Cornell Dupree commented: "I don't know what particular reason why Jimi left, but Curtis had to be in uniform. Every time he performed, he was in uniform. I never heard anything about [Hendrix] not being in uniform."[28]

Jimi Hendrix's roommate at the time, Dean Courtney, claimed an alternative version of the events leading to Hendrix's exit from the band. One evening, shortly after leaving for a gig with King Curtis at the Sheraton Hotel, Hendrix returned to the apartment to borrow Courtney's tuxedo. Soon after leaving for a second time, Hendrix abruptly returned again. "Jimi," Courtney recalled, "in his Snagglepuss voice, said, 'He pissed me off. I told King Curtis go kiss my ass ...' He said King was talking down to him about coming back late and not having a tux. He reprimanded him right onstage, right in front of the crowd, so Jimi just walked out."[29]

Hendrix did have a history of wearing out his welcome with bandleaders and having challenges with punctuality. Shortly after leaving King Curtis and the Kingpins, he became the guitar player for Stax Records's duo, Sam and Dave, who had hit gold with their song "Hold On! I'm Comin'" in June 1966. Hendrix's very first date playing with his new band was at a midtown New York club. Lead singer Sam Moore recalled Hendrix's brief tenure with the band: "He plugged in," said Moore, "We start doing 'Hold On! I'm Comin',' and he starts doin' this *nawaaaaahhh*. You know how Jimi played. I cut my eyes over at him. Next time I go over to him and said, 'There is no solo there, Jimi. Stop.'"[30] When Hendrix repeated his interpretation of a solo yet again, Moore fired him on the spot.

While Courtney's version of Jimi being fired by Curtis is certainly feasible, other, more probable versions of Hendrix's departure from King Curtis and the Kingpins note that Hendrix realized the time had come for him to strike out on his own and pursue his own personal freedom to play music his way, not unlike Curtis eschewing Capitol Records for the artistic haven that Atlantic Records finally provided. Remember, Kingpin drummer Ray Lucas had been invited by Hendrix to join him in England for a new opportunity, so it would appear Hendrix had already strategized and set in motion his next career step. Rather than being fired, he chose to leave the group on his own for a better creative opportunity. Though Curtis was a noted stickler for rules and consistency from his band, it seems ridiculous that he would jettison such an extreme talent over nothing more than a superfluous uniform-code violation.

Curtis had spoken to Percy Sledge earlier, mentioning that he hoped to keep Jimi in the band for, at best, a year. But after that, he realized, "nobody would be able to hold him down." Curtis envisioned no realistic long-term prognosis for Jimi staying with the band.

Jimi Hendrix's creative musical oasis lay across the Atlantic Ocean, in England, where he would make his fame and fortune. With the immediacy of his resultant superstardom, who is to argue with his logic?

Chapter 10

Queen Aretha

With no time to rest from the exhausting, exhilarating 1965 Beatles tour, the new year opened with Curtis back in the Atlantic recording studio, now producing songs for Atlantic's subsidiary Atco with the Coasters, as well as recording his own Atlantic album, *That Lovin' Feeling*. But the landscape for King Curtis and the Kingpins was now, in Curtis's view, very fluid. Concerned with creative stagnation, he wanted to change things up with his band again, both in the studio and on the road.

A June 16, 1966, Atlantic Records date for Solomon Burke would match Curtis with a new drummer that would soon become not only his mainstay on the road but also in the recording studio, as well as a dear friend. Born in Elkton, Maryland, Bernard "Pretty" Purdie was playing drums in bands at the age of fourteen. He left for Baltimore at age eighteen and attended Morgan State College for two years, then remained on the Baltimore music circuit for a few more years. Purdie arrived in New York City in 1961 and got his first job with the duo Mickey and Sylvia.

Purdie, yet another member of Mickey Baker's family of prodigies, would soon meet with King Curtis, already a well-established mainstay on Mickey and Sylvia recordings. Purdie told me: "I just got a lucky break, and I met Mickey and Sylvia at Sylvia's nightclub, and they asked me to play on 'Love is Strange.' They did a re-release of 'Love is Strange' [on the Willow label], a hit they had in 1957. They put it out again ... and it was a hit all over again."[1]

After his first week in New York City with Mickey Baker, Purdie met King Curtis. While Curtis had always been an ardent supporter of new artists, he never neglected to challenge musical neophytes, as he had been tested. If you wanted to play with King Curtis, you had better be prepared to *play*. Purdie laughed loudly, never having forgotten that humbling experience: "I mean, he had his band, and he had already heard of me through Mickey. All I wanted to do was sit in. That was the cause of it. Because in my profession, you gotta be ready and you gotta hang around. You really had to hang around for a long time to get your chance. And that's what I did. I hung around. I hung around. And then when I got a chance, he [Curtis] made me look like a fool."[2]

The cocky Purdie, thinking he could easily step in right away with King Curtis, received a rude awakening to how unprepared he really was. He elaborated in his autobiography:

When Curtis finally said, "Yes, come on!" I jumped up, came down, and was getting ready to sit down at the drum. As I was putting my leg across, Curtis started calls for "Sister Sadie." Curtis counts off "One, two" at a super-fast tempo. All I did was get my leg down. By the time I got my leg down he was already into the tune, and so the only thing I could do was hit cymbals, you know, I'm hitting cymbals. I haven't sat down yet. I hadn't sat down and wasn't able to adjust the seat or adjust anything. When I finally got a chance to sit down thirty-two bars later, he said, "You got it." Everybody in the band knew what was going on and they all walked off the stage. They all walked off the stage. I couldn't find one—I couldn't believe it. I couldn't believe it. All I could do was look at him and get mad. I couldn't say anything, because I was supposed to be ready. I kept telling him I was ready. I kept telling him I was ready, you know, "I can do it, I can do it." That son of a gun got me. So when I fumbled and stumbled and fell on my face and—you name it—I did it wrong, he goes back to the top of the song, and the song's over. Curtis says, "Thank you." I had to get up. I was so upset that I could have killed. I said, "I'll be ready next time that you play. I can do it. And I will be ready when you ask me again. And eventually you're going to ask me again because I'm going to worry you to death." There was nothing that I could say that night. The damage was done. I didn't stay around. I was totally humiliated. I was so upset, I cried all the way home. I had blown my shot. And now I got to figure out a way to get another one. I had to tell myself, "You'll be back. You'll be back every night that he's there."[3]

Purdie and Curtis would forge a mutual respect and musical collaboration that would take the two of them to the highest peaks of the music world. Purdie would be a critical building block to the next iteration of King Curtis's band, one of the great live concert and studio bands of the era.

Long-standing King Curtis and the Noble Knights drummer Ray Lucas would stay with the band and nearly finish out the year with Curtis in the recording studio. Initially, he was despondent when replaced in the Kingpins touring band by Bernard Purdie: "When Aretha came on the scene and Curtis started working more with her, he decided to dissolve the band and change things around. I thought the world was over. But I didn't fit. It had nothing to do with my drumming. There are certain things some drummers do and certain things other drummers do. I felt bad. But when I look back on it, it was the same thing as when I came in the band and replaced Belton Evans. I was the young upstart drummer then."[4]

Lucas was soon comforted by the discovery that, despite his unexpected exit from King Curtis and the Kingpins, he was still very popular with record labels:

Cool ain't nothin' when you go in the studio. When you go in the studio you've got to know how to make things work. You've got to find the part that works for the song and you have to set the pace of the song. Without that it's just a bland song. [*Lucas looks at a list of his recordings*]. Honestly, I forgot how many things I played on. I just played and went on to the next session. When I look at this list I really can't believe it. I was lucky. I had a chance to work with some of the best musicians. So if my landlord gets on me for not paying the rent, I should show him this list right? [laughs][5]

By 1966, Aretha Franklin's contract with Columbia Records was coming to an end. Her experience there was coincidentally similar to King Curtis's

experience with Capitol Records: a significant talent with inconsistent recording success. The daughter of a very visible Detroit preacher, the Rev. C. L.
Franklin, and an alumna of the church choir, Aretha had previously moved to
New York from her Detroit home at the age of eighteen to pursue her musical
career, much like Curtis. In 1960, Franklin had signed a five-year recording contract under the famous Columbia Records producer John Hammond,
which was extended one additional year. Having achieved only modest
success for the label by recording primarily jazz and pop songs that rarely
took advantage of her gospel roots, Aretha's commitment to Columbia had
come to an end by 1966. Jerry Wexler once more launched into the fray,
intent on landing the next notable member of the Atlantic Records group of
soul and pop talent. This time, he correctly envisioned that Aretha would not
just become a top performer for his label but would launch Atlantic into the
awareness of everyone within earshot of her music.

After signing Aretha Franklin to a contract, Wexler's focus was to
quickly get her into the recording studio. The backing musicians and location for this first Aretha and Atlantic collaboration were crucial, and Wexler
had in mind the perfect location: Rick Hall's Fame Studios in Muscle
Shoals, Alabama. Atlantic had recently enjoyed a tremendous run of quality
work with Fame's backing group of musicians, something akin to the early
cohesive bond shared by Jim Stewart's Stax Studio artists in Memphis,
Tennessee. Standard Fame musicians Jimmy Johnson on guitar, Spooner
Oldham on keyboards, and Roger Hawkins on drums, were augmented
with guitarists Tommy Cogbill and Chips Moman of Memphis, and Wexler
arrived with ace Atlantic engineer Tom Dowd in tow.

Jerry Wexler had a particular recording studio philosophy for working
with Aretha Franklin, as opposed to other Atlantic artists:

Well, I was the producer, so whatever I produced with Aretha, every
song had her full concurrence. There was no such thing as, like,
"Ya have to sing this song," or "You have to use *this* player." Also,
she would bring in songs; she probably brought in more material than
I did. So, when she brought in the songs, we would do it. So now, that
"Save Me," if you listen to the lick there, it's the same as Etta James's
"Tell Mama." And of course, "Tell Mama" was done in Muscle Shoals
[Fame Studios] several years before. See the parallel there?[6]

Moving forward from her Columbia experience and now able to explore her gospel origins more deeply as well as merge them with soul music, following a path not unlike the trail that Sam Cooke had blazed, Franklin felt rejuvenated. She and the band began to work out her song, "I Never Loved a Man (the Way I Love You)." Though frequently underestimated for her keyboard ability, Franklin covers piano on this first song for her debut Atlantic album. Keyboardist Spooner Oldham graciously yielded to cover the electric piano. While most in the studio knew precious little about the young Atlantic prodigy, they froze the minute her hands first hit a legendary "magic chord" at the keyboard to start their session that day. In Peter Guralnick's *Sweet Soul Music*, Spooner Oldham recalled: "I was hired to play keyboards, and when she came in the studio and hit this one masterful chord, I stopped and said, 'Now look. I'm not tryin' to cop out or nothing. I know I was hired to play piano but I wish you'd let her play that thing, and I could get on organ and electric."[7]

After hours of work and recording, the song was complete, and everyone in attendance knew it would change the world of soul music. Ask any of the musicians in the studio at Fame on that fateful day. Ask Dan Penn, writer of such Southern soul classics as "The Dark End of the Street," "Do Right Woman–Do Right Man," "Take Me (Just as I Am)," and others, one of the few in attendance who had any previous knowledge about Franklin, who had just happened along to watch history unfold. Ask Spooner Oldham, who gave up his seat at the piano to ensure Aretha covered the keyboard. Ask Jerry Wexler, who knew his new star had instantly charted her own ethereal constellation with his (and Tom Dowd's) critical direction. It was one of those once-in-a-lifetime moments that are so rare and timeless for any musician that everyone who was in Fame Studios that day still remembers it like it was yesterday.

Liquor quickly emerged, and the celebration began. But, as soon as the euphoric musicians settled back into the studio to record a second song, written by Dan Penn and Chips Moman, the session disintegrated. There were many people—Aretha and her husband, Ted White, included—that were deeply concerned, and had been before the session began, that there were no Black musicians other than Aretha in the studio.

According to Red Kelly of the "Soul Detective" website, Jerry Wexler
"used Chips Moman as his 'contractor,' as he had for the previous sessions at
Fame with Wilson Pickett, and it was up to Moman to put together the horn
section, a task which he would then delegate to Charlie Chalmers. In this case,
Charlie said, for one reason or another, he was unable to get his usual go-to
Memphis horn players (like Floyd Newman, James Mitchell and Bowlegs
Miller), and so had to hire a couple of white 'reading' players that worked at
Pepper Sound Studio in Memphis."[8]

Couple the euphoric emotions of the moment with the massive
amounts of alcohol, then turn up the heat on the simmering racial undercurrent coursing throughout the studio, and suddenly you have a pressure
cooker ready to burst. The lighter to the fuse of this impending explosion
was one of the backing band's horn players, who now ignited a near riot
in the studio with Aretha's husband, Ted White.

The Pepper studio's horn player Ken Laxton has been widely
rumored to have insulted or offended Aretha in some way. Red Kelly
stated that what Laxton said was: "'Man, she sure sings her ass off.' It was
White who was the aggressor, saying something like 'What you say about
my wife's ass, white boy?' from which there would be no turning back.
Wexler had Rick Hall fire Laxton on the spot, but nothing was going to
calm White down."[9]

Sufficiently angered, Ted White whisked his wife back to their hotel in
a huff. Rick Hall went to the hotel in an attempt to smooth over all the high
emotion, but his efforts at diplomacy with White immediately escalated to
loud arguing and fisticuffs. By the next morning, everyone was headed back
to New York City, the session now cancelled. The previous day's euphoria
was now replaced by a deep and dark disappointment for all. A brooding
Jerry Wexler returned to New York City with only one complete song and a
monstrously foul mood to go with it.

Back home in New York City at Atlantic, the cowed but not defeated
Wexler sought to smooth the racial imbalance in the studio as well as
complete the remaining production of Aretha's album. His first decision
was a natural solution: transition King Curtis to be Aretha's new bandleader
as well as saxophone player. Ruth Bowen, Aretha's longtime booking agent

who would work with her for over years, had known of King Curtis earlier, but as she told me: "When Aretha went to Atlantic Records, I got to know Curtis better and more personal, and then when he came on as her bandleader and conductor, we became very close."[10] So close, in fact, that Curtis asked Bowen to represent him, as well.

Jerry Wexler was quickly elevating Curtis's presence and promoting new responsibilities for him in the Atlantic hierarchy, getting him to produce artists as well as back them in the recording studio. He correctly judged that some of the many Black artists at Atlantic would prefer to record under the watchful eye of one of their brothers from the South rather than Wexler, a Jew from New York City. Wexler's strategy of integrating King Curtis more deeply into the workings of Atlantic Records evolved into a resounding success, not only for artistic performance but especially for studio harmony.

Curtis brought a new, more comfortable atmosphere to Atlantic, as well as order and organization to the studio. While he had long since been transplanted from the Fort Worth area, as his new booking agent Ruth Bowen noted, the southerly sax man had kept his genteel manners: "To me, Curtis was one of the most courteous musicians I have ever met. He was a perfect gentleman always, always. Now, he had his other moods, but those moods he kept in front of other people and not with people he respected and loved. You better not say anything wrong in front of the ladies that he loved, or you would get your ass kicked for sure—that was Curtis."[11] Curtis absolutely championed respect and etiquette when women were in or nearby his studio and never tolerated foul language if a lady was present.

When I spoke to Cissy Houston, a wonderful singer in her own right and a member of the backing vocals group the Sweet Inspirations, which supported both Aretha Franklin and King Curtis on many of their albums, she concurred: "We sang with Aretha, all the things he [Curtis] played for Aretha. He was the leader for Aretha's band at one time, and we were in the room [studio] with him for a while. We were all like a big family." Houston also noted that Curtis was always a "gentleman and a protector of women, you know that kind of stuff, he just really treated everybody like they were human."[12]

Curtis shared an immediate connection to Aretha and became the "big brother" she'd never had while growing up. Author Gerri Hirshey noted that Curtis "shored her [Aretha] up with the sassy horn and relentless good humor. Aretha said his horn spoke directly to her. On the road he backed her as no one could. Aretha says she sang and felt her best when King Curtis stood to the side with Bernard 'Pretty' Purdie on drums, Cornell Dupree on guitar and Richard Tee on keyboards. It was the same in the studio. 'Going Down Slow,' in particular, on her *Aretha Arrives* album is a beautifully choreographed chase between Curtis's horn and her voice. 'King Curtis could make me laugh so hard', she says."[13]

In her autobiography, Aretha Franklin continued to appreciate the otherworldly connection she shared with King Curtis from day one at Atlantic: "King was a key part of my music at Atlantic; he thoroughly understood soul and accompanied me, as saxist and bandleader, with exactly the right kind of funky flair. He was the man that could cook up that 'Memphis Soul Stew'; his 'Soul Serenade' is a permanent part of the soundtrack of my Atlantic years."[14]

For Jerry Wexler, the groundwork had been successfully laid to ease the earlier tensions that arose on the part of Aretha and her husband in response to the lack of diversity at Atlantic Records. With Curtis's commanding authority in the studio, Wexler's challenge now lay in getting the critical studio musicians from Fame Studios up to Atlantic's New York City recording studio to finish Aretha's album. There was no doubt in his mind that Fame owner Rick Hall, after all the bad blood of that infamous first Aretha session, would never allow Aretha to return to Muscle Shoals to record with his house band again. Wexler could feel the electricity that all the musicians shared with Aretha, but going back to Fame was out of the question. And Hall was still steaming over the whole initial Aretha session debacle and adamantly against allowing his musicians to travel up to New York to complete their work on this desperately important album for Atlantic.

Undeterred by the Fame Studios fiasco, Wexler hatched a plan. He called Rick Hall and asked for Hall's musicians to come to New York to record a new King Curtis album, *King Curtis Plays the Great Memphis Hits*. Grateful of the offer to repair the unfortunate damage done in Muscle

Shoals to the relationship between Atlantic and Fame, Hall leapt at Wexler's perceived olive branch. Hall's musicians were off New York to record with King Curtis on February 10–12, 1967.

It's unclear if Hall would have had any reason to know of the songs that were to be covered in the King Curtis session. If he did, one would think alarms of suspicion would have rang out as he would quickly realize they were all Stax Records hits—with, curiously, no Stax studio musicians invited to New York to reprise any of their successful earlier backing support on the original songs. While Jimmy Johnson, Spooner Oldham, and Roger Hawkins were dispatched under the auspices of recording with King Curtis, Hall was completely unaware that Jerry Wexler had "conveniently" scheduled the remaining Aretha Franklin recording sessions in New York for February 14–16, just a few days following the King Curtis recording schedule in the Atlantic studios.

With the Fame musicians back in the studio with Aretha, the group could now return to making great music. Aretha had been working on a cover of Otis Redding's "Respect" and thought it would work well on the album. Through her genius at interpreting and massaging the cover of a tune to make the song her own, Aretha transforms Redding's plaintive male plea to his lover into an empowering feminist anthem for women everywhere. Jerry Wexler concluded that at the song's instrumental break featuring King Curtis, they not only needed Curtis's horn but a very distinct melody.

Producer Arif Mardin, famous for his lush string accompaniments on so many of Atlantic's catalog of songs, assisted with the production of the album. He recollected to me:

> "When Something Is Wrong with My Baby," was the song recorded in the morning [by Sam and Dave]. In the afternoon, Aretha Franklin's session started. We're doing "Respect," and Curtis and I said, "You know, this song needs a bridge." You know, put a saxophone solo in there. And I think it was me or him: "But, wait a minute, remember that song, 'When Something Is Wrong with My Baby?' He goes to F-sharp minor and then he goes down to G. So why don't we put those chord sequences in 'Respect,' and the G7 will lead us to what the song is." Ah, so we did that, and you have now in the song, "Respect," a very strange modulation with where the tenor sax goes in. You have to listen to it.[15]

The song's writer, Otis Redding, just happened by Atlantic Studios when Wexler and Mardin were mastering the record. Author David Ritz wrote about Redding's reaction in his Aretha Franklin biography: "He broke into a wide smile," Jerry Wexler remembered, "and said, 'That girl has taken that song from me. Ain't no longer my song. From now on, it belongs to her.' And then he asked me [to] play it again, and then a third time. The smile never left his face."[16]

Bandleader King Curtis was not surprised in the least with Aretha's uncanny ability to take another artist's major hit song, turn it around, and make it entirely her own. He told Charlie Gillett: "When Aretha records a tune she kills a copyright. Because once she works out the way to do it, you're never going to be able to come up with a better approach. And it's damn sure you aren't going to be able to improve on how she's done it, her way."[17]

Wexler also suggested Aretha cut a cover of Curtis's hit at Capitol Records, "Soul Serenade," as well as "Save Me," a song Curtis co-wrote with Aretha's sister, Carolyn. Author David Ritz noted what Aretha thought about the song, as well as her early impressions of the collaboration with Curtis: "She called him a gentleman because, even though she described the musical contribution by her and Carolyn as minor, King gave them full credit as collaborators. She also sang King's blistering 'Soul Serenade,' another testimony to the great horn man's pivotal role in helping Aretha become Aretha."[18]

The King Curtis album that enabled Jerry Wexler and Arif Mardin to finish Aretha's first album for Atlantic was also a significant studio work. This was not simply throwaway-album bait used to camouflage the strategic ploy of luring Rick Hall's musicians away from the confines of the Muscle Shoals studio. *King Curtis Plays the Great Memphis Hits* also happens to be Jerry Wexler's favorite collaboration with King Curtis: "That album was such a joy;—that was, like, a great experience."[19] Curtis and Atlantic had earlier created a wonderful relationship with Stax Records in Memphis, cofounded by brother and sister Jim Stewart and Estelle Axton, which is why on the album Curtis covers such soul tunes as Eddie Floyd's "Knock on Wood," Otis Redding's "Good To Me," "I've Been Loving You Too

Curtis and Jerry Wexler sharing a laugh at Wexler's twenty-fifth
anniversary celebration, Ahmet Ertegun's apartment, 1966.
Courtesy of Jerry Wexler / Paul Wexler.

Long" and "Fa-Fa-Fa-Fa-Fa (Sad Song)," "Green Onions" by Booker T. and
the M.G.'s, William Bell's "You Don't Miss Your Water," Wilson Pickett's
"In the Midnight Hour," Rufus Thomas's "The Dog" and "Jump Back," and
the popular Sam and Dave tunes "Hold On! I'm Comin'" and "When Something Is Wrong with My Baby."

By itself, it was an excellent decision to mix these Stax songs led by
Curtis's horn with backing by the Muscle Shoals studio group of Jimmy
Johnson on guitar, Tommy Cogbill on bass, Spooner Oldham on piano and
keyboards, and Roger Hawkins on drums. Throw in the horn section of
Melvin Lastie, Charles Chalmers, and Floyd Newman, and you have a major
soul work with the insightful interpretation and energy that only King Curtis
and his saxophone can bring.

Wexler himself penned the liner notes to the album, and his effusive
praise for Curtis is not lost on anyone. He opens with: "On this album King
Curtis, the greatest saxophone player in the world of rhythm & blues and
pop, offers his tribute to the new Memphis blues sound."[20] He then concludes

with: "His solos are incomparable. His saxophone re-fashions the story originally told in words by the singers who made the hit recordings, adding an unforgettable something all his own."[21]

At the time, Stax's in-house song writers, Isaac Hayes and partner David Porter, had just written both of the Sam and Dave hits highlighted on the album. Hayes, too, vividly remembered the ebullient King Curtis and his sincere support for everyone in the Stax recording studio on East McLemore Street in Memphis. He told me: "King Curtis was a funny guy, a really funny guy and a real gentleman. He always was makin' us laugh in the studio. He was a big star, and anytime he came down to Stax, he *always* gave us constant validation. Constant validation as writers and artists."[22]

Jerry Wexler couldn't have been happier. In addition to cutting his personal favorite King Curtis album, he had also cleverly salvaged and then finalized Aretha Franklin's inaugural Atlantic album, *I Never Loved a Man the Way I Love You*, a recording that would become one of the seminal albums of the soul music era. When word of Wexler's manipulative ploy reached Rick Hall back at Fame Studios in Muscle Shoals, Alabama, he hit the roof, realizing he had been totally outplayed. His musicians were signed to contracts with his studio, and he controlled their recording efforts around the country, not just at Fame Studios. He angrily recalled his musicians back home to Muscle Shoals, but it was too late. Atlantic, Aretha Franklin, and Jerry Wexler would not be denied.

Making up for lost time, Aretha Franklin and King Curtis, now united at Atlantic, exploded onto the pop and soul music landscape together. When asked what Atlantic did differently than any other record label to elevate the careers of Aretha and Curtis, as well as the rest of their portfolio of soul music performers, Ruth Bowen, the booking agent of both stars, had a simple answer: "They gave an artist the freedom to do more of what they felt, and they could give it their all. I remember after Aretha had her first hit with Atlantic, I got a very nice note [from Atlantic] saying, 'Tell Aretha thanks so much for all those records on the shelf we sold now.'" Bowen further recalled, "I loved the material on Columbia, but that wasn't 'it'—Atlantic brought it out."[23]

Chapter 11

Cookin' in Memphis

Just when it seemed his career could not get any better, Curtis was thrilled when King Curtis and the Kingpins were nominated for a Grammy Award for "Best Rhythm and Blues Group Performance, Vocal or Instrumental" in early 1966 for his version of "Spanish Harlem." The competition in this category that year was astoundingly stiff, with such other worthy nominees as James and Bobby Purify's "I'm Your Puppet," the Capitols' "Cool Jerk," Sam and Dave's "Hold On! I'm Comin'," and the eventual winner, Ramsey Lewis's "Hold It Right There." Just to be mentioned in the same breath as the other nominees heightened Curtis's sense of accomplishment and creativity, legitimizing more than ever his move to Atlantic Records, which allowed him to write and interpret music exactly as he wished. Having such early recognition for his new record label transition made Curtis more eager than ever to get back into the recording studio.

The year 1967 also saw the departure of Chuck Rainey as bass player for King Curtis and the Kingpins. Deeply respected to this day for his talents, Rainey sought out bigger and better challenges for himself. As mentioned earlier, he had become tired of always playing the same music. He realized—possibly not unlike Jimi Hendrix earlier—that, creatively, the time had come for him to move on. He approached Curtis and, what with Curtis wanting to "shake up the band" with some new blood anyway, recommended that his bandleader check out another local talent that already had something in common with Curtis, a connection with Small's Paradise.

"Chuck Rainey was leaving at the time and told King Curtis to check me out," noted bassist Jerry Jemmott to me. "I was working out of Small's Paradise, so he came down. I was working with Frankie 'Downbeat' Round. By that time, I had gotten married and started a family, and my old dream of becoming a studio musician had started to fade. I was working in the First National City Bank during the day as a document checker, and I wasn't interested in making music a full-time thing, but the bank thing wasn't working either. I was tired of getting off playing at four a.m. and getting to the bank by eight a.m."[1]

After hearing Jemmott play on his home turf at Small's, Curtis had seen enough. He offered Jerry Jemmott the open Chuck Rainey spot in the band. Shockingly, Jemmott *refused*. "I said, 'Nahhh," Jemmott laughed sheepishly. "In fact, I turned him down several times. Then, in March 1967, I had a vacation scheduled, and I went to visit my father in New Jersey. Curtis called me down there, and I said, 'Well, if he's going to call me all over the country trying to track me down, okay, I'll give it a shot."[2]

Once installed as the Kingpins' new bassist, Jemmott quickly realized the foolishness of his initial ambivalence towards joining the band. "I've never been in awe of people—I respect their ability, but I've never been in awe of them. And since, coming from a jazz tradition, King Curtis wasn't that prevalent in my mind, although I enjoyed his music ... But when I started playing with him, I got to experience the magic—the man was a giant. Working with him opened me right up. He showed me how to perform in front of an audience. His enthusiasm, his ability, his spontaneity—all created magic on the stage."[3]

And Jemmott, too, was deeply impressed by Curtis's support for young artists coupled with the sax man's innate talent to follow his fellow musicians, onstage or in studio. Things just clicked: "It doesn't matter what type of music you're playing, when you start to move step-to-step with somebody, when you start making the same moves at the same time, that's when you make magic from the music. We went on some musical voyages together that were incredible, very spiritual; I'd never experienced anything like that."[4] Jerry Jemmott was overwhelmed by the cohesiveness he felt as the newest member of King Curtis and the Kingpins.

If the allure of playing with King Curtis wasn't stimulating enough, Curtis also tossed Jemmott the carrot he coveted most, studio time: "One of my dreams has always been that I would be a studio musician. I had this vision of myself going from studio to studio carrying my acoustic bass. King Curtis promised me studio work, so it looked like everything was coming together for me."[5]

Alas, the recording studio side of Jemmott's dream was neither as concrete nor as immediate as he hoped. Curtis plunged back into the studio without allowing his new bass player to tag along, for whatever reason. Maybe Curtis felt that Jemmott was better suited for his "live" band and not the studio version (it wasn't unusual, as previously discussed, for Curtis to have two separate bands: one for the studio and one for live performances). Alternatively, maybe Curtis wanted Jemmott to get more experience and polish with the live band before solidifying him in the recording studio environment. Leaving an indignant Jemmott behind in New York, Curtis headed to Memphis and American Sound Studios.

Jim Stewart had started the Satellite Records label in his Memphis garage in 1957. The new label featured rockabilly, pop, and straight country music. In 1958, Stewart's sister, Estelle Axton, invested in her brother's company. By 1959, the company had moved to Brunswick, Tennessee, to a small garage studio, where Stewart met up with a hot-shot guitarist from Memphis named Lincoln Wayne "Chips" Moman. The two decided to work together, with Moman bringing Satellite their first Black rhythm and blues group, the Veltones, who recorded "Fool in Love."

Chips Moman had hitchhiked from his home in LaGrange, Georgia, to Memphis as a fourteen-year-old boy in 1951. Having played guitar since he was a child, Moman was spotted by Sun Records rockabilly star Warren Smith while strumming his guitar in a local drugstore. Smith asked Moman if he wanted a job, and the youngster accepted. Moman quickly became a sought-after local artist and traveled with the brothers Johnny and Dorsey

Brunette to the Gold Star Recording Studio in California to support their songs. It was here that Moman was exposed to engineer Stan Ross and his record production style. He quickly became consumed with not only playing on records but producing them as well.

It was Moman who stumbled across an old empty theater on East McLemore Avenue in Memphis and found it to be available for rent to the sweet tune of fifty dollars a month. Rushing back to his new partner, Stewart, with the news, the two rented the building and built it out. Stax Records was born. After initially recording hits with early Stax artists Carla Thomas, Rufus Thomas, and William Bell, Moman's relationship with co-owners Jim Stewart and Estelle Axton deteriorated. By the end of 1961, a royalty dispute with the Jim and Estelle left Moman on the outside looking in, and he severed his ties with Stax. Moman lost everything he had due to the rancorous split. "Sometimes you can get hurt bad enough that you don't forget it," he said. "What happened to me at Stax caused me to lose my house. I lost everything I had. I remember that year—for Thanksgiving, my wife and child, all we had was a box of corn flakes and some milk. You don't forget those kinds of things."[6]

Moman threatened Stax with a lawsuit, and the nominal $3,000 settlement he received was adequate to enable the start of his own recording facility at 827 Thomas Street in 1964. Moman called his new digs American Sound Studios. Success was hard to come by initially, and Moman kept afloat financially by doing recording engineer work for studios and backing recording sessions on his guitar at Fame Studios in Muscle Shoals, Alabama, for the likes of Aretha Franklin, Wilson Pickett, and others. He also met his songwriting partner, Dan Penn, and co-wrote such major songs as James Carr's "The Dark End of the Street" and Aretha Franklin's "Do Right Woman, Do Right Man."

Moman signed contracts locking down a local white rhythm section for his new studio, consisting of guitarist Reggie Young, bass players Mike Leech and Tommy Cogbill, Bobby Wood and Bobby Emmons on keyboards, and Gene Chrisman on drums. While excited to be signed to a studio contract, drummer Chrisman remembers the newly created American Studios wasn't in the best part of town, as he told me: "It was a kind of a rough place to play, I think. Somebody broke into somebody's car one night and tried to break into the Ranch House [restaurant located next door] one night, and Chips took a gun and fired it down, you know, or up, and that guy took off like a bullet."[7]

King Curtis steamed into Memphis for the first time to play with the American Studios musicians for Atlantic's Wilson Pickett recording session on July 1, 1967. Drummer Roger Hawkins told author Roben Jones how stunned he was the first time he met King Curtis, who was fitting seamlessly into the studio with all the other musicians, chameleon-like as usual: "A ray of light. A guy comes in—everything's cool, everything's fine. He just walked in; you could feel the talent. He came with open arms. It was never a feeling of 'let's see if these white boys can play.' I don't like to bring up the racial issue, but there was a racial issue back then. He was one of us, we were one of him."[8] When King Curtis was in the studio, established color barriers evaporated and all seemed to be equals, all on the same status level. Everyone could now just concentrate on making great music.

Four days later, Curtis would be back at American to cut his own solo album, produced by Atlantic engineer Tom Dowd and Tommy Cogbill under Jerry Wexler's supervision. The four tracks recorded that day were "When a Man Loves a Woman," "Blue Nocturne," "C. C. Rider," and the rollicking, "Memphis Soul Stew."

During a break between the earlier Pickett session and his solo session four days later, Curtis went to lunch at the Ranch House restaurant with the American house band. Curtis took one look at the menu and muttered, "Today's special is Memphis Soul Stew."[9] Lightning bolts went off in his head, calling to mind a piece he had been working on back home in New York. When I spoke to keyboard artist Bobby Wood, he remembered it well: "There was a little card thing, I believe, sittin' on his table, that said ... 'Today's Special,' I believe that's the way it was—I'm not sure, as specials go. That's what he saw, man, and went next door and wrote it, actually, and I think he scribbled down a few things on a piece of paper while he was sittin' there.[10]

All the musicians raced back to the studio to capture Curtis's vibe.

If "Soul Serenade" was Curtis's signature tune while at Capitol Records, "Memphis Soul Stew" was most certainly his anthem for his new tenure at Atlantic. Lasting nine weeks on the *Billboard* pop chart (achieving a ranking high of number 33) and ten weeks on the R&B Chart (topping out at number 6), the song is a bubbling booya of masterfully blended individual solos.

To begin the song, after a brief Tommy Cogbill bass intro to set the funky pace, Curtis lists his tasty ingredients in the song's recipe: "Today's special is 'Memphis Soul Stew.' We sell so much of this, people wonder what we put in it. We gonna tell you right now; give me about a half a teacup—of bass." Cogbill began with a pulsing bass note line that elevated to an upward riff. No wonder Jerry Jemmott later admitted his deep bitterness at not being included on the recording date: the bass line alone is the roux that binds the entire production together.

"Now I need a pound of fatback drum." Drummer Gene Chrisman storms right in, crisply announcing his entrance with a machine-gun run on the snare drum, keeping the pace up-tempo. Curtis was always impressed with the sheer power of the man, considering he was so slight.

"Now give me four tablespoons of boilin' Memphis git-tar, this is gonna taste alright." Lead guitar Reggie Young enters with a swooning, twangy, country-style line. Bass, drums, and guitar now start to form a savory, simmering broth.

"Now just a little pinch of organ." Organ player Bobby Emmons jumps in with a fluttering trill, enabling the song to almost break the simmering combination and burst into a bubble. Things are heating up.

"Now give me a half a pint—of horn." Curtis enters on his sax, circling between the two notes and whisking back and forth several times, then screams a spicy squeal offering a brief taste of what's to come.

"Place on the burner … and bring to a boil … that's it, that's it, that's it right there." Who says a "watched pot never boils?" Under King Curtis's attentive direction, this main course is about to be served, and he commands, "Now beat … [Chrisman sharply machine-guns again] … well!"[11]

Curtis starts to honk and blow, roaring up the scale, and the band explodes right along with him. The call-and-response song between chef and individual ingredients, culminating in a lip-smacking result, is reprised later on the *King Curtis Live at Fillmore West* recording, hard-boiling the

San Francisco hippy crowd into a drooling frenzy. It's no wonder this song is still incredibly popular.

Interesting that, at the time, several of the American Studios musicians weren't particularly familiar with Curtis nor any of his earlier studio work as a solo artist or backing musician (although according to Red Kelly, Jerry Wexler had brought Reggie Young and Tommy Cogbill to New York City a few months earlier, in April of 1967, for recording sessions with Solomon Burke and Patti LaBelle, at which time they may have met Curtis.)[12] They were, though, like so many other strangers who worked with King Curtis for the first time, immediately won over by Curtis's infectious personality and professionalism: "It was a pleasure to get to work with King, and, you know, to listen to him all these years, and [I] didn't know him at the time. [I] didn't know he had cut with the Coasters and, you know, whoever else they had out at Atlantic recording at the time," recalled Gene Chrisman. "All those people. You know, it was great, and I really enjoyed being with him."[13] Bobby Wood was one of the few who had previously heard of King Curtis: "When I came to American, we used to go to dances, and my band and I learned the top 10 and a bunch of that stuff that he [Curtis] had played sax [on]. I knew he was established already, even before he got there. He was just such a cordial, down-to-earth, nice guy that we, you know, just kinda fell in love with him as a musician; we respected him highly. I mean, he was welcome to be a part of the band; whatever he wanted to do, it was okay with us. He was like one of the guys."[14]

An argument can be made that "Memphis Soul Stew," in particular, was not only King Curtis's trademark Atlantic Records effort, but also the definitive showcase for the individual talents of the American house band. From 1967 to 1972, American Studios churned out a staggering catalog of approximately one hundred and twenty hit records, a startling volume of production and chart success.

Back home in New York, a seething Jerry Jemmott didn't just stay home and feel sorry for himself. "We were working together in the band, but there was no studio work," complained the irritated Jemmott. "I said, 'Hey, what's going on? I want it *now*.' That was my goal, and I was disappointed because he didn't include me on his recording of 'Memphis Soul Stew.' That was done with Tommy Cogbill and the [American Studios] cats from Memphis, 'cuz everybody else in the band was making records. I was like, 'Gee, this is what you promised me, and the record comes out, and I'm not on it.' So, I told him, straight up, you know, and he said, 'Okay, that's fine.'"15

Jemmott refused to be ignored. "A friend of mine who was Lionel Hampton's bandleader asked me if I wanted to play with them. So, I said, 'Curtis isn't giving me studio work, so later for Curtis. I'm going to play with Lionel.' He was going to Japan, where I had never been, and after all, he was Lionel Hampton, the great jazz musician, and jazz was my thing."16

Though angered by some initial broken promises by King Curtis, Jemmott would continue his pursuit of consistent recording work, with or without the Kingpins. One month later, Curtis acquiesced and extended Jemmott a long overdue invitation into the studio. This was Jemmott's chance at his dream:

> Curtis called and told me, "You don't have to be in the band anymore, just make my records." So I said, "Cool!" He asked me to come down to Atlantic Records because the bass player didn't show up. That was the beginning. I'd done some dates for RCA Victor and Columbia, but nothing really major, nothing consistent. I was always trying to get into the studio scene and break through, which was a hard nut to crack. At that time, he [Curtis] helped me fulfill that goal when he gave me that offer. So, I've always been indebted to him, and I would always make any session he called me for. This was *it!*17

King Curtis had such a positive initial experience with American Sound Studios in Memphis that six weeks later (now with his mollified bass player, Jerry Jemmott, in tow) he quickly amassed his Kingpins and sped back to American to cut an entire album on August 24, entitled *King Size Soul*.

The band covered such hits as Aretha Franklin's "I Never Loved a Man (the Way I Love You)," Procol Harum's "A Whiter Shade of Pale," Buffalo Springfield's "For What It's Worth" (a minimal hit for Curtis, achieving number 87 and lasting a brief four weeks on the *Billboard* Top 100 chart), and Stevie Wonder's "I Was Made to Love Her" (occupying the *Billboard* pop chart for six weeks and the R&B chart for two). Curtis also included his successful hit cover of Bobbie Gentry's "Ode to Billie Joe" (reaching number 28 on the *Billboard* pop chart and number 6 on the R&B Chart) and repeated his previously recorded hit, "Memphis Soul Stew."

When the band returned to New York, Jemmott then backed the inimitable Wilson Pickett on his song, "Deborah," in the Atlantic studio on January 4, 1968. This was the opportunity of a lifetime for the ever-confident Jemmott, and he didn't disappoint. "Bernard Purdie and King Curtis were on the date. It was an all-star lineup," recalled the thrilled Jemmott. "Well, I took care of business. I took it *out*. I followed the chart until I saw a place where I could put a little something in. I put it in, and they *loved* it. That was it. After that, they started asking me for work, and my studio career was happening."[18] The world of consistent studio work for Jemmott was even better than he could have imagined: "It was all through the King Curtis connection that that occurred. I would go down to Muscle Shoals. Actually, Jerry Wexler was the producer. Once King Curtis introduced me to the company, then other producers started calling me—mainly Jerry Wexler."[19]

Wexler also recognized something uncanny in the young bass player, something that separated him from the standard bass-playing competition. Jemmott remembered, "He was able to detail what it was about me that he thought that was special that made him want to hire me all the time, and that was my use of syncopation, and my phrasing. So, because of that, I was able to work with Wilson Pickett, of course, Aretha Franklin, Jerry Jeff Walker, the Rascals—the whole Atlantic lineup, basically, in New York and in Muscle Shoals. In Muscle Shoals it was Wilson Pickett. It was Arthur Conley, Clarence Carter."[20]

Happily creating innovative bass lines in the recording studio, his dream now fully realized, Jerry Jemmott soon recognized that working with King Curtis not only taught him how to record but also how to perform:

> It came from his spontaneity and his reaction— relationship, I should say: interaction with the audience, getting the band involved, his stage presence, his showmanship—all these things he did live. He was able to actually transfer [them] into the studio setting, and all the recordings we did in the studio, they were always live. There was no overdubbing. We would fix some things up if necessary, but his whole

thing was, you know, catch it when it was ripe, and you know, record it—you know, capture the moment. But, it came from his ability to put the people together to begin with, making the right telephone calls to come into the studio, to have this chemistry that's important to make a record.[21]

Jemmott learned that there was significantly more planning and thought required to perform and record music. And King Curtis was an excellent teacher.

King Curtis took the opportunity to opine on his definition of "soul" when he recorded "This Is Soul" on December 5, 1967, in, appropriately, Memphis, Tennessee. Utilizing the standard American Sound Studios musician roster of Bobby Emmons (organ), Reggie Young (guitar), Tommy Cogbill (bass, instead of Jerry Jemmott), and Gene Chrisman (drums), he added Spooner Oldham on piano and Bobby Womack on guitar. In the song, he opens with the statement: "It's been said that only *some* people have soul. I don't believe that. Because, in my travels around the world, I found that *everybody* has soul. Now some people may say it different, depending upon the way they may have been reared. It's best said through music. And if this music makes you feel like you want to dance, or if it makes you feel like you want to cry, that music has soul."[22]

Though it seemed as though Curtis's luck couldn't get any better at this point in his career, a dear friend's good fortune was about to run out. Though 1967 had begun with a bang, Atlantic Records and the entire soul music world would soon be painfully reminded of the frailties of life.

Otis Redding had become the face of Stax Records, an international superstar. Curtis and Redding had met earlier at the many Apollo Theatre productions they worked together and had become fast friends. The two had tried to negotiate a new tour together, but for whatever reason, they could not agree on the contractual terms. Nonetheless, Redding decided to pursue the tour.

After recording "Sittin' on the Dock of the Bay" at the Stax recording studio days earlier with guitarist Steve Cropper and bass player Donald "Duck" Dunn, Redding flew to Cleveland, Ohio, and played two sold-out shows at Leo's Casino. The next day, December 10, 1967, he boarded his

Jerry Wexler, Otis Redding, Eddie O'Jay, King Curtis,
and Nesuhi Ertegun. *Michael Ochs Archives / Getty Images.*

private plane, a recently purchased twin-engine Beechcraft H18, and headed
for Madison, Wisconsin. Despite the rain, fog, and intermittent snowy condi-
tions, Redding, his band, the Bar-Kays, and the pilot took off from the airport.
One hour later, the plane would crash into Lake Monona outside of Madison,
a mere four miles from the Madison Municipal Airport, killing everyone
aboard but trumpet player Ben Cauley. Curtis had similarly lost his friend
Buddy Holly in a plane crash and then his dear compatriot Sam Cooke to
suspect circumstances. Now Otis Redding was killed in a plane that had
plummeted into the icy winter waters of a Wisconsin lake.

Curtis and Modeen had just gone to bed for the evening. At eleven p.m.,
the phone rang: "Curtis and I were in bed and the phone rang, and Marlena
called (who worked for Curtis as a part-time secretary). She called and woke
us up and told us that the plane had gone down. I can remember Curtis
saying, 'I'm supposed to be on that plane with them.' We both knew he had
talked about doing a tour with Otis, and had he done the tour he would have

been with them."[23] Horrified, the two would not sleep well for days, heartsick about losing a friend while haunted by the possibility that Curtis could have been on that same fateful trip.

Much like in his previous musical eulogy for his fallen friend Sam Cooke, Curtis grieved publicly. He immediately set to covering Redding's last hit song, "(Sittin' on) The Dock of the Bay." Recorded at Atlantic Studios in February 1968, the song would last five weeks on the *Billboard* pop chart, achieving an unspectacular number 84 ranking.

With Otis Redding's death still weighing heavily on his heart, Curtis and Atlantic Records producer Arif Mardin traveled to Memphis, Tennessee, returning to Chips Moman's American Sound Studios to record a new album entitled *Sweet Soul* on April 1, 1968.[24] The only charted hits from the album would be minor ones, with a cover of Marvin Gaye's "I Heard It through the Grapevine" lasting a minimal three weeks, only gaining to number 83, and "Theme from 'Valley of the Dolls'" lasting even less time at two weeks, also topping out at number 83. On the album, Curtis also reprises his earlier Capitol hit, "Soul Serenade." This time, however, Curtis eschews his previous saxello and chooses a tenor saxophone, which gives the song a brassier, more melancholy tone, far from the bright, dreamy emotion his previous Capitol version elicits. Mardin was transfixed by Curtis's unusual, trademark ability to carry a melody on his saxophone that was initially meant for the human voice:

> King Curtis was very important—he was like a rock. His rhythm sections became the engine for many sessions. We're talking about Bernard Purdie, Cornell Dupree, Chuck Rainey, Ray Lucas—he even had Jimi Hendrix in his band. For me, a melody designed to be sung by a human voice, played by saxophone or trumpet, reminds me of Muzak. I'm not talking about Gershwin or Porter standards; I'm talking about pop songs. Curtis, however, was able to transcend that and make the melodies sing. So he covered a lot of melodies, and we relied heavily on him for his musical expertise.[25]

Memphis at the time was rife with deep racial tensions, as a few months earlier, on February 12, 1968, local sanitation workers had gone on strike for better wages and equal benefits for Blacks. Martin Luther King Jr., as well as

Latife and Arif Mardin, King Curtis, and Nesuhi Ertegun.
Courtesy of PoPsie Photos.

numerous other civil rights sympathizers, were swarming into town to aid the strikers' stance, making headlines across the nation. The city was in a state of lockdown for many weeks, and everyone was on a razor-sharp edge.

Arif Mardin recalled the deep anxiety that he felt in Memphis like it was yesterday:

> They had a curfew. Now, Curtis and I were on the same plane going to Memphis, and he couldn't find a regular compact car at the airport, so we rented a huge white Lincoln. Okay? So, when we were in the studio, we realized that we passed the dinner hour, and we got into the "Pope Mobile," should I say—you know, huge white car—and we started towards our hotel. Our hotel was at that time—was called the Holiday Inn-Rivermont. I think that building was like a condo or an old people's home, but they changed it and made it a hotel with a river view. Beautiful! And we didn't realize that there were no cars in the street, and Curtis being a big guy—he was very hungry.

We were rushing to the hotel to have something to eat, but we were stopped by state troopers, and we looked like Northern agitators. Here was a huge Black guy and a white guy sitting next to him, you know, and they stopped us, and they said, "Okay, who are you?" And maybe they used like "boy" or things like that, you know. Curtis being very savvy, very intelligent, said, "We are musicians. I am King Curtis," and I think one of the policemen said—what was it at that time?—"Yakety, Yak?" He says, "Yes, I'm that King Curtis. If you allow me to open the trunk, I can show you my saxophone." So, he showed the saxophone. They said, "Okay, we believe you, and go to the hotel right away." So, we went to the hotel and found out that the dining room was closed because there was no cook, nobody. So, they said, "You have to drive to our other Holiday Inn and the kitchen is open there." I mean, Curtis was *so* hungry.

So, we crossed the bridge by mistake. We ended up in Arkansas. Now, today it's all built, but at that time, 1968, there were all corn fields, nothing. So, when we ended up on the other side of the river, I said, "My goodness, some farmer's gonna come out with a shotgun and shoot us." We were so, you know, scared, we made an immediate U-turn, going back to, you know, Tennessee. Found a hotel. We ate half-frozen/half-cooked steak, and we were able to go back to our regular hotel.[26]

Arif also remembered his wife, Latife, who feared for his personal safety, calling him on April 1: "Now, my wife is calling me, 'Something is happening, something is happening. Come back to New York.' 'Oh, no, no, we're cutting great tracks,' I said to my wife. Latife responded, 'No, leave it. Come back!!' You know, because we don't care; we are in the studio cutting great tracks! But, we had to leave, I guess, after that."[27]

Curtis and Arif returned home the very next day. Two days later, on April 4, 1968, the Rev. Martin Luther King Jr. was struck and killed by single bullet as he stood on the balcony near his second-floor room at the Lorraine Motel. The city of Memphis instantly combusted into a racial fireball, exploding with protests and demonstrations. American Studios drummer Gene Chrisman remembered it all too well:

We had to cancel the next night or somethin' because of all the riots and stuff [that] went on. In fact, we were sittin' in the restaurant eatin', and I heard police cars and I thought, "What in the what?" I never heard so many police cars in my life, because it was downtown, you know, we was in a bad section of town anyway. Man, when those police cars come runnin', I thought 'What in the world is goin' on?' And it finally came on [the] news, you know, what happened. Then everything started riotin' in different parts of the city, and so we had to get ourselves outta there, because, where we were, you know, they set a lot of places on fire. I don't think it was right there where we were, but down there on Park Avenue I think—somewhere down in there. And it was getting pretty bad that night, so I think, after that, everybody had to start takin' some weapons with them, which none of us had licenses [for] at the time, but, you never knew what was goin' to happen in that area [near American Studios] of town.[28]

The assassination of Martin Luther King Jr. launched equal rights for African Americans to a higher level in the nation's cognizance. And amid all the success that was Atlantic Records, all the accolades received by Aretha Franklin and King Curtis, all the harmonious integration and emotional synergy that Ahmet Ertegun and Jerry Wexler had championed in their studios, the pervasive undercurrent of racial tension in the recording industry remained, mirroring the current racial upheaval of society. There were still, for example, deep-seated frustrations about the scarcity of opportunities for Blacks in management and upper management careers in the music industry.

These frustrations would reach critical mass in the music industry and erupt in Miami, Florida at the end of 1968. Jerry Wexler never forgot the event, chronicled in his autobiography:

It was on Aretha's behalf that I was supposed to accept an award from the National Association of Television and Radio Announcers (NATRA) at their 1968 convention at the Sheraton Four Ambassadors Hotel in Miami. I arrived at the Bayfront Auditorium tuxed up and feeling fine. I was at a table with our promo men, Dick Kline, Joe Galkin and Juggy Gayles. The speakers were calling for Black takeover of the record companies and R&B stations. Emcee Bill Cosby was a vociferous advocate, whipping it up. Black power was on the agenda, and I'm all for it—Black political power, Black economic power, Black management jobs, Black ownership, Black run labels.

But these shakedown artists had no program; it was just old-fashioned take-what-you-can-get blackmail. Suspicious characters had been running around the hotels hitting on label and station owners. Under the guise of concerned citizens, hoodlums were camouflaging extortion with the rhetoric of the movement.

It might seem ironic that the moment of terror arrived when my cohort, soul brother and longtime collaborator, King Curtis, leaned over and whispered in my ear, "We're getting the fuck out of here."

"Why?" I wanted to know.

"Someone's after you with a gun. You're marked."

"*Marked*! Me? What the fuck!"[29]

There was not a moment to lose and the streetwise, imposing King Curtis was not about to stand by with his dear friend in imminent danger. Recognizing the immediate severity of the situation, another Atlantic artist now rushed to Wexler's aid, the blues singer and songwriter Titus Turner, meeting the two at the Atlantic table. Both Turner and Curtis were packing revolvers and were poised, ready to move. Together, the armed men's goal was to quickly and, most importantly, safely escort the terrified Wexler from the event: "To have two Black men in the business volunteer as my bodyguards was comforting, but no less scary. They obviously knew what's happening; my life was on the line. With Titus showing his piece, they whisked me out of the auditorium in nothing flat."[30]

The sheer panic of the moment was never forgotten, and Jerry Wexler remained grateful for both his friends' loyalty at the time—but he felt no less indignant at vague accusations levied at Wexler that he was ripping off Aretha Franklin: "Curtis loved me. We were like brothers. He didn't go for that bullshit. Neither did Titus Turner. Neither did anybody who knew me … all the ones I worked with. These were some street cats, some hoodlums, from the outside."[31] "This was not a natural demographic attitude, because there were some street people, you know, just hoodlums, got into the business. They really didn't get into the business; they attached themselves to the Black disc jockeys. And sorta took them over. Took over their [NATRA's] association."[32] For Wexler, the ugliness of the incidents in Miami were due to a few isolated bad seeds that had wedged their way between the recording executives and the disc jockeys in attendance.

Chapter 12

The Kingpins and the Three M'Skeeters

C ontinuing his whirlwind 1968 schedule, somewhere between April and June Curtis jetted off to Los Angeles to record with his friend Fats Domino on Domino's new album for the Reprise label, *Fats Is Back* (although Richard Perry, the producer, is quoted as saying that most of the tracks were recorded in New York). Summer had Curtis touring in Germany from June 6 through 9 and then home by June 14 for a stint at the Apollo Theatre featuring O. C. Smith, Vivian Reed, and Bill Cosby. Two weeks later, Curtis participated in the Soul Together concert at Madison Square Garden with Joe Tex, Sonny and Cher, Sam and Dave, the Rascals, and Aretha Franklin.

May 7, 1968, found Aretha Franklin in Paris, France, recording her first live album for Atlantic Records. While the recording shows Aretha in fine vocal form, there were problems. Her backing musicians, the Donald Towns Band, left much to be desired. A fuming Jerry Wexler would not wait until the release of the album in October to make changes; significant improvements needed to be made—now.

While King Curtis and the Kingpins were established as Aretha's standard backing group for all her Atlantic recordings into the next decade,

Aretha's husband and manager, Ted White, had other ideas for her touring band. After witnessing the inspiring cohesiveness between Aretha and Curtis in their initial foray into the recording studio, Jerry Wexler would have none of it: "He [White] brought in a band for her live appearances—I forget their name. That's one thing ... Ted White never interfered in the studio about ... you know, never got in my face about my decisions. But of course, he had everything to say about her live performances. But I was politicking for King Curtis and the Kingpins to become her live band as well and get rid of this bebop band. And finally, it happened (as you may know): they became her live band."[1]

Aretha Franklin biographer Mark Bego's interview captured Wexler's emotion, holding nothing back: "While her singing on *Aretha in Paris* is crisp and exciting, her accompaniment is a bit bland and the arrangements a little Las Vegas–like. That album embarrassed me! Ted White's only interference, at this time, came not in the studio, but in the fact that he selected the band that accompanied her on live appearances, which was a *horrible* band!"[2] According to Wexler, the Donald Towns Band was even disliked by club owners: "I went to Las Vegas with [Aretha and] that Donald Towns band. And the manager or the entertainment director of—I forget which of the casinos it was—came up to me and started vilifying me for this band. I said, 'Hey man—it's not my band. Give me a break!'"[3] Wexler despised the band so much that, on the back of the *Aretha in Paris* album he was listed—at his request—as "Supervisor," not "Producer": "I was the one who finally brought about ... how should I say ... I don't want to say 'the demise of Donald Towns' ... but I brought about the institution of King Curtis and the Kingpins—who by that time were working with her in the studio—to be her regular band out on appearances."[4] Then it was settled. King Curtis and the Kingpins was now firmly installed as the Queen of Soul's royal court, in the recording studio as well as on the road.

In July Curtis and his band toured Italy with Deon Jackson and the Sweet Inspirations. Looking for a replacement for Jimi Hendrix since his exodus from the group, Curtis had decided to add Phillip Leno Wright on guitar. In his autobiography, Wright described his process of becoming a Kingpin:

> I met Luther Dixon [producer of the Shirelles], who said he was a songwriter, producer and talent scout. He wanted me to join a recording band called King Curtis and the Kingpins, who were also joined by Cissy Houston and the Sweet Inspirations singing group. King Curtis did call me and we spoke about what he wanted of me, yet I still couldn't decide for another two months. When I picked up the phone again, he said my plane ticket was at the airport and all I needed was to go to the airport and get on the plane. I finally decided to say yes, and I flew excited and ready to go to Europe as King Curtis had promised me.[5]

For whatever reason, the relationship was tense from its inception and the two never hit it off: "After arriving at King Curtis's residence, the first thing he showed me was all his shoes, furs, suits and variety of expensive jewelry. I wasn't impressed the least bit with his assorted fiasco display of stuff. He noticed I was not impressed. I wanted to get down to business, so he angrily threw a newspaper on the dining room table, right in front of me, and said to me in an unfriendly tone of voice, 'Here, find you some place to live.'"[6]

  Jet magazine reported that sometime that summer Curtis "was jetted to Lisbon to play for 1300 guests at the estate of tin magnate Antenor Patino."[7] Patino, a wealthy real estate investor who owned property in many places, including an exclusive estate in the US, apparently paid top dollar to have Curtis play for him. *Billboard* magazine reported on September 21, 1968, that "King Curtis and his group received $10,000 and 15 round-trip tickets for his Lisbon date a few weeks back."[8] Then it was a return to the studio for Curtis, covering sessions with Freddie King for Atlantic's subsidiary label, Cotillion.

  Once home, although the tour of Europe and the Patino engagement were exciting, as was the experience of playing Madison Square Garden for the Soul Together benefit concert for the Dr. Martin Luther King Jr. Fund, Wright was thinking of moving on from the Kingpins. He had seen enough of King Curtis: "I was, however, extremely disappointed with King Curtis's way he conducted business. I had been desperately trying to figure out would I be able to leave the band with no other plans to follow."[9] As soon as Wright received an offer from Junior Walker and the All Stars, he was as good as gone:

I had terminated my guitar position with King Curtis and the Kingpins for good. I'm sure King Curtis must have understood why. I had many reasons for leaving the organization. One of the main reasons was, I had previously recorded a guitar rhythm sound on a reel-to-reel in a rehearsal with bass player Mervin Bronson, of the King Curtis and the Kingpins band. My guitar creation, with Mervin playing the bass, became the precise guitar part and rhythm played in the tune called 'The Ghetto' by Curtis and Donny Hathaway. I didn't know Curtis had taken my guitar creation from the reel-to-reel at rehearsal on Broadway and recorded it precisely with Cornell Dupree, the other guitar in the band with me, playing it as I played it on the reel-to-reel. Lyrics were written for the recording, but I was excluded from any copyrights, and thoughtlessly left out of any type of credit for my guitar rhythm creation. The song 'The Ghetto' should have included my name for a percentage of the copyrights.[10]

September 1968 saw Curtis helping out Jerry Lewis for his annual Muscular Dystrophy Association telethon, then flying to a concert in Montreal on September 14, next supporting the *Soul!* television show on New York Public Television, and then getting back into the studio with Aretha Franklin for her album *Soul '69.* This latest Franklin album would rocket to number 1 on the *Billboard* R&B album chart and number 15 on the *Billboard* Top Album chart, despite containing singles that, by themselves, were only moderately successful: "Tracks of My Tears" (which reached number 21 on *Billboard's* R&B singles and number 71 on the pop singles) and "Gentle on My Mind" (which topped out at number 50 and number 76 on the R&B singles and pop singles charts, respectively).

The following month, Curtis and the band spent a week back in Montreal at the Sahara Club beginning on the seventh, and then they traveled back to New York and the Philharmonic Hall to support Aretha Franklin and the Sweet Inspirations. Curtis returned to the Atlantic recording studio to back

Ben E. King for some Atco tracks, including the King Curtis/Christopher Jackson composition, "When You Love Somebody."

Curtis then promptly left for a tour with the Four Tops from November 7 to 17. Jerry Wexler returned to New York and got back to the business at hand. In December, he released King Curtis and the Kingpins' next album, *King Size Soul*.

However, there was something new on the horizon. Jerry Wexler called it "swamp music." The music man was at it again, having previously been credited with originating the term "rhythm and blues" for the Black music of the 1950s while a reporter for *Billboard* magazine. He now coined the term "swamp music" to describe the white roots music played by artists from the South in the mid- to late sixties and into the early seventies. From Dr. John's Louisiana bayou sound in New Orleans all the way to the Allman Brothers in Macon, Georgia, this musical homage to soul and gospel music engulfed the southeastern United States, from Corpus Christi, Texas, along the Gulf Coast to the Florida panhandle, and northward. And the man at the epicenter of this Southern backwoods musical maelstrom was Delaney Bramlett.

Hailing from Pontotoc, Mississippi, Bramlett quickly rose from destitution to the recording studios of Los Angeles, arriving before long at the front door of Ahmet Ertegun's New York City apartment. After moving to Los Angeles, it was love at first sight as Delaney was completely smitten by the first white Ikette for Ike and Tina Turner, Bonnie Lynn O'Farrell, who had similarly picked up from East St. Louis, Missouri, and relocated in the West. Their initial meeting was followed by a passionate two-week courtship after which the two married. The Bramletts then formed a band, Delaney & Bonnie and Friends, and the contagious nature of their Southern white bayou-cultivated music and captivating stage presence enraptured all who heard and saw them, from fans to fellow artists alike.

Stax Records in Memphis had signed a distribution deal with Atlantic Records, and Atlantic often sent artists to Stax to record. Jerry Wexler remembered the fateful call he received one day from Ahmet Ertegun: "Don Nix had discovered them [Delaney & Bonnie], Stax Records had signed them, and their first album excited everyone at Muscle Shoals, which is where I was when Ahmet called me to say they were available. 'Grab 'em,'

I yelled, 'Grab 'em quick!"[11] Delaney & Bonnie and Friends was now a signed Atlantic Records recording act.

Jerry Wexler expanded on the impact of Delaney & Bonnie in the evolution of swamp music: "The Southern whites, the music they played was organically the same as the black's music, because they were from the same culture—there was no difference. Certainly, there was Jim Crow and separatism in the South, segregation and so on. At the bottom of the agrarian ladder, however, which was where these musicians lived, black and white, they came from the same place. There were many things they shared; they did the same things and squished the same red mud between their toes. When Delaney and Bonnie hit, they were so exciting, there was nothing more exciting out there."[12]

By 1969, it seemed every musician wanted to play in Delaney & Bonnie's band, and Delaney & Bonnie always had a standing request to whomever might be available. Over the years, this unpredictable "open invitation" entourage included at one time or another the likes of Leon Russell, Eric Clapton, Duane Allman, George Harrison, Carl Radle, Jim Gordon, Bobby Whitlock, Jim Price, Dave Mason, Bobby Keys, Sandy Konikoff, Jim Keltner, and many others. "At the time," laughed Delaney to me, "I never knew who was going to be in the band. Sometimes we'd have a two-piece horn section, sometimes we had a thirty-piece horn section, and it just grew and grew."[13]

While touring England and warming up for Eric Clapton and his band, Blind Faith (one of rock and roll's first "super groups," consisting of Clapton, Steve Winwood, Ginger Baker, and Ric Grech), Delaney and Eric became close friends—so much so that Clapton came to prefer playing with Delaney & Bonnie and Friends over his own bandmates. In his autobiography Clapton noted the reason for his change in focus:

> For me going on after Delaney and Bonnie was really, really tough, because I thought they were miles better than us. Their band was made up of all these great Southern musicians, who had such a strong sound and performed with absolute confidence ... needless to say it wasn't long before I dropped all my responsibilities as being part of Blind Faith and started to hang out with them.

Their approach to music was infectious. They would pull out their guitars on the bus and would play songs all day as they traveled, while we were much more insular and tended to keep to ourselves. I took to travelling with them and playing with them. The truth is I was the man in the hallway, who has come out one door, only to find it has closed behind him while another one is opening. Through that door were Delaney and Bonnie, and I was irresistibly drawn towards it.[14]

Blind Faith broke up shortly after the tour with Delaney & Bonnie and Friends, and the English press immediately assailed Delaney, charging that he had strategically aligned himself with Clapton to undermine, and ultimately sabotage, the group as well as pilfer the guitarist for his own devices. Delaney bristled at this suggestion; as far as he is concerned, it could not have been further from the truth:

At that time, Gerry McGee played guitar with me, and Dave Mason started playin' guitar. Man, they were all wanderin' around. Eric didn't join the band then; I didn't know Eric at that point. Eric was in Blind Faith, and they asked if Delaney and Bonnie could open the shows for them here in the States. We did and got terrible press over there [England], sayin' we broke up Blind Faith, which is not true. Blind Faith couldn't stand to ride with each other. So, Eric's sittin' there one day and he says, "Can I just mess around with you guys? Do you mind if I come and play with you?" He did and was up there for every show.[15]

Delaney and Eric would forge an enduring friendship, with Delaney widely credited by Clapton himself with teaching him to sing. Delaney recalled his vocal formula for helping any of his friends sing well:

Well, I would show some little things; it's like I would see something in their voice I would really like. I would tell them, "You're over-lookin'; you're throwing away your best quality. You're using the garbage, and you should throw that garbage away and use the best quality." And so we talked about it, and I would sit and sing the same line to him, or something like that, in that order. And he would say, "I see what you mean."
     You know, opera singers sing from the diaphragm, and that's why you don't hear—some of 'em use a little throat, not many of 'em. But I said I like to use both, throat for the tone, diaphragm for the power.[16]

And he could indeed generate power, for no microphone manufactured yet could withstand Delaney's intense, forceful vocal delivery: "I can bust any mike there is. And then—here I am, a hundred and eighty years old, I can still break mikes, you know—and I did break 'em all the time. You can ask my wife," he said with a grin. "She gets mad."[17]

Returning to the States, Delaney & Bonnie got back to recording, showing up at Fame Studios in Muscle Shoals, Alabama, but minus one guitar player. Delaney requested Ry Cooder, who was unavailable. Jerry Wexler had a solution: "Ry was booked, so I recommended Duane Allman."[18]

Hailing from Macon, Georgia, Duane Allman had been playing in the backing band for producer Rick Hall at Fame Studios in Muscle Shoals, Alabama. When Wilson Pickett recorded his cover of the Beatles classic "Hey Jude" (reaching number 16 on the *Billboard* charts), Jerry Wexler was struck by the talents of the lead guitar player. "Wilson calls him 'Sky Man,'" Hall told Wexler, "'cuz he likes to get high. He's got hair down to his butt. He's a hippie from Macon, but I'll be damned if he didn't talk Pickett into singing the song. Wilson said a Beatles tune didn't fit him. The hippie said, 'What's wrong, you don't got the balls to sing it?' That's all that Pickett needed to hear."[19] Despite Allman being a neophyte in the industry, Wexler was so impressed with his performance on the song that he bought Duane Allman's contract from Rick Hall for $15,000, a tidy sum at the time. Everybody won in this transaction, as Hall and Wexler each felt they had emerged victorious over the other.

At first look, Delaney was put off by his friend Jerry Wexler's recommendation for a new guitar player. "Delaney was suspicious," Wexler noted. "But when Duane came down they formed an instant and intense musical bond."[20] Wexler planned to use Allman as a session player at Atlantic Records, where he would meet, along with Delaney, Aretha Franklin's bandleader, King Curtis.

Curtis, who always had complete confidence in Jerry Wexler's opinions, took Wexler at his word and booked Duane Allman in Memphis on January 2, 1969, to support Curtis's newest album, *Instant Groove.* Playing with the American Studios backing band of Jimmy Johnson on guitar,

David Hood on bass, and Roger Hawkins on drums, the album would also feature the trademark string accompaniments of Arif Mardin. Curtis and Duane would quickly join forces again six days later to record three songs for Aretha Franklin, featuring her popular interpretation of the The Band's hit song "The Weight," which lasted seven weeks and topped out at number 19 on the *Billboard* chart.

Impressed with the young guitar player's incredible talent, Curtis rushed Allman back to Fame's Muscle Shoals studio to finish work on more tracks for his album *Instant Groove*, featuring Curtis's own version of "The Weight" and a cover of Joe South's hit "Games People Play." Allman simply replicated what he did on his previous "The Weight" effort with Aretha and added some brief slide guitar work to the tune.

Finalizing the album in late April in New York with the standard Kingpins ensemble, the group cut the only tune that would crack the record charts, the title track "Instant Groove," which would debut suddenly at number 35 on the *Billboard* R&B chart but disappear almost as quickly, lasting only two weeks.

Once introduced by Jerry Wexler, the trio of King Curtis, Delaney Bramlett, and Duane Allman hit it off immediately, with Curtis now playing big brother not only to Aretha Franklin but to Delaney Bramlett and Duane Allman. Wexler fondly recalled the cohesiveness between the three men, as well as his own growing fondness for Curtis: "The only thing I can say is we became very good friends," smiled Jerry Wexler. "And he [Curtis] became friends with my family, too—with my kids and, when I had a house in East Marion on the North Fork on Long Island, I mean, he would come out on his motorcycle and stay over. Delaney Bramlett would come and stay there, Duane Allman would come—they sort of formed this trium-virate, you know? They acted as a musical troika, and they would come together at my house, more than anything. I remember when those three would play together in this incredible freestyle mode, playing soft Delta blues in my backyard together."[21] Wexler has often said that one of his biggest regrets was not having his tape recorder rolling for these sublime, impromptu sessions between Delaney, Duane, and Curtis. Delaney fondly remembered it like it was yesterday: "We got some clams—we dug some

Curtis perfectly outfitted (of course) on his beloved Honda
CL450 Scrambler. *Courtesy of Modeen Brown.*

clams and baked 'em and just sat out there and played music. We played
music twenty-four hours a day."[22]

Bonnie Bramlett recalled Jerry Wexler telling stories about Billie
Holiday on these Long Island escapes. She also remembered King Curtis's
motorcycle. One night at the Wexler home, Duane wanted to take Bonnie for

a quick spin on Curtis's bike, despite Delaney's protestations to the contrary: "Well, I don't know … don't go fast with her."[23] Bonnie, however, felt perfectly comfortable with Duane. As she told me, they had earlier become trusted friends: "Duane was my friend years before I ever met Delaney … I knew Duane in St. Louis years before I ever met Delaney."[24]

Wexler's driveway was particularly long, providing a safe haven from traffic as long as the two stayed on the driveway. This lent small comfort to Delaney, who, almost as though he experienced a foreshadowing of Duane's fate, worried about having Bonnie on a motorcycle at all. Bonnie felt like having a little fun:

> Well, the driveway was about a quarter of a mile from where they were. The house was right on the beach. And so, you had a minute to get out to the hard road. Which is, like, just a two-lane, regular hard road in a straight line. By the time—I kept sayin' [to Duane] "Will you take me," and Delaney said, "Now don't take her fast," you know, "Don't take her fast." And I went, "Take me a *little* fast, you know? C'mon, I won't tell." He [Duane] said, "You're gonna get me in trouble"—he's yellin', all scared, "I'm gonna be in trouble!" I said, "I won't tell anyone, just take me a little fast."[25]

As the pair crept down the driveway, Bonnie urged, "Take me just little fast, Duane."[26] Duane suddenly revved the engine, speeding off with Bonnie clutching Duane around his waist, all the while screaming at the top of her lungs. When Duane reached the end of the driveway, he pulled over and Bonnie quickly hopped off, terrified by the sudden sprint: "So, he gets out on the pavement, and he goes, 'Reeeeeeeeeeeeeeee,' then 'REE a REE a REE a REE.' We were goin' SO fast, I was just goin' 'WAAAAAAAAAAAAAAAAAAAA!!' I was screamin' bloody murder all the way down, and then he stopped, and I say, 'STOOOOOOOOOOOOOOP!' He stopped it and I got off, and I say 'I ain't NEVER gettin' back on …'" Bonnie told author Galadrielle Allman what happened next:

> [Duane was pleading] "Git on this motorcycle Bonnie, we gotta go back … if I go back and tell them you won't come they'll get so mad at me."

Duane Allman at Atlantic Studios with mentor King Curtis, January 10, 1969. *Photo by Steven Paley / Michael Ochs Archives / Getty Images.*

"You promise me."

"I'll *never* do that again. I promise you to God I will never do that again, just get back on this motorcycle."[27]

Bonnie screamed, "You son of a bitch! You scared the hell out of me!" "Oh my God, Bonnie. I promise, I never would have done that if I knew how upset you would be," Duane pleaded. "Please just get back on the bike. I promise, I'll be careful, just come on now."[28]

Hesitantly, and still visibly upset with tears streaming down her face, Bonnie carefully climbed on the back of the bike and muttered, "Oh, all right, you better not—" and Duane immediately zoomed off at top speed back down the driveway, spewing rocks everywhere, Bonnie shrieking with laughter all the way back to the house.[29] As she told me: "He did the *same damn thing*, because he knew he had that quarter of a mile to pat my red eyes—no problem, just tryin' to get my eyes not red [from crying]."[30] Bonnie still laughed about her moment of terror with Duane and how the master salesman talked her into getting back onto Curtis's motorcycle: "Oh, he could look *so* sincere. Shit. Gave me whiplash all the way home!"[31] Duane Allman had safely negotiated Jerry Wexler's long driveway on a motorcycle. A few years later, he wouldn't be so lucky.

Curtis's girlfriend, Modeen, remembered the closeness of the trio, even as she kept her distance from their free-flowing musical experimentation: "I knew them all and I was there; I would see them play their instruments or whatever they were doing, and it meant nothing to me. I did not get involved, because I was not a musician—I could see them sit there until the sun would come up—singing, playing, trying new things—and maybe preparing some food for them, whether at my house or their house."[32] Modeen also became very close with Bonnie, as Bonnie fondly remembered: "I hung with Modeen: like, the wives. Because they [all the men] would ditch me whenever they could. And they did that. The guys stuck together … and I reached out to Modeen on a couple of occasions."[33]

In fact, Duane, Delaney, and Curtis became so close that Duane and Delaney kept their own private, locked rooms at Curtis's apartment in New York, and Duane and Curtis had a standing invitation to stay at

Delaney's spread in California. Modeen noted that "[when the Bramletts or Duane were in town], they were our guests and when we went to California we were theirs."[34] Bonnie, always glad to have any company in the house, at the same time suspected the men had ulterior motives for staying at each other's homes: "It wasn't, like, *just* Curtis and Modeen's room; it was his and Cornell's [Dupree]. They stayed at our place—we liked company. Yeah, we like company; we didn't go to the hotels. You get your feelings hurt if somebody stayed at a hotel and not … at your house. Besides that, if we stay at the house, they can ditch us women a lot easier; they can't leave us in a hotel room—we'll find them in a heartbeat."[35]

There were special and intimate moments exchanged between the friends when staying at home with each other, especially when Curtis was in town. Bonnie smiled sweetly when reminiscing about this time:

> When Curtis and Modeen came to the house, and I had my two little girls that lived with Delaney and I—Suzanne … Suzanne was, like, about five … five years old maybe by now. And we lived out in the Valley. And so, Curtis is sittin' on Delaney's big easy chair in a den, and our den is like three steps down. The easy chair fits two people. So, Suzanne was sittin' in the easy chair next to Curtis. And she's so little and he's so big, and his arms are like this [demonstrating large arms], and he's got his arm around her right here.
> Curtis looked at us and smiled, saying, "Look at us," and we're sittin' there talkin', you know. It was so sweet. She loved her some King Curtis.[36]

And Bonnie agreed with Modeen, who said children in general loved Curtis—everyone loved being around Curtis: "'Cuz he was funny. But he was firm, and that made me feel safe. I knew there were boundaries that you didn't want to cross, which made me feel safe. And I also knew that if I was hurtin' in any way, shape or form, he was gentle."[37]

Delaney recalled the magical musical bond he shared with King Curtis and Duane Allman:

> We used to sit and talk about it: he said he was "me" and playing sax like I sang, and I tried to sing like he played sax—me and him, we used to talk about that. Same thing with Duane: we used to play what

we thought one of the three of us would do, and we'd do it, like what we thought the other one would have done, and that's what was golden about that whole thing. You have no idea—nobody will ever know—what the whole thing was about. Nobody will ever know. See, me and Duane and Curtis would sit in one room, by ourselves, and we'd play, and we'd sing.[38]

In light of their intense relationship, labeling these three artists as the Three Musketeers of Atlantic Records would have been accurate, but Delaney had already christened the trio himself: "We all made a pact—I'm tellin' ya, we were 'The Three M'skeeters,' [muh-SKEET-ers] man, you get us three together, you're not gonna need nobody else. I'll tell you right now; we'd walk in and sit in a nightclub, and people didn't know what to think. We didn't need no drums, we didn't need no bass, we didn't need no nuthin'! Just us three, just sittin' there."[39]

Kingpins bassist Jerry Jemmott also recalled working with Allman on Atlantic sessions:

We used to call him "Sky Man" [later called "Skydog"] because he had that long, blond hair, and well, he was *out* there. I think maybe Wilson Pickett named him. Anyway, he'd come up to New York to do sessions, I'd go down to Muscle Shoals to do sessions, and so we played together a lot. He was great to work with: great insight into music. Call it insight, intuition—all the great players have it. They listen ahead. It's all about knowing where it's going. He was one of those people that could do that. The last time I saw him, he told me he was leaving to get a band together with his brother, and he sure did it.[40]

On the many occasions that Duane Allman would come to New York City, he and King Curtis also would hit the town with Atlantic producer Joel Dorn, always sharing friendly banter:

When I would be done working and Duane was done and Curtis was done and we'd have some time, you know—like late in the evening—we'd just hang out. Mostly get high and laugh. That's really what it was about.
     Duane and Curtis and I talked about doing some stuff. Curtis was another guy—I mean everybody knows him for those solos on that

R&B shit he did, but Curtis could *play*. We'd have these reefer conversations and say, "Yeah, how about if we get this front line together and this rhythm section and do it." And I would say, "*You* can't produce! Why don't you just sit there and have some lunch or something?" And we would start with that kind of stuff.[41]

Regarding the touring and socializing Delaney, Duane, and Curtis did together, the subject of their shared drug use is an understandably keen topic. While both Delaney and Duane were known for using cocaine often, Modeen insisted that this wasn't Curtis's main habit—gambling was: "Oh, he used it and whenever he did, it wasn't around me. It didn't control him. It wasn't his favorite thing to do, but yes, he did it socially."[42]

However, Duane Allman's brother Greg contended that Curtis was the one who introduced him to cocaine: "I was turned on to cocaine by King Curtis, during the [Allman] Brothers' trip out in Los Angeles. I had done a fair amount of speed before I tried cocaine, and to tell you the truth, coke didn't really work on me. It seems that people who had taken speed, when they tried coke, it wouldn't work, and the people who took cocaine, when they tried speed, it wouldn't work. When I first tried coke, it just gave me cottonmouth, and not much else."[43] And in a 1971 interview with *Rolling Stone* magazine's Ben Fong-Torres, producer Bob Krasnow, who convinced Tina Turner and her husband Ike to record a cover of Otis Redding's "I've Been Loving You too Long," had this observation of what he felt was Ike's introduction to cocaine: "That night he [Ike] made his first deal—bought $3000 of cocaine from King Curtis, and he bought it and showed me, and I laughed and said, 'That's not coke, that's fucking *Drano*!' Since then, he's learned.' What—to lighten up on drugs? 'No—to tell what good coke is and what bad coke is.'"[44]

To be fair, the streetwise, confident Curtis also cared enough to educate his friends about drugs, as Joel Dorn recalled:

You know what? King Curtis was a real smart guy. As a musician he had everybody's respect. When I came to New York I was really a brash kid. One night, he said, "You working tonight at the studio? I'm gonna pick you up later." So I knew we were going to smoke some reefer, we were going to do some drinking, and we were going to end up in a good club. Curtis always had a Cadillac with a leather roof, and it was fun; we'd go uptown and hang.

So he came up this night and took me in the car and said, "I'm gonna take you someplace." I'd been to the Apollo and to the clubs in Harlem, but I'd never been on this scary street. It was pitch black; there wasn't a light on in any window, and it almost looked abandoned. He took me into this place and down a hallway, there was a guy guarding the doorway who was big as the door. I knew we were in a new place. The guy said, "Hey Curtis," opened the door and let us in.

It was a cut house where all these old Cuban ladies were smoking cigars, some of them cutting cocaine, some of them cutting heroin. There were guns all over the place and I mean, it was far out. So Curtis went over to one of the tables, and he put his finger into this white powder. He said, "Stick your tongue out." It was the tiniest little bit of something. He said, "Can you taste it?" I said, "Yeah." He said, "Remember that taste." It was so tiny, I didn't catch a buzz off of it, but I know now, unfortunately, it was coke.

So I got this coke taste in my mouth, Curtis waited about fifteen minutes, and we took a drink of soda or water. We went over to another part of the place, and there was more white powder, more Cuban women, more flipping of stuff. He said, "Stick your tongue out again." Again, a tiny bit. He said, "You got that taste?" I said, "Yeah." He said, "Rinse your mouth out real quick."

After a few more minutes, he said, "You remember that taste of the first one?" I said, "Yeah." We waited a few more minutes and left. He looked at me—Curtis was a real funny character, but he was serious this time—and he said, "That first thing you tasted was cocaine, the second thing you tasted was heroin. Stay away from all this shit, but if you ever do it, look for that taste first. I don't want you to die."[45]

King Curtis enjoyed his recreational time with friends but was always looking out for their best interests. It was one thing to have fun but entirely another to be out of control and dangerous. He valued his friends and took their safety seriously.

Chapter 13

Donny and Slowhand

As if playing and socializing with Delaney Bramlett and Duane Allman did not keep Curtis busy enough, he also began branching out into producing records at Atlantic Records. Atlantic's top producer, Tom Dowd, gave me his review of Curtis's abilities in the control room: "Curtis was a great producer. He knew how to relate to the musicians and keep everyone comfortable. He was a great horn player, but many people don't know he was a very talented producer."[1]

Curtis still loved to record in the studio, and July 9, 1969, found him back at Atlantic playing on a Shirley Scott album entitled *Shirley Scott and the Soul Saxes*. The Soul Saxes, the band backing the accomplished Scott and her Hammond B-3 organ, were three of the most noteworthy sax players in the business: Hank Crawford (Ray Charles's former music director), David "Fathead" Newman (another top Ray Charles sax player), and King Curtis. On paper, this looked to be another successful sax supergroup, akin to Curtis's previous collaboration with Oliver Nelson and Jimmy Forrest on *Soul Battle*. With Eric Gale on guitar, standard Kingpins pianist Richard Tee, Jerry Jemmott on bass, and Bernard Purdie on drums accompanying Scott and the sax trio, this album certainly had all the star-powered ingredients for success.

The album consisted of soul and pop music covers such as the Isley Brothers' "It's Your Thing," Aretha Franklin's "(You Make Me Feel Like) A Natural Woman," Ben E. King's "Stand by Me," and the Beatles' "Get Back." Unfortunately, on many songs, Ernie Royal's trumpet drowns out many of the other musicians. Producer Joel Dorn, filled with optimism for the assembled band and the album's potential, bemoaned the fact that the outcome missed the mark:

> For the album *Shirley Scott and the Soul Saxes*, it was my idea to put King Curtis, Hank Crawford and David Newman together, but I'll be honest, I was a little disappointed with the result. I think if the arrangements had been better, it would have helped, but I wish that I'd known more about what I was doing then, because I would have made a better record. The idea was great, but it just didn't come off right, and it was such a great opportunity because it was the only time those three guys were on the same record.
>
> It was early in my career, I was twenty-six years old, I'd had a great idea, but I didn't set it up to work properly. Shirley and her sax-playing husband, Stanley Turrentine, were going through their divorce at the time. I knew Shirley from my days as a D.J. in Philly. She was very intelligent, but soft spoken, very sweet, and low-key. She was a pianist originally but moved into the organ because that provided work in the clubs, on what used to be called the "chitlin circuit." The organ's like an orchestra in a box, and organ/tenor trios or quartets were really in demand. It was a genre that was looked down on by the orthodox jazz crowd, but if you like to have fun, it's incredible music.[2]

Saxophonist Trevor Lawrence, famous for co-writing the Pointer Sisters' "I'm So Excited" and playing on Stevie Wonder's "Superstition" and "Sir Duke" along with other hit songs, was now called in to the recording studio to help support a King Curtis–produced session for bluesman Freddie King on the Cotillion label. Lawrence was stunned at how kind his idol King Curtis was to him and shared many of his favorite memories with me:

> The big thing was with King Curtis: I met King Curtis! We, as kids growin' up—as a matter of fact, one of the first R&B songs I learned was "Soul Twist." So naturally, me meeting King Curtis, that was, like, a remarkable thing. The thing that's even more remarkable is that he was so nice to me! The very first time I had sushi, King

Curtis took me to a sushi restaurant. And were settin' down eatin' raw fish—I had never even heard of sushi. But that's the kind of guy he was, man, if he liked you. I know Curtis, and I hung out with him. We became friends, and I was one of his close circle of friends ... He really showed me the way.[3]

And while Lawrence has always been grateful for King Curtis's support in the recording studio, he's even more appreciative of the learning experience Curtis extended to him in the production booth:

I played on the records with him where he was being a producer. I'll tell you another great thing about King Curtis. First of all, you gotta figure out the correlation between it—I'm a saxophone player and I wanted to be an arranger. And as I got into the record business, I seen what a producer did, and to me, I could be a producer because I was an arranger ... I knew musicians.

But the thing is, what King Curtis did for me, let me tell you what he did. He knew that I wanted to be a producer and that I was an arranger, so you know what he did? He allowed me to actively do the sessions. I'd come in the control room, and I'd sit in that control room all the time while everybody's working. I got a chance to see the engineers work: Tom Dowd (can you imagine a young man like me, just from Brooklyn, and in five years I'm sittin' there, I'm sittin' at Atlantic?), Tom Dowd is there, King Curtis is there, everybody is in there working, and I'm there watching and taking it in. Understanding how they splice tape, you know? I mean, I got my education from King Curtis.

I don't think he knew he was doin' that; I just think he liked the people that he liked around him. You know what I mean? I don't think he was intentionally saying, "I'm going to teach this kid to be a producer," I think he had me hangin' out there, but by allowing me to hang out there I got a chance to see how he worked. What you learn immediately is the give-and-take of the producer. You gotta pick everybody's brain.[4]

For Lawrence, King Curtis's influence wasn't just about playing the saxophone properly or becoming a great producer. It was also all about how to become successful:

King Curtis was a very, very important part of my life. King Curtis was very beneficial to me in a lot of ways, not only in music, but in me seeing what type of person I wanted to look like. He was a successful saxophone player; I never thought saxophone players could make a living, but it wasn't until I saw him that I really saw what it would look like.

As a matter of fact, there's another great thing that King Curtis did. I mean, one day out of the blue, King Curtis comes up to me and says, "Hey, I got this for you." He gave me this tenor saxophone mouthpiece. The Otto Link 150/2 mouthpiece, the kind that he played [sources say Curtis preferred a Berg Larsen 150/2 mouthpiece]. He said, "Yeah, man, I got you one of these." And just out of the blue! And I used that mouthpiece, oh Jesus Christ, I think I used that mouthpiece from then, I think that might have been 1968. I used that mouthpiece up until maybe ten years ago. I still have it! I used it when I played [Marvin Gaye's] "Trouble Man" [in 1972], and all of those albums that I did, I used that mouthpiece. You know, King Curtis just gave it to me ... just out of the blue: "Hey man, you should try to use this." I don't know what his thought pattern was about, I don't know what he was doin', but you know what? He did it. He didn't give me no story about it, and I wasn't beholden to him about it; he never made you feel like you owed him anything. He was that kind of a person. He was just, to me, just a great inspiration and a great person to pattern myself after. Well, I patterned myself after King Curtis. He kept himself; he was very sharp, very well dressed, very classy. And that's the kind of person I tried to be.[5]

Lawrence, too, had his own story about King Curtis's cherished motorcycle and how self-sufficient and determined Curtis could be:

I remember one time we had a gig, a gig somewhere in Washington, DC, and he decided he was going to ride his motorcycle. I think he had one of those famous cars. It wasn't like the Cadillac El Dorado; it was the competition to that.

And so, we're going down, and I'm in this car ... and he's on the motorcycle, and unfortunately it started to rain. And oh, man, it was a mess. And you know what? He rode the bike all the way. He didn't stop; he didn't make somebody else take the bike. He did it. Once he said he was going to do something, he was there.

I mean, *this* guy, he was always driven; I mean you want to *become* this guy. I mean, the respect level was very high. I looked up to this guy. Of course, I'm a saxophone player and he's the great King Curtis, but he didn't even treat me like I was "just another saxophone player." Once he liked you, he treated you like you were somebody.[6]

While attending a convention in Palm Springs in late 1969, Curtis was approached in his hotel lobby by a young man with a dream. The man handed Curtis a demo tape of some original songs that he had written and sang, begging Curtis to listen to them. Ever sympathetic for the struggle of a young artist and recalling his days as Mickey Baker's prodigy and its impact on his own career, Curtis took the recording up to his room and listened to it with Modeen. What he heard made Curtis run straight to the phone and call Jerry Wexler at his home on Long Island. Screaming that he had found a stone-cold star, the next morning Curtis jumped on the first plane back to New York City and hurried the tape to Wexler's office. After hearing this tape-recorded performance of "The Ghetto," Wexler agreed to sign the young artist at once. Donny Hathaway was now an Atlantic Records artist.

Donny Hathaway would go on to become one of the stars of the soul music movement. In addition, he would make major contributions to jazz, blues, and gospel, most notably for his solo work and duets with Roberta Flack on such hits as "The Closer I Get to You" and "Where Is the Love." Modeen recalled:

> We met Donny Hathaway in a hotel at the BMI dinner in Palm Springs, and Donny Hathaway had taken a tape from the hotel and handed it over. I didn't know Donny, and Curtis called me from the lobby—I was upstairs in bed—and said, "I'm bringing somebody upstairs" (he always traveled with a tape recorder) and said, "I have a tape over here," and Donny and Curtis came upstairs. It was the one with "The Ghetto," that was the one it was. He listened to that, and he left it with Curtis. Curtis brought it home and he took it to Jerry, and it is history after that. He signed with Atlantic, and Curtis had a contract with Atlantic with a piece of Donny. When he played the reel-to-reel tape—I remember Curtis bringing that back and he said, "This is a star!"[7]

Jerry Wexler and Curtis agreed to get Donny Hathaway into the studio as soon as possible. Curtis produced Hathaway's debut album while sitting in (on, of all things, guitar) for the cover of Ray Charles's "I Believe to My Soul." In addition to the talented Hathaway on piano, Curtis flexed his Atlantic muscle by requesting Aretha Franklin also sit in at the piano. The album, *Everything Is Everything*, features Hathaway's debut hit single, "The Ghetto" (achieving number 87 on the *Billboard* Hot 100 and number 23 on the *Billboard* soul singles chart). It also contains a wonderful interpretation of the Nina Simone classic "To Be Young, Gifted and Black." But particularly hair-raising is Hathaway's gospel/soul interpretation of Erroll Garner's jazz standard, "Misty." Donny Hathaway took a song that has been covered as often as any in popular music history and changed the feel and tone completely, making it entirely his own innovative and stunning composition (not unlike what Aretha Franklin created with Otis Redding's "Respect").

As diplomatic as King Curtis could be in the recording studio for bringing together white and Black musicians, he was not immune to mistakes. Joel Dorn told me of a particularly famous faux pas Curtis made when working on a Roberta Flack recording session:

> I get a call from Wexler, and he said, "Roberta Flack is using Donny Hathaway to write charts on the album you are making." I said, "Yeah, I know." That is like someone calling you to say the sun is going to come up. He said, "Look, Donny doesn't want to work with a white producer, so I have an idea. Can you work with Curtis?" I said, "Of course." He said, "Okay, Donny will relate to Curtis, you just keep your mouth shut and let Curtis figure out who to talk to." So, Curtis calls me up, and he said, "You got a problem with that?" I said, "No problem at all. It will be fun, man." So, Donny wrote two charts, "Reverend Lee" and "Gone Away," and he, Curtis, and Roberta sang background.
>
> Here is the system that we developed: I would stay in the control room; I wouldn't look at Donny, and I wouldn't talk to him. Curtis would go from the control room to the studio, and I would keep the monitors on so I could check out what was going on in the studio (I could see everybody talking), and then Curtis would come in and we would talk. If Donny were around, I just sat on the sofa and Curtis would talk. The whole thing was: Donny had his Black producer and I was going to be kept in tow—I'm happy to do it. I'm keeping my mouth shut, and I don't say a word—nothing. Donny comes in, and he had a bad scene on the plane. Donny was very heavy [in body weight], and they bought him a coach ticket, and I don't think he had enough money to upgrade it or didn't know how to get into first class. So, he came and he was embarrassed 'cuz he had to squeeze into the seat, and with the whole scene, he came in and he was livid. He gets off the elevator and Curtis says, "Hey Donny, welcome to Salt and Pepper

Productions"—a little ice breaker. Donny said, "I've had enough of salt and all I want is pepper." He went off on a thing that was insane. He could have done that anywhere, but he was pissed off about the flight because the seats were too small.

So, we're working and Donny insists on certain things, and we are letting him do whatever he wants—usually you put the rhythm down from seven to ten and then ten to one, you bring the strings and horns in, but Donny wanted everybody there at seven o'clock whether they were playing at two o'clock in the morning or not. That session must have cost three billion dollars and we are doing it, and the string and horn players are in heaven because they are getting paid to play cards, making phone calls, reading the paper— it's a regular lunatic session. Donny lays everything down and he keeps coming back between the control room and the studio, and I'm staying on the dummy [quiet].

Every time Curtis would get into the control room [without Hathaway present], he would call Donny every fuckin' name in the world. I won't even go into it, but trust me when I tell you, he ripped Donny to shreds. I don't think it was [as] malicious as it would trans-late, but he said it. We finished the session and I get home about five o'clock in the morning—we got the two tunes and they were fine, everybody went home—and about eight o'clock in the morning I got a call from Noreen Woods, who was Wexler and Ahmet's gatekeeper [secretary]. She was the best. She was like the master politician gate-keeper (information dispenser if she liked you), and she said, "The shit just hit the fan. Remember that session last night?" I said, "How can I forget it?" She said, "Donny had a hidden tape in the cassette player in the control room and taped things being said about him." All he got was Curtis doing that shit, so he went berserk, and I remember Curtis had to apologize to the Atlantic executive board for quite some time."[8]

Curtis began to record new songs for another album, *Everybody's Talkin'*. The album's title track, Curtis's cover of the Temptations hit, was recorded on August 12, 1969, at the Criteria Studio for Atlantic Records, and it would debut at number 46 and last two weeks on the *Billboard* R&B list. And not unlike the generous support he showed for his wife Ethelyn earlier when he formed Kilynn Music Publishing (as Ethelyn had no music writing experience), Curtis gave Modeen songwriting credit for two original songs on the album, "Central Park" and "Wet Funk (Low Down Dirty)." Curtis also started in parallel an album called *Get Ready* produced by his friend Delaney

Bramlett. While in Los Angeles recording with Delaney on January 26, 1970, Eric Clapton and Duane Allman were called in to the studio by Delaney to help record the King Curtis single, "Teasin'."

Playing just one song with King Curtis was more than enough to stun Clapton. Clapton biographer Ray Coleman wrote:

> Eric is sparing with his praise of other musicians, a trait which makes his nominations as his favorites particularly significant. He thinks long and hard before naming the people who have been special to him. On non-guitarists who have been important to him, Eric says, "Steve Winwood is very high on the list. Also harmonica players like the guy who used to play with Muddy Waters [Jerry Portnoy]. Saxophone players, too: I once worked with King Curtis, and that was frighteningly good, something I wanted to repeat forever. He had exactly the same idea about what lines to play as I did. It was like another instrument with the same person playing it."[9]

In a 1980 interview with BBC radio personality Tommy Vance, Clapton elaborated on his only recording opportunity with King Curtis. Vance asked, "Of all the recorded material that you've been involved in, and that's really an extensive amount, which to you is the most gratifying; which do you ever play at home or maybe even hear on the radio and think, "Yeah, I really gave it all I had at that moment in time?"[10] Caught off guard by the question, Eric emitted aloud a thoughtful sigh and responded:

> "Ahhh. The first thing to hit me then when you asked me that was a recording I did with King Curtis. Not necessarily because I gave all I had, but the memory of it is so vivid, just the spontaneity of the recording. It was just so quick ... it was ... I think he [Curtis] was doing sessions with Delaney in LA. And they were fed up with what they were doing, they were doing something for hours and hours and it was getting nowhere so he said, 'Let's just do something else.' And he sang the line he wanted to play, and I played it with him. And we did it in about ten minutes ... it was great, it was perfect. And it was called ... God, what was it called ... 'Teasin'. And it's still one of my favorite performances ... it's not, there's nothing spectacular about this, it's just very sweet."[11]

Bobby Whitlock, who played keyboards with Delaney & Bonnie and Friends and later for Eric Clapton with Derek and the Dominos, was also there in the studio covering organ and confirmed to me the connection all the musicians shared in their one and only collaboration: "I was there. It was magic. He [Clapton] and Curtis, they were both right on the money. They played exactly together. It was magic. Like they call it down here, 'FM.' Whenever there's a session and somebody does something incredible down here, they call it FM; it stands for 'fucking magic'!"[12]

Aside from the musical symbiosis displayed in the studio between Eric Clapton and King Curtis, in his autobiography Whitlock also has other fond memories of the recording date and the evolution of the song:

> Ahmet Ertegun had introduced us to King Curtis when we were in New York one time. Ahmet played a big role with Delaney and Bonnie as well and was very good at hooking different artists up. He knew who and what would work well together. King Curtis was a gracious, kind, and gentle man. He was who you see when you see a picture of him laughing or smiling.
>
> Thanks to Ahmet, Delaney was asked to produce a track for the forthcoming King Curtis *Get Ready* album at Sunset Sound [Wally Heider Recording Studio III is listed in the Atlantic Records Discography] in Los Angeles. As Eric [Clapton] was in town, he was asked if he would like to play on the track. "Teasin'" was pretty much made up on the spot with Curtis and Eric playing twin parts. The band was really cooking. It is one of my favorite tracks. Eric's wah-wah guitar and King Curtis's soprano sax playing in unison together sounded like one completely unique instrument.[13]

Though the recording session was finished, the memories were to continue: "When we had finished recording, Eric and everybody else left and went back to the hotel. As usual I had to hang around and wait until Delaney was finished. For some reason he would always keep me there with him no matter where we were and not let me leave until he said so. He really was a father figure, and I looked at him that way many times."[14]

The lasting, unforgettable image left in Whitlock's mind for the day, however, may not be what you imagine:

> Delaney and Curtis were overdubbing their parts again after Eric had left and out came this huge bag of blow ... I have a very clear picture of King Curtis sitting in a chair with his sax across his lap and Delaney

standing right next to him and they're laughing. Curtis has an ounce of cocaine in his left hand and a $100 bill in his right hand. It's folded in the shape of a large scoop and he just rammed it in the bag and without looking, stuck it under that great hole of a nostril, and every bit of it went up his nose. Then what wouldn't fit up there just spilled down his face and onto his chest.

Then he did the same thing again to the left side. He never broke stride. It was like he was doing it without even noticing that he was doing it or even giving it any thought whatsoever. He just kept talking and laughing and shoveling that stuff up his nose. I had never seen anything like it. He had a huge grin on his face and looked like he had a white Fu Manchu mustache. He just sat there holding that bag of cocaine and that $100 bill, smiling. I thought for sure that he was going to explode or go into a cardiac arrest. But it never happened … that was the one time that Delaney was outdone. Even he marveled at what Curtis had just done. That is the last picture that I have in my mind of Curtis, sitting there in the chair with cocaine running down his face.[15]

While producing the album may have come easily to Delaney, he was challenged not by Curtis's powerful horn or strong personality but, surprisingly, his insecurities with his singing voice. In earlier recordings Curtis had not been shy about singing, but after so many years of playing the saxophone, Curtis had developed a substantial lisp. This made the self-confident horn player completely self-conscious, shying away from any vocal parts. Not to worry—Delaney applied the same formula to Curtis that he had so successfully ingrained into Eric Clapton: accentuating the unique qualities, not burying them. As Delaney put it:

I produced Curtis the last thing, and I made him sing. Beautiful singer! He just had a lisp, and he didn't want to—but that's what I thought was wonderful about it. The lisp.

I made him sing "Lonesome and a Long Way from Home" [recorded on April 29, 1970, unissued]. He didn't want to sing because he thought he had a lisp (because he had such an embouchure built up playin' that sax). He could play up so high in the melody up there, and people just couldn't believe that it was a tenor, and—because his embrasure was so big.

He said, "No, don't let me sing, I've got this little lisp here."

And I said, "That's the part of the character I like," so he went ahead and sang.[16]

King Curtis accepting his Grammy Award from Herbie Mann
(Eubie Banks presenting). *Soul.*

It's well established that Curtis was always in control in the studio,
be it at the microphone or the mixing board. So, I asked Delaney if Curtis
was difficult and temperamental to produce as a featured recording artist.
"Shit no, he was so easy," Delaney said, smiling. "All I had to do was sit
there and add a suggestion, and he would do it and try it and if it didn't work,
we'd try somethin' else. No shit, he was a joy. I mean, if I hadn't known
him, I would have been so intimidated, but we were friends and had written
songs together."[17]

Curtis, in addition to working with Aretha Franklin, continued his
solo career at Atlantic and out of the blue received word that his earlier
interpretation of Joe South's "Games People Play" had been nominated for
a Grammy Award. While he was thrilled by his nomination, Curtis was
no less puzzled as to why this specific song had even been considered.
"He was shocked—he had no idea, and the song wasn't that big," noted
Cornell Dupree.[18] The other nominees included Ike Turner's "A Black

Man's Soul," Albert Collins's "Trash Talkin'," Junior Walker and the All
Stars' "What Does It Take," and Richard "Groove" Holmes's "Workin'
on a Groovy Thing." "Games People Play" would win the 1969 Grammy
for Best Rhythm and Blues Instrumental Performance. It would be King
Curtis's first and only Grammy Award.

The award itself, while a crowning achievement for Curtis and his
career, also carries with it bittersweet memories. The very next day, a beaming
King Curtis proudly strolled into the PBS studio set of the *Soul!* television show
in New York City with his new Grammy Award in tow. He was ready to
celebrate his unexpected victory with host Ellis Haizlip as well as the studio
and television audiences. Just before the tape would roll for the show,
a triumphant Curtis leaned forward from the stage to show his trophy off to
the impressed studio crowd. Suddenly, a woman lunged forward, grabbed
the award from Curtis's large hands, and fled the studio. Sadly, the award
has never been recovered.

Modeen was horrified: "He was doing Ellis Haizlip's show and took the
Grammy to have it on the show, and some lady in the studio grabbed it and
ran out the door. He tried to get a new one, but they [the Grammy Award
committee] said they didn't replace them."[19]

So yes, King Curtis won a Grammy Award. And, tragically, he held this
coveted trophy of recognition in the palm of his hand for just one day.

Chapter 14

Sam Moore and the Fillmore West

In 1970, Curtis looked to broaden his talents by branching out into writing and performing film and television scores. His friend Ellis Haizlip approached Curtis about being the musical director for PBS's *Soul!* variety television series, and Curtis jumped at the opportunity. What with Curtis's previous successes directing Aretha Franklin's band as well as producing Donny Hathaway, Roberta Flack, the Coasters, and others, Haizlip's nomination was an obvious choice. The weekly show featured a soul artist performing their recent hit single accompanied by an introspective analysis and interview with Haizlip on the impact their music had on current civil rights issues. Adding this new skill and market to his plate (which was overflowing already), Curtis not only maintained his solo and backing work for Atlantic but continued to climb their hierarchy to produce still other Atlantic recording artists.

By 1970, Sam Moore and David Prater had scorched through every soul review performance and recording date as the duo Sam and Dave. Jerry Wexler had signed the pair to Atlantic Records contracts five years earlier and sent them to Stax Records in Memphis. Wexler hit the bullseye again by pairing the vocals of the two with the Stax backing group of Booker T. and the M.G.'s along with the Mar-Keys horn section. Add to this effervescent mix the Stax songwriting duo of Isaac Hayes and David Porter (who penned so many of the pair's hits), and you have the explanation for Sam and Dave's explosive status: a stunning collaboration of cutting-edge songwriting, innovative world-class backing musicians, and of course the pure entertainment and percolating energy that could only be that of Sam and Dave.

Their albums captivated public imagination, especially because the live vocal showmanship generated by Sam and Dave translated so successfully to vinyl. Though the momentum of the live efforts of Delaney & Bonnie and Friends was somehow lost when recorded in the studio, Sam and Dave's histrionics were deeply palpable to even the most casual of music fans. While listening to their records, you could feel them dancing, sweating, urging their audience on every time their songs were played. As noted earlier, the pace of Sam and Dave's live show had blistered the other members of the concert bill during the Stax/Volt tour of Europe in 1967, especially headliner Otis Redding, who could barely keep step when following their warm-up act.

In 1968 Sam and Dave were called home from Memphis by the mother ship, Atlantic Records, to New York City. While they still churned out exemplary material, without the creative, exuberant energy of the Stax musicians and with minimal use of the Hayes/Porter writing duo (although the pair did write several songs during their Atlantic era), the super-hot nova that had been Sam and Dave began to cool. They eventually split in 1970, but Jerry Wexler was adamant about launching Sam Moore as a solo artist. Moore was ecstatic.

Wexler booked the Atlantic recording studio for Sam Moore in late November and early December 1970. Based on King Curtis's recent success producing Atlantic artists, Wexler felt Curtis was ideally equipped to produce this all-important inaugural solo effort. Wexler recalled: "He was a fine producer, and if he was in town when I was recording, he was always next to me in the booth, a fountain of terrific ideas and suggestions. No charge."[1] Ahmet Ertegun also recognized Curtis's creative production influence in the Atlantic Records recording studio: "King Curtis was like a father-figure to all of the other musicians. They all respected him not just for his playing and musical direction, but because he was a monumental person—when he walked into a room, it was like joy had walked into the room."[2]

Jerry Wexler decided to pair Sam Moore with King Curtis out of more than a simplistic desire to assign a Black artist to a Black producer. Sam Moore was in the throes of a horrible addiction to cocaine and heroin. This concerned Jerry Wexler deeply, and he felt that King Curtis's no-nonsense studio personality, in addition to his towering physical presence, could control, motivate, and eventually harness Moore's abilities to create a quality solo album for Atlantic.

Sam Moore, however, was taken aback by the suggested pairing and deeply troubled. No Tom Dowd? No Arif Mardin? No Joel Dorn in charge of the recording booth, *just* King Curtis—a saxophone player?!!? Moore felt it was as if he had been promoted to the varsity, only to be saddled with a "B-squad" coach. He made no secret of his disappointment when I chatted with him: "I respect the man as a saxophone player and a musician, but a producer? When I went to his apartment in New York I was like, he didn't show me nothin'. He was real cocksure. It was like an attitude. It was sort of like a chip on his shoulder ,because this man [thought he] knew what he was doing."[3]

Sam Moore wasn't used to being challenged by someone he perceived to have no credentials:

> I was lukewarm to him, and I couldn't get any warmth out of him, and he was always like, "If you can't do it, I know somebody who can"— stuff like that. He was always talking to me, things that he respected like Ronnie Isley and Donny Hathaway—those were his kind of people. To myself, [I thought,] "If you feel that way, what in the hell are you dealing with me for?" I would go by his apartment and we would sit there and listen to material, and I think one of the first tunes he let me listen to was "Hi Di Hi," [actually the song's title was "That Old Sweet Roll (Hi De Ho)," and it was sung by both Dusty Springfield and The Guess Who in 1969 and 1970, respectively] and I'm going, "Yeah okay, I'm not so sure about this." You have to understand that, at that tim,e I was getting so high myself. Maybe he wasn't so sure about me.[4]

Curtis's response to Sam's pessimism? A terse, "get to work" attitude. The tough love that Curtis showed Moore in the studio clearly left the singer unsettled, which may have been the plan all along: "You are sitting up there, and he was playing tenor on his horn [saying] 'Play the damn thing, Sam.' He would say, 'Let's move on to another song.'"[5] In these early sessions, Moore was genuinely unnerved and confused by the harsh treatment he was receiving: "You would say, 'What is it with this cat?'"[6]

Moore's admission that he was "getting so high myself" was an understatement. Not only did King Curtis have his hands full with the heady Moore's talents and ego, but he also had to wade into and negotiate Sam Moore's addiction. Moore's voice was unforgettable and his talent limitless, but his mind was often addled by drugs. Being the street-savvy man he was, Curtis believed the only way to reach Moore was with tough love, structure, and ultimatums. Curtis began pushing Moore's buttons, shoving challenges straight into his face from the first day together. Curtis would suggest many different songs for Sam to record that Sam felt were not his style. Curtis was trying to broaden Sam's sound for a completely different type of record. Eventually, Curtis wore Sam down, for Sam admitted: "Whatever it was, he still came up with the best."[7]

As the recording sessions progressed and the two dug deeper and deeper into their musical relationship, a begrudging appreciation for each other's talents emerged. Adversarial attitude and doubt were slowly replaced by an air of respect that quickly led to adoration. Finally, this created a trust and cooperation that Moore had not known since his early days at Stax Records in Memphis. This was evident in an interview of the two by Vince Aletti that appeared in the February 18, 1971, issue of *Rolling Stone* magazine. Curtis was effusive in his praise for Moore: "He's one of the greatest singers in the world. I only produce people I like ... and Sam has always been one of my favorite singers."[8] Now delivered from his earlier apprehension toward Curtis's production skills, as Moore described to me, he returned the adulation to Curtis: "We dug each other right away ... with patience, getting to know the artist; there's no rush ... he's just beautiful."[9] As Moore traipses off to the recording studio, Curtis affectionately calls after him, "Take your time, brother-man."[10]

Explaining his production style with Moore to Aletti, Curtis aimed to "clutter up as little as possible—just show the natural flow as opposed to a lot of overdubbing." Moore also explained his evolving style, shepherded by Curtis now that he was a solo artist for Atlantic: "Now I've got a broader chance to make a broader move wherein I can do songs that would exploit my range. Because I do count on my range in the *feeling* that I put in a song. What I do now is start out singing the song on a single track and put a double voice to it. I'll over-dub it myself, maybe two or three times, then I'll just tag it—go on out by myself. It's basically like Sam and Dave, just the fact that I'm singing a little bit higher that I generally have done."[11]

Aletti could not only feel the respect between the two in the room, but the thrill both shared for the quality of their collaboration: "Sam Moore— producer saxophonist King Curtis tight by his side—both grinning like they *know* they can't lose—preparing for the big step: Sam's first solo album for Atlantic."[12] Discussing the album's cover of Howard Tate's "Stop" (written by Jerry Ragovoy), Moore praises Curtis's song choice and suggestions for interpretation: "Can you believe it? Can you believe what King did with that stuff? How do you mess with something that Ragovoy's done? You don't mess with stuff like that. That is like my coming in and messing with Quincy Jones stuff!"[13] Curtis also had Sam cover, as only Sam can, Alan Toussaint's "Get Out of My Life Woman," Smokey Robinson's "Shop Around," Clay Hammond's "Part Time Love," and the Detroit Emerald's "If I Lose Your Love," along with a few others.

Sam Moore was now a convert to the "Gospel According to King Curtis." Curtis was the best option for helping Sam realize the heights of his vocal talents and how to apply them: "I didn't know [my strengths], and I don't think Atlantic knew … this guy knew the strength, and a lot of times he would throw stuff at me in rehearsal, preparing two recordings of doing this song—you can do it—and you're going, 'I don't know, I don't feel it, I don't see what's happening with this song.'"[14] Sam Moore also recalled a conversation he once had with Tom Dowd about the same subject, King Curtis the producer: "I spoke with Tom Dowd and even Tom said he couldn't have done no better, and he is 'the' producer-engineer. If the master himself said he couldn't have done no better than King done, I put my money on Tom Dowd. He told me he always respected King's work."[15]

In our interview, Sam also remembered the impact King Curtis had as a producer on others in the studio: "When they were doing Aretha, King made the job so much easier because he knew his way around the studio—now, Tom [Dowd] told me this. I never spoke with Jerry [Wexler] or Ahmet [Ertegun] about it. What bothered me—and it still does today—is all these people that come around and talk about they're producers of Britney Spears, etc.—if you all had a producer like that [Curtis] and if you could perform, you had the best. I don't know anybody other than Aretha or Gladys Knight, Patty LaBelle, Sam [Cooke], Howard [Tate], Ollie Woodson, David Ruffin, or anybody in that period that could have handled that material. King Curtis was a genius, I would have liked to work with him some more."[16]

Curtis knew how to set the table for his featured artists and the entire studio production. For Moore's introductory solo effort, he called in his "A-Team" to the studio, a soul-satisfying combination of Aretha Franklin and Donny Hathaway on keyboards, Curtis on saxophone along with many from his own band, the Kingpins, and the Sweet Inspirations on backing vocals. "I spoke to Bernard Purdie, and I also spoke to Estelle [Brown], who is with Sweet Inspirations, and I got to tell you, you couldn't have gotten any better than that," trumpeted Sam. "This guy [Curtis] was on the right road, because, you got to understand, [back in the seventies] you had Philadelphia International, Donny Hathaway, Marvin Gaye, all these good 'flatfoot,' standing-at-the-microphone-singing kind of people. Can you imagine, this guy put all that stuff together around me, a 'junky'? Can you imagine what I could have been if I would have been straight?"[17]

Sam Moore feels indebted to King Curtis for all his efforts and still has a huge original portrait of Curtis displayed prominently in his living room: "King gave me so much love. I got a chance to work with the guy—he was such a challenge. He would challenge you for you to challenge *him*. If you would come up to him in a challenge, probably nothing much is happening with you. Not that you didn't have the talent, but your talent stayed outside. If he could take a guy like myself that was all drugged up and do what he did with me, I got to tell ya ... he was a *master*."[18]

True to the lyrics of Moore's 1966 hit with Sam and Dave, "Hold On! I'm Comin'," King Curtis reached out to Moore, refusing to let him drown in his first solo album endeavor for Atlantic Records. The Big Man's emotional strength and production talents rescued Sam Moore from the dulling, debilitating effects of heroin and cocaine's clutches and let everyone (including Sam himself) see for the first time the true expanse of his individual vocal talent.

For reasons that will be explored later, Atlantic Records chose to shelve the master tapes for the album in 1971 just as Curtis and Sam were working on mixing the recorded tracks. Shockingly, due to Moore's out-of-control drug addiction, he soon forgot he ever recorded most of the solo sessions with King Curtis at Atlantic. Many years later, (an astounding twenty-eight years later, to be exact) when contacted by Sam's manager (and wife) Joyce, Atlantic maintained the tapes had been destroyed in the mysterious Atlantic Records fire at a warehouse in Long Branch, New Jersey, in February 1978. Refusing to take no for an answer, Joyce Moore doggedly pursued the history of Sam's master tapes, only to have Rhino Records staffer Dave Gorman come up with a copy of the album, proving that the tapes still existed. Sam and Joyce returned their attention to Atlantic, eventually purchasing the master tapes and finding a European record label to produce the album. Thirty-four years later in 2005, Sam Moore's original album for Atlantic Records, cut in 1971, was finally released—a bewildering tale in and of itself. *Plenty Good Lovin': The Lost Solo Album* is a remarkable testament to Moore's vocal faculty, making a number of covers his own with his unmistakable soulful spin, under the close tutelage of his friend King Curtis.

In early 1971, booking agent Ruth Bowen said it was time for another Aretha Franklin tour with King Curtis and the Kingpins. It had been some time since Aretha's dynamic abilities had been paired in a live setting against the backdrop of her smoking-hot Atlantic backing band, and Bowen went to work coordinating all the necessary arrangements. After nearly finalizing the entire US tour schedule, she suddenly realized she had a gaping hole between California dates. She reached out to Bill Graham, owner of the Fillmore West theater in San Francisco. At the time, she had no idea of the breathtaking results that would follow from her simple desire to plug a void in Aretha's tour calendar.

The first of many challenges that Bowen would soon experience with the Fillmore dates was unexpected resistance from Aretha Franklin. "Aretha didn't want to do it," Bowen told me. "[Aretha said] 'I don't belong in the Fillmore—that is not for me.' I had to hit her over the head almost. Then it wasn't enough money, and I couldn't get Bill Graham to come up with the money. Bill said, 'I can't go any higher than that.'"[19] Aretha's fee was $15,000 for the proposed three-day event. Graham countered with an amount obscenely below that, a mere $5,000 for all dates combined. With nowhere else to turn, Ruth Bowen asked Ahmet Ertegun to put up the remaining $10,000. Ertegun met her halfway and pledged $5,000.

In spite of all Bowen's successful negotiating, massaging and cajoling, she frustratingly realized there still wasn't enough money. "Then I went back to Atlantic," a desperate Bowen recalled, "and I said, 'Ahmet, I got to have some more money. I got to go into the Fillmore West.' Jerry [Wexler]'s ears perked up, and he said, 'Yeah, let's record that live—we are due for a live album—I'll give you the money.' They always came up with it—they never denied me."[20] From Bowen's simple request for Atlantic support came Wexler's innovative solution of a live Aretha Franklin album. The fruits of their negotiations would leave an indelible mark on pop and soul music history.

Tour financing complete, Ruth Bowen was not done. Not by a long shot. She happened to speak to Ray Charles, who she also booked: "I called Ray because I had business with him anyway on some dates. I said, 'You're off for a few days, why don't you come down here and catch the show?' He said, 'Yeah, I think that would be nice and I've never seen her in person.' I told him that I would make the arrangements, and he said, 'OK, good.' I called Joe [Adams, his manager] and I told Joe that I was making the arrangements for Ray to come down—got the hotel and the plane ticket. We were there to get him, and he had a ball."[21] Bowen paid to fly Ray Charles to San Francisco and cover all his expenses. That included Charles's meals: "That man could *eat*," laughed Bowen. "He could eat me out of house and home! Ray came alone; he didn't bring anybody with him. I told him that I would have him picked up. Ray was accustomed to going places alone. If he missed the plane, Joe would say, 'At two o'clock we are leaving,' and if Ray wasn't there, they left and he had to find his own way."[22]

As the concert dates approached, Jerry Wexler's initial enthusiasm for the live recording cooled as he became more and more concerned about

Aretha Franklin's prospective audience: "I considered the musical tastes of the flower children [in San Francisco] infantile […] but I was dead wrong: they were swinging from the rafters, swarming the stage, packed beyond capacity."[23]

King Curtis intended to make the most of the opportunity to record live, and he recruited the cream of studio society for Aretha's backing band. Billy Preston was called in for additional support on keyboards, while the Memphis Horns (led by Wayne Jackson on trumpet and Andrew Love on saxophone) would provide brass muscle. Also added were Kingpins stalwarts Cornell Dupree on lead guitar along with the venerable Bernard Purdie on drums. But something was missing.

Curtis put a call in to bassist Jerry Jemmott, who simply refused. Jemmott preferred to stay in town, where his coveted studio career was flourishing. "I didn't want to go," Jemmott explained. "I was doing my thing, so I said, 'Call Chuck Rainey.' And Curtis said, 'No, I want *you* to do it.' I didn't really want to, but my love for him and the experience of playing with him made me do it."[24] Curtis was calling in all his markers to ensure he assembled the premium musical talent onstage to command everyone's attention, as well as to record what he felt had all the capability for a significant live Aretha Franklin album.

While touring was like bad cough syrup to the hesitant Jemmott, it helped Curtis's cause when Jerry discovered that the three-day event would yield not one but two albums. Jerry Wexler also wanted to record King Curtis and the Kingpins during all three of their warm-up sets for an additional live album before Aretha hit the stage. This was the carrot the recording-hungry Jemmott could not refuse. "The promise of recording finally convinced me to leave New York," noted Jemmott. "Ever since I was a ten-year-old kid, I've had a tape recorder, and my passion has been to get it down on tape, put it on wax. That's why I enjoyed studio work so much."[25]

These concert dates produced two of the most significant live albums in soul music history. In addition to *Aretha Live at Fillmore West*, Atlantic also released *King Curtis Live at Fillmore West*. Though renowned by fans and music critics alike, both albums only hint at the excitement, not only in the crowd but on the stage during the three-night affair. Wayne Jackson,

Album cover for *Aretha Franklin and King Curtis Live at Fillmore West: Don't Fight the Feeling. Rhino Records.*

hired by King Curtis to aid in backing the Fillmore nights, remembered the dates well, but he had a hard time putting into words for me what the concerts meant to him. "It was the single greatest day of my life," he stated. "Man, once we heard Ray Charles would be there as well, we were all 'amped' up!"[26]

As the curtains parted on opening night, the San Francisco audiences adored Aretha Franklin and King Curtis and the Kingpins for every minute of the musical celebration. Bill Graham had correctly chosen the Tower of Power, a local Bay Area favorite, to open the concert and heat up the crowd each evening. Following the Tower of Power, King Curtis and the Kingpins came on for their set, Curtis resplendent in a black leather jacket embroidered with a white horse's head coming through a horseshoe on the back.

Author Michael Lydon and his wife, coauthor and photographer Ellen Mandel, were there for all three nights of the spectacle, beginning Friday, March 5, 1971:

> Friday night went off well. Tower of Power was exuberant and earnest, and nearly dwarfed by what followed them. But they were part of the Bill Graham-Fillmore empire, and the weekend was good promotional exposure. King Curtis and the Kingpins were a knockout, Aretha superb. The song order got mixed up at one point, King Curtis calling for one tune when Aretha wanted another. Aretha did Curtis's song and seemed mildly miffed, but it was just a first-night rough spot, and the crowd went home satisfied.
>
> Saturday night, well, was stupendous. There are many ways for an R&B horn section to play a phrase, but it sounds best if they come in *absolutely* on time and full strength from the first instant, so that there is no ragged fade-up from silence, but a sudden punch of sound. Wayne Jackson's Memphis Horns were as crisp as karate Saturday night ... Curtis and company came onstage Saturday night and started with "Knock on Wood" a Stax-Volt classic. They sounded the way they looked; the trumpets gleaming in the stage lights, [drummer] Purdie rocketing away, his eyes seldom leaving Curtis' swaying back, Jemmott's fingers bounding up and down the long black neck of his bass, Dupree light and pretty on guitar. After three bars you realized what fun it was to be there, one of those paradises everyone hopes will dot their lives.[27]

On Sunday, March 7, the final night of the event, Aretha came onstage glistening in a floor-length white gown with gold accents. The radiant Queen of Soul was unquestionably in the house. All participants, from Ruth Bowen to Jerry Wexler to Aretha herself, had underestimated the crowd's appreciation of soul music. Eschewing a seat in the back of the hall, Ray Charles wanted to sit just offstage so he could, as he put it ironically, "see" Aretha better. Bowen nervously peered out at the raucous crowd from behind the backstage curtain. "Wall-to-wall people," she recalled, "standing up and nowhere to sit. That is why Ray was in the wings. It was a great evening—they went crazy."[28] After all her hard work to pull this event off successfully—feverishly enticing Aretha to play the dates along the way; imploring Bill Graham, Ahmet Ertegun, and Jerry Wexler for critical financial support; flying Ray Charles in for the concert—Bowen smiled triumphantly at Aretha. "She enjoyed it, and I wanted to kill her," Bowen recalled, laughing loudly.[29]

During that last night of the concert, with Charles just offstage, Aretha pulled a fast one on everybody, announcing to the crowd: "And here's Brother Ray Charles!" Nobody was more surprised than Charles himself, who had not discussed with Aretha, much less rehearsed, any duet between the two. Ever the perfect showman, Charles rose to the occasion and was led onstage out before the convulsing crowd by Aretha, who gently sat him on the piano bench beside her. The two broke into a memorable duet of "Spirit in the Dark," with Charles singing as well as accompanying Franklin on piano. The crowd went bonkers. Even Jerry Jemmott had to catch his breath; he told me, "Man, I had no idea that Ray Charles was playin' with us that night!"[30]

Still effusive weeks later, Michael Lydon couldn't get the last night of the weekend, or the intimate relationship Aretha Franklin and the musicians had created with the crowd, out of his mind:

> The band soul-stewed as never before, the whole crowd boogied, and Ray and Aretha traded shouts, licks, breaks, jumps, and howls, suggesting that everybody get, keep, feel, figure, and cherish that spirit.
>
> It didn't stop. We danced, clapped, hugged, kissed, and finally wept, sweating, eyes open and closed, arms above our head—and they sang … finally Ray went off waving to the crowd, leaving Aretha to close her show. She sang a soft song about reaching out your hand to a friend "making this a better world if you can" [Ashford and Simpson's "Reach Out and Touch (Somebody's Hand)," made famous by Diana Ross]. She bowed to all sides, spoke thanks to the band and to the crowd. She said goodbye, goodbye, goodbye. "I love you, I love you." She was gone, the lights went up.[31]

Emotionally spent, Lydon further rhapsodized about the event: "Moments of perfect beauty are brief, impossible to repeat, and ultimately inexplicable. I did that night feel joined in musical-spiritual exultation with Ray Charles, Aretha Franklin, and several hundred other humans. I cannot say how or why. The moment, part of a sluggish time, was instantaneous and spontaneous, and seemed to transcend and illuminate the confluence of processes, large and small, which created it."[32]

Owner Bill Graham filled his Fillmore West facility to the rafters for three consecutive nights, coughing up a paltry $5,000. Atlantic produced two live albums that continue to generate revenue to this day. Aretha and King Curtis, as well as the Kingpins, were all paid handsomely. Ray Charles received a free flight, accommodations, as many meals as he could eat, and a front-row seat for the concert, not to mention a breathtaking unrehearsed spot on the album.

And what of Ruth Bowen, Aretha's longtime booking agent and confidant? What was her reward for organizing arguably two of the greatest live albums and performances in soul music history and bringing soul music to the rabid Bay Area community?

Not a penny.

"I never made a dime," she proudly laughed, "because I had to drop my commission in order for her [Aretha] to go to the Fillmore West because it wasn't enough money."[33]

This was neither the first nor last time Bowen would take nothing for her efforts. She was Black. She was petite. She was a woman trying to survive in a very male-oriented, cutthroat business against the racially charged background of the 1960s and 1970s. And she was trying to exist in New York City, the city that ate dreams and spit them into the Hudson River by the day.

When I asked how she endured the monumental odds against her, Bowen responded matter-of-factly: "I just fought like hell for my artists. And many times, I would take nothing for my efforts. They [the established white booking agencies and recording company executives of the era] kicked my butt up one side of Madison Avenue and back down the other. But I fought like hell for my artists. ... Years ago, I added up what I believe I'm still owed from all the years I've spent in the business, for work I did for people. The total was something like well over three million dollars [laughing]."[34]

Bowen's talent management firm was originally titled the Three Queen Booking Agency (for the three main artists she initially represented: Dinah Washington, Aretha Franklin, and Ruth Brown), then refined to Queen Booking Corporation. Ever true to her artists, first and foremost, Ruth Bowen not only got by but excelled, to such an extent that she amassed the single largest Black-owned entertainment agency in the world at the time, a story worthy of its own book, to be sure.

Chapter 15

Mentoring and Montreux

A young Black man now came into King Curtis's life. He wasn't a musician. He wasn't a producer. What he was, was the boyfriend of Jerry Wexler's daughter, Anita: "Jerry Wexler's daughter is 'going with' a Black person," recalled Jimmy Douglass to me, "and for 1967, that's pretty deep. I wasn't just a kid of color in the place, I was also 'going with' Jerry Wexler's daughter. So, I came in [to Atlantic Records] in '68, okay, so you have that going on in the office and having everybody not knowing how to play it."[1]

Douglass, still in high school while dating Anita Wexler, wanted to get into the record business, and Jerry Wexler was happy to oblige, albeit with a relatively hands-off approach. As Douglass explained:

> I was a Black kid, and you didn't have Black kids doing this. Jerry's cool, you know—at the time, he was there and he was supportive, but he was kind of supportive from the background, like he pulled back some distance. He was like, "Dude, if you can make your own way, kid, make your own way." And everybody else in the office was like, "We don't have to help you because he's [Wexler] helping you." So, I was kind of on an island, by myself. Which was a very interesting

place to be, and I think Curtis recognized that and he was trying to help me navigate those waters a little bit.[2]

Curtis had taken many a musician under his wing over the years, and he now turned toward mentoring a young producer-engineer. Douglass appreciated his support, as well as his patience:

Curtis wanted me to become the next big thing. And every time I would get to do a gig with him, I would fuck up [laughing]. And I mean this. He was using Gene Paul and Lew Hahn as the engineers, and you know, when you are young, you think you can do everything. Of course you can. And every time I would get to work with him, and I would do something really stupid, and he'd go, "You ain't ready yet, man." And we would do this for a while. But he was always around, always smiling. It was something, working with King Curtis; we're doing a bunch of little demo things; it was all cool.[3]

With his many missteps and the steep learning curve that Douglass was experiencing in the Atlantic Records hallways and studios, he was stunned when one day King Curtis asked him for help with a major project:

When he came back from the Fillmore with the Aretha project, he had his record, *Live at Fillmore West*. And he said to me, "Listen man, can you do me a favor? Like, they didn't get to run no 'roughs' [the initial rough mix of the recorded songs] of this from the show. They were in such a hurry, Tom [Dowd] couldn't run no roughs. Can you run a rough of the show for me?" And I says, "Sure!" So, no problem, because it was a rough, I ran it as a seven and a half [IPS, inches per second]. For standard mixing stuff back then it was sixty-nine IPS. That was standard. It kinda was rough, I did it [slower] at seven and a half, because it was a long show and a lot of tape, you know? Okay, so we did the rough. I kinda ran it through them. He [Curtis] fell in love with them, and then he went back to work with all his people. He took the mixes to Lew Hahn; didn't work. He took the mixes to Gene Paul; didn't work. He took the mixes to somebody else, I think it was Bobby Warner—whoever he was working with—it didn't work. He ended up using those rough mixes for the album. That record is an album of rough mixes at seven and a half ... the wrong speed.[4]

Curtis and his producer prodigy quickly became close and would socialize often. Douglass was impressed by Curtis but had no idea of the level of notoriety Curtis enjoyed:

> I mean, King Curtis, he was an amazing artist, but to me it's like, "Man, you're cool, you're really cool, everything you do is cool," but I want to be where the big action is, right? You know, I'd been a big fan of his stuff, but I also didn't know how big he was out in the world. One day, we jump on his bike, and he said, "C'mon, man, I'm gonna take you somewhere." So we jumped on his motorcycle, and I remember it was a nice, beautiful fucking day. I rode on the back of the bike with King Curtis. Life has now changed for me; I'm his "man" and I'm feeling really good. We're lining up town on Broadway on his bike; he had a nice, big-ass bike, it was so sweet. And before we went, everybody around was like, "King Curtis!!" We're on his bike, and we go see people, and every place we went people are just flocking around him; it's a great feeling. They were all recognizing him, and I thought, Wow, he's really kinda big out here. I didn't realize how big he was like that, that people knew him like that.[5]

Curtis remembered his ordinary farm beginnings and encouraged his attentive young friend to set his sights high for the future: "He was just so humble at that moment, and he was really genuine. He said, 'You know what? You can have it all if you want it, pretty much'; 'I got it all,' that's what he was trying to say, not in a condescending way, you know what I mean? Not arrogant. And I absorbed it, and I was like, 'Wow, okay.'"[6]

Jimmy Douglass has continued to feel indebted to King Curtis, who was more than just a major supporter in the beginning of his professional career. Curtis was the adult figure that Jimmy so desperately needed, and the two would become extremely close. Curtis imparted his wisdom on more than just music. He taught Jimmy about life: "It was important to me, because I was so young. I'm going to try to tell you why, because Curtis was there in the studio all the time, and he was King Curtis, and he loved me because there were a number of things going on here. I was a Black kid. You didn't have Black kids doin' this. So, there were a bunch of things. I didn't—I never had a father, and he kinda took over as a father role for me."[7]

About this time, Tom Dowd was looking to expand his stable of producer-engineers. He looked no further than his friend, Les Paul.

Les Paul is one of the great innovators and guitar players in music, building the first solid-body electric guitar. But he was much more than that, he also pioneered multitrack recording and many other inventions. Paul created the first eight-track recorder, giving the second one that was made to Atlantic engineer Tom Dowd. He is one of the very few artists to have a permanent exhibit at the Rock and Roll Hall of Fame. "Tom Dowd is how I got into Atlantic," Paul's son, Gene, told me:

> One day Dad pulled me aside at the home in Mahwah [New Jersey] and said, "A guy called me up and he wants a guy he can mold. He wants an intern."
>
> "For what?"
>
> "For recording, mixing, that type of thing. Would you be interested at some point?"
>
> "Tell me more; what is it?"
>
> "It's a place ... well, the guy is Tom Dowd."
>
> And I said, "Well, who's this?"
>
> "Do me a favor and go in the office and get a Ray Charles record."
>
> And I went out there and I got *The Genius of Ray Charles*. Dad would play it night and day. He loved it. Respected everything that happened with it. It was driven into my brain. So, I go get the record and I come into the control room, and Dad says, "Turn the record over."
>
> I turn the record over and he says, "Read the liner notes on the engineer."
>
> I said, "Wow. Tom Dowd [with Bill Schwartau]."
>
> "That's the guy who called."
>
> I said, "You've got to be kidding."
>
> He said, "No. Atlantic Records needs somebody, and they're asking me, and I'm asking you. Do you wanna go in and take shot?"
>
> I said, "Where is it?"
>
> He says, "New York."
>
> I says, "Well, I've never been to New York."
>
> "Don't worry about it I'll get you in there. Do you want to do it?"
>
> I said, "I'd love to."
>
> And I wore a nice suit and a tie—everything wrong—and I walk into the studio and the control room, and if you're familiar with Atlantic Records' "A" studio, it's got that green and orange paint in the studio. Ugly as hell. And the control room had no modern equipment

in it whatsoever. I'm lookin' at it and I'm saying to myself, "I can't be in the right place ... this is not the right place." So, I call Dad up. And I say, "Dad ..." He says, "Did you get there?" I says, "Well, I got somewhere. I don't know if I'm in the right place." He says, "What color is the studio?" I said, "Orange and green." He said, "Stop. You're in the right place." I said, "Yeah, Dad the console ... " He says, "Forget it. Forget it. Now I want you to do me a favor." He said, "Stand there, close your eyes and open them up, and envision Ray Charles in there cuttin' that record right in there, and Tom Dowd is sittin' at the console right next to you."

I said, "Okay."

"Now, do me one favor."

I said, "What's that, Dad?"

He said, "Eat it up and learn."

That was my "hello," and it took me about a year before I could talk to Tom Dowd on a one-to-one type of thing. Because he got the second eight-track. Tom Dowd and Atlantic Records got the second eight-track, Dad got the first one. Tom Dowd went to the house and got the second one. And so, Tommy was a great influence on me. When we talked, he would really talk to me and he said, "You are here to capture. You are not hear to create; you are here to capture what's in that studio." The balance, the harmonics came from the player. Today it comes from the engineer. And that's the difference, engineering then 'til now."[8]

Gene Paul quickly learned that at Atlantic, it was all about the vibe: "I remember doing one [session] with Aretha, and [Bernard] Purdie's mike fell down on his hi-hat during the take. And I'm runnin' up after the take, I'm running into the studio to fix it. And I'm going by Wexler. And Wexler says, 'What are you doing?' I said, 'I'm going to fix the mike for the next take, it fell on Purdie's high hat.' He says, 'That was the take.' They didn't care about winning a Grammy for the best sound. It was all about the music."[9]

Les Paul was extremely close with King Curtis, and Gene grew up going with his dad to see Curtis perform in New Jersey on many occasions.

Dad was really good friends with King Curtis. And I had no idea that someday I'd be recording him. I just went to the club and enjoyed it. So, I came from an early part of life enjoying Curtis, and working with him was an absolute honor. He was an incredible musician, an incredible human being, and, uh, and not only what I saw, but all the people around him felt the same way.

He [Curtis] was working at some dive in Jersey on Route Three, in the back swamps there someplace, and we used to go to see him. And Dad never stopped talking anything but, "Hey Curtis is in town, let's go see him." And I was there immediately, even as a young kid. To me, you hear the guy and you say, "Wow." And then to one day be sitting there, recording Curtis and working with him, was just an absolute thrill of my life.

I remember one session where we were covering Aretha, and Tom Dowd was there, Arif, and Aretha and the whole band and everything. And we were playing a tune back. And everybody was baffled about, "Okay, what goes in that eight-bar, sixteen-bar solo? What are we gonna put in there?"

They were pondering it over and, lo and behold, Curtis came by and he wouldn't come in the room. He wouldn't come in the control room. Everybody had the utmost respect for one another, and they were very much involved in knowing that there's a certain atmosphere to a recording session, almost a "vibe" that took place. And nobody wanted to disturb whatever zone they were in. So, Curtis cracked the door open, and we were playing back, I think it was "Bridge Over Troubled Water," which was a phenomenal cut of Aretha (and a very ballsy cut for her to do, after Simon and Garfunkel) [laughing]. And when she brought it in the room and noted what she was gonna do, we looked at her like, "What the hell are you talking about?" And by the time they finished the tune, the fade went on longer than the tune. Nobody ever heard it. The only one that heard it was the person that cut the record.

Because back then they had a "law" [rule], which was: you make a record or an album cut "x" amount of times for playing on the radio. So, they didn't stop. The groove was so good that they couldn't stop. So, the ending went on forever. Curtis cracks the door open, doesn't say a word, nobody sees him for a while, and we're playin' "Bridge Over Troubled Water." And Curtis is lookin'—because I can see Curtis, because I'm at the console looking at everybody, my view went to the door, too. And I waved at Curtis. And Curtis shut the door and he took off.

Everybody looked at each other and said, "Get him!" And Arif ran out the door, and he said, "Curtis, come here, come here," and brought Curtis in the room. The control room. And he [Arif] said, "Listen. You got it right here. This is made for you." And Curtis listened for a little bit and he said, "Okay, but I don't have my horn with me." And one of the guys—my buddy [business partner] who I'm with now, Joel Kerr—he's a horn player. And he was out in the hallway, which everybody was when we cut Aretha, and he's standing there, and he said, "No problem." Somebody he knew had a horn. So, he went and got the horn, brought it back to Curtis. Curtis grabbed the horn, went in the studio, put on the earphones, and as we were playing the track down, he put the earphones on, tuned up, walked up to the mike, and Arif looked at me and said, "When we get to the solo, punch in [record him]."

I said, "Well, I gotta set him up."

"Just punch him in."

And that's the way they ran this. It was all about the vibe and the music and the moment. And Curtis is just noodling around in the studio, and when the solo came up, I punched in. He played the solo. I punched out. And that was it. One take. That was the take. And it was just, that was the thrill.[10]

After he returned home to New York, triumphant from the Fillmore West experience, Curtis's phone rang with more good news: innovative "Wall of Sound" music producer Phil Spector wanted Curtis to help John Lennon on an album the two were working on, called *Imagine*. Spector and Curtis had met back in early 1961, during an Atlantic studio date for the Top Notes during which they recorded four songs. With Curtis's previous work with the Beatles during the Shea Stadium concert and subsequent tour of 1965, Lennon and Curtis had hit it off both personally and professionally. The Beatles had even rewarded Curtis post-tour with a signed twenty-four-page Beatles tour booklet as a souvenir of their time together (with a cryptic "To Curtis-Boy, it was great. Thanks a lot. Keep taking all pushers," written by Paul McCartney).

Conflicts within the Beatles had begun in 1968, and the band formally disbanded with Paul McCartney's announcement of leaving the group on April 10, 1970. Shortly thereafter, John Lennon released his first solo album, *John Lennon/Plastic Ono Band*, to great critical acclaim but with little commercial success. He set out to create a more universally appealing second solo album, *Imagine*.

According to press reports in early 1971, Lennon laid down some recording tracks at his studio in England and sent them to King Curtis in New York, who returned the tracks back to Lennon along with twelve different saxophone solos to choose from. Lennon followed later by coming to New York and heading to the recording studio June 4–5, 1971, to work with Curtis on overdubbing for "It's So Hard" and "I Don't Wanna Be a Soldier, Mama."

Meanwhile, basking in the glow of the Fillmore dates, the ever restless Ruth Bowen decided it was now time for an international tour for Aretha Franklin with King Curtis and the Kingpins. While on this new European tour, Bowen ran into Claude Nobs, the architect of the famous Montreux Jazz Festival. Bowen said, "We were on tour, and we went to Amsterdam, London, and so forth, from one hotel to another. We worked two to three days there [in Amsterdam] with Claude Nobs. He called me and said, 'Include me on the tour, whatever it costs.'" Laughing, she said, "He never should have told me that 'whatever it costs.'"[11]

Of Nobs, Bowen marveled: "He was a collector. ... He had every record that Aretha's father had ever made. He is a remarkable guy. He loved Curtis as well. He had a knack for putting people together—showing musicians the right blend of something and it always works."[12] Known as the "Man with the Million Dollar Voice," Aretha Franklin's father, the Rev. C. L. Franklin, was the pastor of New Bethel Baptist Church in Detroit, Michigan, from 1946 to 1979. He recorded numerous sermons during his career, which Nobs had collected.

Nobs would expend any amount of energy to get Aretha Franklin to perform at Montreux, to the point of exasperation. "It was hell trying to arrange the date," Nobs told author David Ritz, "She [Aretha] must have canceled four times. But I was determined. I'd come back to her and beg. Then she'd make another demand—a bigger dressing room, an extra hotel suite—and I'd cave every time. I sent her flowers, candies, and chocolates. She said it was the chocolates that won over her heart. She agreed to come!"[13]

Despite his enthusiasm for landing Aretha Franklin on the concert bill, Claude Nobs still had some deep concerns with Aretha's earlier backing band for live performances: "I was afraid she'd arrive with that terrible orchestra she had used before in Europe. When I learned that she'd be

Album cover for *Blues at Montreux. Atlantic Records.*

using King Curtis and the Kingpins, I wept with joy. Cornell Dupree was on guitar."[14]

Despite everyone's unalloyed faith in Nobs, his impressive abilities would soon be put to the test. Upon hearing that King Curtis and the Kingpins would be backing Aretha, Nobs now proposed the strange pairing of Champion Jack Dupree, there for a solo performance, with King Curtis and the Kingpins for a stage duet at his festival. The gasps from Atlantic Records in New York City could be heard all the way back across the Atlantic Ocean in Montreux. Everyone in the States was immediately against the idea. Dupree was a blues pianist, originally from New Orleans and noted as much for his rough-edged lifestyle as he was for his musical talents. The gruff, coarse, and growling Dupree, living a hard-drinking existence, paired with the refined and urbane saxophone of King Curtis?!? This combustible pairing seemed destined for utter failure.

Most of the women on tour, including Aretha Franklin, Ruth Bowen, and Modeen Brown, were repelled by Champion Jack's physical appearance. In the end, though, they all found great humor in the situation. When they were together talking with me about the subject, both Ruth and Modeen instantly broke into cackles of laughter at how repulsive they found Champion Jack. "Aretha said he was ugly, but he could sure play," laughed Ruth. "Oooooooooh ... he *was* ugly," Modeen chimed in happily amid more laughter.[15]

This would be the first opportunity for Joel Dorn, as a new Atlantic producer just in from Philadelphia, to work with King Curtis on a live album. The two had earlier become friends while hanging out with Duane Allman. Curtis mentored Dorn in navigating the rivers of diplomacy at Atlantic, including how to survive their famous hierarchy. Curtis was the buffer with management at Atlantic, not only for Black artists but also for more than a few new employees who were white. "My thing was, I didn't get along with Wexler," Dorn recalled:

> I spent so much time trying to be a great record producer that there was a lot of shit that I didn't understand, and the politics of a company—I didn't get it. I was a bigmouth, and I had a lot of success early. One of the things that Curtis was doing with me was telling me to "shut your fuckin' mouth"—it was like that—I was cocky, and I was winning. Wexler and I just never made it. The few times I got around Ahmet, I just didn't know how to behave in front of him. It was Ahmet's company, no matter what contributions other people made.[16]

Dorn's quick and caustic wit, though it put him in the doghouse with Jerry Wexler, had landed him instantly into King Curtis's circle of friends. True to form, the ever irreverent music producer quickly picked up on how to irritate his sax-playing friend. Dorn continually jabbed Curtis by referencing Boots Randolph, another saxophone player whose most famous hit song from 1963 was called "Yakety Sax"; it had reached number 35 and stayed on the charts for a nine-week run (and became Benny Hill's theme song for his comedy television show).

Decades later, a still gleeful Dorn remembered needling Curtis: "A lot of times where there would be a lot of people around and Curtis didn't want to be fucked with, I would stand behind him and he would be talking to people and I would say, 'Telegram for Boots Randolph. Is there a Mr. Boots Randolph in the audience?' We always said, 'Delivery for Mr. Randolph— Mr. Boots Randolph.' Sometimes I would see him in the hallway or some shit, and I would say, 'Hey what's happening, Boots?' It was the only time he would say, 'Shut the fuck up.'"[17]

The biggest concern Dorn and others at Atlantic Records had with the pairing of King Curtis and the Kingpins with Champion Jack Dupree was that at first blush it looked like a total disaster. Mike Hennessey's album liner notes for *Blues at Montreux* illustrated the marked contrast between the two artists:

> Musically the two seem to have little common ground. On the one hand there was Curtis, 37, a house musician and producer with Atlantic, a major black musician, a highly regarded and sophisticated exponent of contemporary soul music and a player and composer who shared with Sam 'The Man' Taylor most of the credit for inventing that saw-edged kind of soul saxophone that has become an indispensable element in modern rhythm and blues.
>
> And on the other hand, there was Dupree, 60, a self-taught barrelhouse piano player and instant composer of salty blues with a sly earthy humor, intensely mobile eyebrows and a grin as wide as a keyboard … Dupree the simple, unsophisticated bluesman, unable to read music and not given to respecting such musical conventions as that, for example, which requires that 12-bar blues choruses are 12-bars long.[18]

Just on Hennessey's review alone, there would not be many in the music industry that would have had the foresight, much less the courage, to pair such extremely different artists, especially for a recorded live performance where absolutely anything can happen at any time. Indeed, it was not uncommon for Champion Jack Dupree to abruptly end a twelve-bar chorus after nine or ten bars and begin another twelve-bar phrase all over again. Curtis and his band were famous for their ability to follow any musician onstage, but Joel Dorn feared the worst, namely that the King may have finally met his match.

Nevertheless, jazz maven Nesuhi Ertegun convinced Dorn to record the session, and once the duo appeared together, a relieved Dorn realized that Champion Jack's unpredictable musical personality paired with Curtis's note-perfect backing would be a magnetic combination. An impressed Dorn recalled:

> There is no rehearsal. I think they rehearsed while they were setting the mikes up. First of all, he [Jack] told everybody that he was a middleweight boxing champion of the world. He was just one of those guys—he had a million stories—he was a good singer and player. Curtis said they were rehearsing for something else—I forget what it was—but they ended up playing with him. He said, "Why don't we make a record—how could we get hurt?" We real quick put together a session, and Jack Dupree sang with Curtis. They weren't really blues players—they were rhythm and blues players. The spirit was great. Jack Dupree is one of those guys who gets up in front of an audience and he just nails them.[19]

It may be this specific album that ultimately defines the depth and breadth of the true global talent of King Curtis (and also of his well-schooled Kingpins). Without a moment of rehearsal, the Atlantic tape rolled and what was created is nothing short of spectacular. The coarse and unpredictable Champion Jack bantered back and forth with his audience, tinkling the ivories, starting and then suddenly changing what should have been predictable blues phrases, while oblivious to his saxophone player and backing band. Curtis and his majestic Kingpins magically shadowed Champion Jack's every move. Run and dodge as he might, Champion Jack Dupree never shook King Curtis and the Kingpins throughout the entire live performance. It was as if Champion Jack and Curtis were the same person playing through two different instruments, as Eric Clapton had described it earlier.

Joel Dorn's early concerns about potential disaster were not without merit. In the album liner notes, Mike Hennessey recalled the challenges of following the self-taught Dupree's helter-skelter lead piano during many of the songs. On the opening number, "Junker's Blues," Dupree was chatting with the audience during a chorus when "suddenly, after seven bars, he begins a new twelve-bar chorus. Note how quickly the other musicians pick this up. Jack then goes into the vocal and by the time he gets to his second vocal chorus, he's one bar ahead of the band. They adjust by missing out a bar and then, after another chorus, Jack sings against stop chords for what should be an eight-bar passage. He only manages seven—and again King Curtis and Co. get things back in line. Jack has the final word, however, by contriving to get 13 bars in the last chorus!"[20] Curtis had led off the song with a bluesy intro that graduated to snorting and squealing back and forth with Dupree, then growling and moaning as Dupree shouted encouragement, letting the audience know they are in store for something very special.

Dupree followed with "Sneaky Pete," a fast-paced number that showcased the nimbleness of Curtis's band. And what of the title Dupree gave this song? He told the crowd: "This one's about the wine you used to buy for fifty cents a gallon. The cats would stand on the corner and drink that wine all night. We called it 'Sneaky Pete.'"[21] The crowd lapped it up.

Another up-tempo tune "Everything's Gonna Be Alright" is followed by "Get with It," which, Dupree told the crowd, "is what some cat would holler when we had what we used to call a 'function' in the United States. People would start dancing and let their hair down. If you didn't have any hair, you just let yourself go anyway."[22] During this number, Dupree suddenly goes from a twelve-bar chorus to a sixteen-bar chorus, but the band again quickly recovers.

"Poor Boy Blues" is a personal lament, as Dupree told his audience: "That's me. I've been poor so long I can't get over it." Grinning, he adds, "It's women that make you poor, you know … she promised me my money, would lead me astray. So just to protect me, she took it all away."[23] Curtis contributed an appropriately melancholy accompaniment that evolved into squeals and honks with Dupree yelling in response. Cornell Dupree also added a bluesy guitar solo for good measure.

Dupree refused to wallow in his self-pity for long, ending on a high note with the swinging "I'm Having Fun," which Dupree dedicated to when "you get a little drunk, play the piano, and really enjoy yourself."[24] Curtis contributes raucous banter with Dupree. In the end, you gain a tremendous level of appreciation for the spontaneous talent on display during a live King Curtis event, as well as for his (and his band's) innate ability to deliver exacting performances tailored to each specific featured artist's direction, no matter how off-track and challenging. The album is stunning.

The rest of the tour was not without additional adventures, with Curtis equal to these challenges. Upon arriving in Italy, Ruth Bowen, Aretha Franklin, and others ran into trouble: "As we toured the coast, when we got to Rome is where we got into the problem. Aretha got arrested [for breach of contract], and I was on a house arrest. Poor Curtis, bless his heart, got me out of that one,"[25] smiled a grateful Bowen.

Aretha Franklin, along with King Curtis and his band, had committed to play at the tenth annual Cantagiro, which was Rome, Italy's most popular music festival at the time. The event was ten shows long, lasting from June 22 to July 10. For 1971, the festival format changed, and it was called Cantagiro Cantamondo. Each show was divided into four parts. The first highlighted local Italian music talent. Next followed foreign folk groups. Then, the big Italian acts played, such as Gianni Morandi, Milva, and Lucio Dalla. The last portion of the concert featured international artists such as Donovan, Sam and Dave, and Led Zeppelin.

According to *Billboard* magazine, Aretha Franklin went to leave the country without performing in the last two shows in Rome due to illness. She was detained by airport officials and was prevented from taking her flight to Paris. She returned to festival organizer Ezio Radaelli the $40,000 in advance fees that had been paid to her and to King Curtis's band, and she was then allowed to leave.[26] Aretha maintained that Italian police had manhandled her and then arrested her without provocation. She and her two sons, Clarence and Eddie, were alleged to have been interrogated for four hours before being released.[27]

Not unlike his friends, Curtis also could not resist creating a stir when in Italy. One night Norman Dugger, Curtis's chauffeur and valet, went out on the town with Curtis to get a bite to eat. Possibly antagonized by Aretha's situation there, or maybe just because he was in a surly mood, Curtis tried to start trouble at the restaurant. "He just started throwin' napkins and ice cubes at people—just throwin' stuff at anybody," a disgusted Dugger recalled. "I told Curtis, 'Why do you have to be like that? Why do you want to start trouble?' He was just like a big kid, a big bully, tryin' to start stuff."[28] People rarely stood up to Curtis, and the Italians were no exception. Nobody wanted to mess with the big man from New York City.

Curtis always wanted to be sure that his beloved Modeen was protected, not only physically, but financially. This was one of the few times, due to the length and distance of the tour, that the two lovers would be apart for an extended period. Before he left for this latest European tour, and maybe because Curtis had lost a number of dear friends to plane crashes, Curtis had a discussion with Modeen:

> Curtis was going away on this latest trip, and he always said to me, "I have to get these things straight, because God forbid something happened to me," and I always believed he had a feeling that something was going to happen to him. He was sitting at the dining room table before the trip to Italy, and he said, "If anything happens to me ... [separated wife] Ethelyn will be here to take the curtains off the windows." So he said, "I want to give you these papers, and if anything happened to me this is what you do."
>
> He said to me, "Here's the paper which the judge had given me." He said "all you do is bring these papers out" and said she [Ethelyn] waived all rights to inherit anything from his estate. Noreen [Woods, Ahmet Ertegun's secretary] was sitting there, and we kind of laughed it off. And I said, "Nothings going to happen to you." And he said, "I'm telling you, Modeen, that woman is crazy. If anything happens to me, she will pull the curtains off the windows or try. You put this in the safe, and if anything ever happens to me ... " He said, "I'm going to Europe, and I am going to be in a lot of planes, up and down." He was going with Aretha, and I think they were going for three weeks and they were going to be all over."[29]

Curtis returned safely to the States, relieved that his premonition of a premature demise had not come to pass.

Just a month after his homecoming, Curtis was overjoyed when his pal Delaney Bramlett called asking Curtis to join a performance with Delaney & Bonnie and Friends for a live broadcast concert at the WPLJ radio station in New York on July 22, 1971. Duane Allman was on guitar, with Chuck Morgan on drums and Sam Clayton on congas.

On the day of the concert, everyone was in high spirits and fine form. Curtis and Delaney especially interacted with the crowd even more than usual. To everyone's joy, from musicians to spectators, the "Three M'sketeers of Atlantic Records" (Delaney's nickname for the trio) were reunited once again. The genuine affection and sense of camaraderie the Atlantic threesome shared along with everyone else in the Delaney & Bonnie and Friends band, both on- and offstage, was on full display for all. Delaney fondly reminisced, "I remember that! We were sittin' onstage, we were sittin' there, and I said, 'Hey, hillbilly' [to Duane]. What I wanted him to do was get up closer to me, 'cuz he was sittin' too far away from me. I said ... I said, 'Get your fuckin' chair over here in front of me.' I said, 'I can't see your hands.' And he said, 'Okay, bro!' And then (what you'll probably hear on that [recording]) he said, 'I gotta go pee!' And I said, 'Scuse me folks, but Duane Allman's gotta go take a piss.' You probably won't hear it all on that tape."[30]

Trying to cover for his friend as Duane exited to the backstage bathroom, Delaney, unsure of what exactly to do next, suddenly put the entire moment on Curtis's broad shoulders by telling the crowd, "And now, King Curtis is gonna tell a joke,"[31] catching the always well-prepared saxophone player, for once, completely off guard. Speaking to author Mitch Lopate, Delaney recalled:

I did! And he—Curtis didn't have a thing to say! He didn't have nuthin' to say! Curtis didn't have a thing to say, 'cuz I was waitin' on—for Duane you know. Duane says, "I've got to pee." See, what it was, they had been sittin' there waitin' and waitin' and waitin', because it was a live radio show from New York, you understand? And I said, "Well, there he goes, folks!" I said, "I ain't playin' another song because Duane's gotta take a piss." [laughs] I said, "I don't know when he's gonna be back, but I ain't gonna play one note until he gets back." And when he got back, I said, "Duane, now move your damn chair over closer to me 'cuz I can't see you!" He says, "Okey-doke!" and he said, "Okay, bro!" So he moved over there and we started playin'—oh, yeah, and I said, "While he's gone, Curtis, tell a joke! We're losin' time, here!" And Curtis went, "Wha-a-a-t?" [*laughs*].[32]

Modeen remembered that whenever the three ever got together, it was nothing but music, music, music: "Wherever those guys were, they would eat and sleep and play music, and they wouldn't do too much sleeping. They loved music. They would wake up in the morning and play music."[33]

It was good to be home.

Chapter 16

The End of the King's Reign

The August 8, 1971, issue of *Jet* magazine featured a picture of King Curtis in their "The Week's Best Photos" section. Unsurprisingly, Curtis was dressed immaculately, looking like a gangster, in a striking black suit and vest with a white necktie and white fedora, proudly showing off his latest purchase. The caption read, "Vintage Car: Showing off his $18,000 Cadillac convertible in New York City, bandleader King Curtis commands the rapt attention of young fans, (l-r) Karen McPherson, Edward Franklin, son of Aretha Franklin, and Tina Treadwell, daughter of the late George Treadwell."[1]

Four days later, August 12, 1971, was always a significant date for Curtis, and that year it fell on a Thursday. The next day, August 13, was Curtis's dear friend and confidant Aaron Watkins's birthday. Never losing sight of his friends back home in Fort Worth, Curtis called Fort Worth on the twelfth, as he did every year, to wish his "big brother," affectionately known as "Long John," another early happy birthday. "Curtis always remembered my birthday," Aaron Watkins said with a smile, "and he called and would always send me nice stuff. He called me in the morning and told me, 'I'm sending you thirteen pieces of clothing,' as he was laughing, ''cuz your birthday is on the thirteenth.' He was always very thoughtful, always remembering us."[2] The clever Curtis would always put a little extra into his efforts for his long-term friends to maintain his gratitude. He was never so important or busy as to forget who had helped him along the way from Fort Worth to New York City.

This August 12 was also much like any other day. Happy with Jimmy Douglass's work on his *Live at Fillmore West* record, Curtis had earlier begun recording his next studio album, *Everybody's Talkin'*, with engineer Gene Paul. After a lengthy period (over a year), Curtis turned to Douglass to assist in finalizing the album. Douglass recalled:

> I think Gene was recording a lot of it, and then he switched in the middle to start to work with me. We work on that album, and we went and did this for a while. And then I started mixing stuff with him, finishing off the album, and a lot of it wasn't finished. It was just a lot of overdubbing and stuff. We kinda cut it, and he was going to rehearse with the band at the apartment on West Eighty-Sixth Street for the evening. So, when I left, Norman [Dugger] was there 'cuz Norman was always with him, right? So, Norman was there and I don't remember who else, people were milling around, so I ended up coming back home to change to go back out and meet them.[3]

What Jimmy Douglass didn't know was every Thursday night was "bowling night." There would be no rehearsal this evening. To beat the heat of New York City's sweltering summer evenings, Curtis and others formed a co-ed bowling team that competed at the Madison Square Garden bowling alley. Curtis, Modeen, Ruth Bowen, Erma Dupree, Norman Dugger, and others (Aretha Franklin among them, from time to time, when available) tradition-ally went bowling on the off Thursday nights when Curtis did not have any professional commitments. Not surprising to anyone, Curtis was team captain. Ruth Bowen, as well as all the teammates, loved bowling night: "We sort of formed a little organization, and Curtis was the captain of the team. We would go and bowl against another group at Madison Square Garden bowling alley. We would go anytime we were home—every Thursday."[4] Joel Dorn was there for some of Curtis's earliest bowling experiences:

> The first night Curtis and I met, he played Pips; it was a jazz club. So, he is there for the week, and he had just gotten into bowling. I was a 160-average bowler, nothing special. Somehow, he got into bowling, and he

got the most expensive ball, shoes—the best of everything. There was a dwarf that was a waiter at Pips—they called him "Tink," which is short for "Tinkerbell," and I never knew his name, always Tink; I think he was three feet, nine inches, stocky little guy. So, one night that week after the gig Curtis wanted to go bowling. So me, him, and Tink went bowling, and that ball must have cost seventy-five dollars (and it would cost four-hundred dollars now). The shoes were sharp and matched his outfit. He bowled, like, a seventy-one and an eighty-three, and Tink kicked his ass (I beat him) ... we laughed about it ... the more I am sitting here talking about him, the more I wish he was here 'cuz it was really fun."[5]

On this particular Thursday "bowling night," Curtis had a tour coming up over the weekend in Chicago, and instead of leaving on Thursday as usual, he chose to wait until Saturday so he and Modeen could pick up his son, Curtis Jr., from Ethelyn and take him on the trip. Curtis adored his little boy and made great efforts to spend time with him, in spite of having a busy schedule. "Curtis Jr. had said that he wanted to come home [to live with Curtis and Modeen] because Ethelyn would play games [cause trouble]," Modeen said with a wistful sigh. "I would say that if it was his birthday, I would go up to the school. I would never go if she was going. And I would say, 'If your mom is coming, I won't come.' She would tell me she was coming and she wouldn't go, so he would have wound up with nobody. Curtis said, 'We'll pick him up and we'll take him to Chicago with us.' He [Curtis] didn't have to be there until Saturday, and we would pick him up that morning."[6]

Ruth Bowen remembered that Curtis wasn't available to bowl that evening: "This particular Thursday, Curtis said, 'I don't think I'll be goin' with ya.' And I said, 'Why not, how can we go without the captain?' He said, 'I hurt my finger and I don't think I will be able to bowl, but I'll be waitin' here for you when you guys get back.' So, we went and we came back happy because we won, and he was happy that we had won."[7]

Modeen has never forgotten the splendid mansion they had just purchased and were in the process of remodeling, just a half a block west from Central Park on West Eighty-Sixth Street.

We had just purchased the house. Our plans were, we were going to get married, because when I met him New York State had a law where you

Curtis at home with Curtis Jr. *Courtesy of Modeen Brown.*

couldn't get a divorce (and Jackie Gleason set new precedence when he got his divorce). Curtis would have had his divorce, I think it was May of 1972, and then we were going to get married. His wife was not in the picture when I met him. She was a strange lady. She was from Nassau [in the Bahamas]. Young Curtis lived with her and used to come to us on weekends, and then one day she just said that she was not going to keep him anymore, we were going to keep him: "Let Modeen keep him."

As soon as she sent him to us and I had him at home and in school in New York, I would drive him to school every morning. That [having Curtis Jr. live with them] was not going to break Curtis and me apart. She just wanted to be evil. She went down to the courts, and she said, "He [Curtis] has this woman living with him." I never gave my apartment up. Curtis and I lived together, but I always keep another address. Curtis said to the judge, "I travel and I work, and, yes, she lives there, but she has her own separate room. I have a room, and the boy has a room." The judge threw it out, because what was he [Curtis] going to do, take him [Curtis Jr.] on the road with him? That was her reason. So then after that didn't work, she left him with us. Curtis decided, or we did together—Curtis brought the subject up—we should find a boarding school for him. I thought: New York Academy—a wonderful school. I looked into that and put him there, and he was doing fine. He was doing terribly in school when we took him. He was confused between his mother over there and his father over here. She was a strange lady and she believed in voodoo. We never sent him back.[8]

Arif Mardin, for one, was thrilled to hear that Curtis and Modeen had purchased the dwelling at 50 West Eighty-Sixth Street, as he and his wife lived nearby: "We rented an apartment at Central Park West and

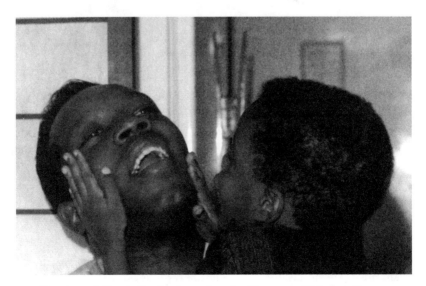

Curtis and Curtis Jr. sharing a laugh. *Courtesy of Modeen Brown.*

Eighty-Sixth Street, and I said, 'You know, there's a building there, why
don't you go and look at it?' And we were so glad that we were going to
be neighbors."[9]

This particular dwelling was more than just a house; it was a mansion
made from limestone in the early 1900s for the Gimbel family (of Gimbels
department store fame). Ironically for Curtis, it had also supposedly been
a speakeasy where many would congregate to drink and gamble in the
1940s. It would later, at different times, house several young, struggling
actors, such as Tom Cruise and Sarah Jessica Parker and her boyfriend,
Robert Downey Jr.[10]

Upon returning victorious from their bowling competition, Modeen,
Ruth Bowen, Erma Dupree, and Norman Dugger found Curtis in the
basement of the mansion, which was still undergoing renovation. Curtis
wanted to pull out all the stops on the remodeling, making the swim-
ming pool in the basement the focal point of the residence. Jerry Wexler

50 West Eighty-Sixth Street. Past the gate on the right is the basement
entrance. The access door to the utility room is on the left. Both are
a few steps down from the sidewalk. *Timothy Hoover.*

recalled: "Man, Curtis just *loved* that pool. He was so proud of his home."[11] Bowen concurred, "He just loved it and couldn't wait for it to get finished."[12]

Modeen remembered: "I had gone bowling with Ruth Bowen and some other friends and Norman. Curtis didn't go bowling with us. We had a brand-new air-conditioning unit installed in the building that we had bought, and something was wrong that made it kick the electricity off, like the circuit breaker."[13] Modeen continued:

> He [Curtis] had a flashlight in his hand, because he had a new air-conditioner put in and it wasn't working. We were all downstairs and we came in, and Curtis started playing pool—we bought a pool table—with Norman. He came out and said, "I brought the final plans for the house of what it's going to look like when it's finished." We had them on the floor, and he and Ruth Bowen and all of us had them spread out, and Ruth said, "King, this is really going to be nice." And he had a flashlight in his hand and was standing up over us, going in this subbasement, and he said, "Yes, I hope I live to see it finished."
>
> At that, he walked out of the door—this particular townhouse had two doors on the street level: one is into the area where the pool was, and then you had another door which brought you in to where the utility room was.[14]

Curtis, flashlight in hand, and Norman exited the basement towards the street to access the utility room in order to examine the fuse box, looking for a tripped circuit breaker. Norman said, "We heard some commotion up on the street at the front of the house. Sounded like a man and a woman arguing on the stoop of the house. Instead of going into the utility room, we both walked up to the front to see what was goin' on."[15]

On the front steps, a young girl was arguing with a young male, twenty-six-year-old Juan Montanez, who was wearing a red bandana covering his forehead. Curtis was incensed that his front stoop had uninvited company and walked straight up to Montanez. According to Norman Dugger, the only other person present, Curtis said, "You better get your trash [yourself] outa here."

Montanez replied with a smirk and a half-hearted *"No hablo inglés ... "*

Further agitated by the slender Montanez's smart-aleck response, Curtis walked closer, now towering over him and getting right in his face, yelling, "Man, you better get your SHIT outta here !"[16]

Unimpressed, Montanez smirked and responded again, "*No hablo inglés*." Enraged, Curtis threw himself into Montanez. "Curtis was *so* angry," noted Dugger. "And he raised his hand and broke the flashlight right over the kid's head! Man, batteries went flyin' everywhere, broke the flashlight in half right over that guy!"[17] The two started fighting. The slight Montanez was no match for the hulking Curtis. The big man from Texas would certainly make quick work of his much smaller opponent.

Horrified, Dugger continued: "They took to fightin', and I didn't see what was goin' on, and all of a sudden, I see blood all over the sidewalk. I didn't see no blade, no nothing. Then King stumbles back and pulls a knife outta his chest. He grabs the guy and slashes him three, four times, then falls down on the ground."[18] While the two struggled, Montanez had pulled a knife and stabbed Curtis once in the chest.

Sam Moore, who on his way to Curtis's house to go over potential album mixes on his solo album that was just being finalized, recalled witnessing the scene from across the street:

> I went by there, and I don't know what was going on, except as I was headed up to the apartment, I saw him [Curtis]—you couldn't miss him because he was a big man, and a Puerto Rican or Mexican or whatever he was. I just know he was a little guy, and they were fussin'. I couldn't hear what they were saying, but I knew they were fussin'. As I got closer I saw him [Curtis] stagger away and I thought, "them were fightin', man—what's going on?" Understand I had illegal stuff on me, so I couldn't get any closer. I couldn't turn around and run, because I was about the only one on that street (there were a lot of people on that street, but the street was so wide it would have looked like I was the one who did it). I just backed up. And I got a chance to get the [subway] train, and I came on back to my apartment.[19]

A now hysterical Norman raced down the steps from the sidewalk back through the basement entrance to get help. "King's been stabbed! … King's been stabbed!"[20] Norman screamed to nobody in particular as he burst back through the door.

Modeen, completely perplexed, was thinking that not more than a second or two had passed since Curtis and Norman had casually walked outside to check the house circuit breaker: "I said, 'Stabbed?' I'm confused because he just went out of here."[21] Just as incredulous, Ruth Bowen leapt to her feet and yelled, "What do you mean he's been stabbed?"[22] It was an almost surreal, horrible nightmare. Moments before, good friends had been sharing a simple evening and an easy laugh, all romancing together about Curtis and Modeen's bright future, their impending marriage, and the new home. The year 1972 was going to be an even better year than 1971, if that was possible. The basement and the evening had been filled with such optimism.

Modeen rushed upstairs to the street from the basement: "I dashed out the front door. And I'm looking for him, because I think he's fighting or running. And he [Norman] said, 'Here ... *here!*' When I look down, Curtis was laying in front of me and blood everywhere. I'm trying to get him up, and I said, 'Norman, get the car keys.' They said, 'Don't move him, we'll call 9-1-1.'"[23] Modeen, in no uncertain terms, imparted her mounting sense of urgency, shouting to everyone: "I said, Get me the car keys!' I insisted that Norman get the car keys. And Norman was going to drive, and I said, 'No, I'll drive.'"[24]

Ruth Bowen was now at the front of the house with Modeen, Erma Dupree, and Norman: "When we got up there, he was laying there bleeding, and Norman said he [Curtis] managed to stab the guy back."[25] Still shaken by the memories, Bowen recounted to me: "Luckily, Mo had the car in front. And by the time we got him [Curtis] into the car, she said, 'I'll drive.' So, somebody was saying, 'Don't move him, don't move him,' but we had to. And we eased him as lightly as possible, and the guys lifted him up and put him in the backseat with his head in Norman's lap, and I got up front with her and I'm trying to calm her down.[26]

Indeed, Curtis had fought back. And unbeknownst to anyone at the time, Juan Montanez escaped down the street, only to collapse due to his own wounds one short block away.

Bowen knew there wasn't a moment to lose: "By the time we were leaving, the cops saw us going and they said, 'He's got to go to the hospital,' and the escort took us right through. She [Modeen] was driving frantically."[27]

On the way to Roosevelt Hospital, Modeen refused to let mere red lights slow her mission of mercy: "I took every light to the hospital."[28] Bowen still marveled at the fact that everyone riding in the car made it to the hospital in one piece: "How she ever got there, we will never know. We could have all been killed, the way she was driving."[29]

They careened wildly through Manhattan towards the hospital, desperately trying to save Curtis's life. Ruth Bowen grimly recalled what happened next, like it was yesterday:

> Before we got there, I heard a gurgle and a sigh [from the back seat] and I thought, Oh my God, he's dead." When I got out of the car and they were taking him out on the stretcher, I told them to please take her [Modeen] inside and give her a shot because she is going to go berserk on us. I knew he was gone. They took her inside and sat her down, and they came over and the nurse was sitting next to her. She [Modeen] said, "What are you doing? I don't need this. Look after Curtis, look after Curtis," and the nurse said, "Wait just a second and it will be fine," and they gave her this shot and it was the only thing that kept her half calm.[30]

Modeen remembered, "We were sitting in the waiting room waiting on the doctor to come out to tell us how Curtis was doing."[31] Though Ruth Bowen had her fears based on what she had heard from the car's backseat, she kept them to herself to give Modeen strength. Modeen had no idea if Curtis was alive or dead when they had arrived at Roosevelt Hospital: "All we know, we got in there and I ran inside and got people and they came out and they took him and we were waiting in the waiting room. Norman said to me, 'And I got blood from here all over me because I've been tugging with him,' and he had *so much* blood on him."[32]

So, the three friends waited, desperate for any good news. And prayed. The stunned, tense silence was suddenly broken; thirty minutes after arriving at the emergency room entrance, something caught Norman Dugger's eye. Modeen remembered: "Norman was sitting in the emergency waiting room, and a stretcher comes in with two police and the guy had a headband on his head. And Norman said to me, 'Mo, Mo, that's the guy on that stretcher, that stabbed King.' Of course, I dashed for the police and told them the story and told them I was waiting for them to come out. And it turns out [Montanez] had been stabbed three times, but he was okay and he didn't die, he was fine."[33]

Montanez, Curtis's combatant on the steps of the mansion, was arrested on the spot. The arresting officer, Detective Herbert Stein, badge number 563, advised Montanez of his rights. The weapon used in the assault was recovered at the scene.[34]

His assailant now identified and safely in custody, everyone's attention turned back to the doctors working feverishly to save Curtis's life. The emergency room physician came out shortly after Montanez was arrested at the hospital and told Modeen the news. Just after midnight on the morning of August 13, 1971, the magnificent, meteoric reign of King Curtis was over—Curtis Ousley was dead.

The assistant medical examiner, Dr. Emile Tibere, listed the cause of Curtis's death as: "Stab wound of chest, heart and lung. Hemothorax. Hemomediastinum and Hemopericardium."[35] The single stab wound to the large chest of King Curtis had been perfectly, if unintentionally, placed and had pierced his heart.

Modeen went into shock: "It turns out this man should have never been in the streets. He [Montanez] had a rap sheet with everything. He had stabbed somebody else ... busted for drugs ... he had all kinds of things on his record. He should have never been walking the streets. They do that. Of course, that was a turning point in my life. I didn't know where I was going from there. I don't know where I got the energy to continue to go on that night."[36]

What Curtis had worried about so deeply had suddenly, horribly come true: an untimely tragedy had befallen him. Finally collecting herself, Modeen returned to their mansion, Curtis's blood not yet dry, still soaking the pavement. Modeen and Ruth slowly entered the lovely home, so full of energy and laughter just hours before. Now there was just stunned, lonely, suffocating silence. Modeen and Ruth then went to Curtis's condo at 150 West Ninety-Sixth Street, where Modeen and Curtis had been living during the mansion's remodeling.

Modeen vividly recalled when her dear friend Ruth Bowen came to her aid: "I remember that night she said, 'You're not staying by yourself, Mo.'

They wouldn't let me stay home, and I would have my bag. They wouldn't let me be by myself, which was really good for me."[37] Aretha Franklin dropped everything and rushed to the mansion to meet Modeen, making sure Modeen was never left alone.

Tragically prophetic, Curtis's earlier worries regarding Ethelyn were right on target. Modeen remembered:

> I thought nothing about it, but sure enough he wasn't lying. He died, I bet you, before twelve o'clock, and before one a.m. she [Ethelyn] was at my house. She came to the house with her attorney, and she said, "I came to get the keys for this house."
>
> It was before one o'clock! I opened the door for her. In the meantime, Ruth Bowen is still with me, because they were with me when Curtis died so they all stayed there. I said to her, "Ethelyn you need to see who owns the place," because it was bought in both of our names. If anything happened to him it was mine, and if anything happened to me it was his—this was not the house—this was the condo. So anyway, her lawyer took the information, and I said, "They open up at nine a.m. downstairs." Because they had an office, and I guess she found out there was not steps she could take. She couldn't get the keys and throw me in the street, which is what she wanted to do. She went away and she said, "I will pick my son up tomorrow." I said, "Okay." She heard it on the news, and she lived right near where we lived. She lived at Seventy-Second Street, and he was killed at Eighty-Sixth Street, so she said, "I'll be picking my son up from that school tomorrow." I said, "Okay." She said, "Don't bother to go get him, and don't tell him." So, the people at the school had kept him [Curtis Jr.] away from the TV, where he wouldn't hear it until his mother got there. She picked him up and she told him. I didn't see him until the day before the funeral and his uncle, the one who lived in Long Island, had called and asked her if Curtis Jr. could come over.[38]

Upon legally separating from Curtis in 1964, Ethelyn had unwisely relinquished all rights to any of Curtis's publishing or recording royalties in lieu of a monthly cash payment as part of their separation agreement. Chuck Rainey was well aware of the settlement details: "One thing I will tell you, Curtis paid his alimony. Four hundred dollars a week. Four hundred dollars a week was sixteen hundred dollars a month. In that day, that was a lot of money, but I know he paid four hundred dollars a week, because he was always bitching about it."[39] Ethelyn's financial support from Curtis had suddenly come to an abrupt halt. Fortunately for Modeen, Ethelyn's immediate attempts to lay claim to Curtis's entire estate, something that Curtis had feared so deeply, were rejected.

Four days after Curtis's murder, records show that someone (that could only have been Ethelyn) submitted a death claim with the US Social Security Midtown New York Field Office, claim number 66272143097, on Tuesday, August 17. The claim would be issued on September 25, 1971.[40]

Chapter 17

Requiem for the King

On Friday, August 13, 1971, Delaney Bramlett was home in Sherman
Oaks, California, getting ready to pick up his friend Duane Allman,
who was flying into town to go on tour together. It was not all that uncommon
to get a quick, last-minute call and subsequent visit from Duane, regardless
of any potential legal issues with the Allman Brothers band: "I got sued about
ten times for soliciting Duane, you know? And I didn't solicit him, he just
popped up every time I was gonna go on tour, and he'd leave his band
out there. That's the truth," Delaney laughed.[1]

As he dressed, Delaney heard the phone ring. "I was just gettin' up and
Duane was flyin' into town. The phone rang and my mom answered and
screamed—she almost fainted; she just set right down and started cryin'.
It took her the longest time to tell me what was goin' on." Hysterical,
Delaney's "Mamo" could not speak. "Modeen called Mom and she told me
that Curtis had been murdered! Of course, I just forgot everything else. I just
went to the airport [with Bonnie] as fast as I could get there, and I got on a
plane to New York as soon as I could. As a matter of fact, I did pick up Duane
and we just got right back on the plane is what we did. And I went right to
Curtis's house where I had my room, and there Duane and I got dressed."[2]

Curtis and Modeen were living in a large condo on West Ninety-Sixth Street while the mansion on West Eighty-Sixth Street was being remodeled. Bursting through the front door of the home at West Ninety-Sixth Street together the next day, Delaney, Bonnie, and Duane were shocked at the utter chaos that greeted their eyes. Delaney recalled the pandemonium:

> It was a … everyone was running around, and Modeen said it was the awfullest thing. People were sayin' they were cousins and their relatives and just takin' things of Curtis's, you know? "He wanted me to have this, he wanted me to have that … " One of them picked up his saxophone, and I said, "You better put that sombitch down." Modeen said, "No, he doesn't want you to have his saxophone." I just put it in my room and locked the door. So anyway, it was pretty horrible, and Modeen was goin' crazy, and I was goin' crazy.[3]

While poor Modeen was still in shock, "relatives" of King Curtis were looting their residence on West Ninety-Sixth Street. Delaney and Duane tossed everyone out, both making sure nothing else left the condo that day or any day thereafter. Notified of the pandemonium, Jerry Wexler sprang into action to protect Modeen, calling police to the scene to secure the area. Bonnie Bramlett also remembered the horrible confusion. She said that she could still hear Modeen asking, "How we gonna get these horns outta here? What are we gonna do with everything?"[4]

Later in the day, the phone rang at the Watkins's house in Fort Worth. Aaron Watkins could not believe his ears: "King had called me in the morning [the previous day] to wish me a happy birthday, and now he was dead. It just didn't make any sense."[5]

Shockwaves reverberated throughout the music industry. This was what many, from his horn teacher Garvin Bushell to his early friend Doc Pomus, had feared who had experienced Curtis's sometimes hair-trigger, belligerent nature. Others who had never seen that side of Curtis were even more disconsolate. Regardless of the cause of the situation, Curtis was gone.

Ahmet Ertegun was speechless upon learning of Curtis's death: "I was in New York. I couldn't believe it. He was not somebody who would ever be involved in fights. First, to begin with, he was a very big man, and he was not somebody you would take a shot at because he looked like he could kill you. As it really was, he was a sweet, gentle person and he wouldn't hurt a fly. I loved him dearly and to lose him is to lose a brother."[6]

Jerry Wexler was no less despondent: "When I got the call, I was dumbfounded," said Wexler. "Couldn't speak. Couldn't move. Didn't know what to do. Didn't know how to process it, because it came from out of nowhere. King was at the top of his game—a healthy man, vibrant man, a fabulous artist, a great guy."[7]

Cornell Dupree was in disbelief: "I was in Brooklyn, and my wife called me. She said he was stabbed. I said, 'Okay, call me later to let me know what's going on with him.' The next day they said he had passed."[8]

Chuck Rainey was at home when he received a call: "I was in my apartment and Al Fontaine, a local guitar player, called me at 7:30 in the morning. He was going to work or doing something. He said, like, 'What happened to your boy?' And I said, 'What are you talking about?' He said, 'He [Curtis] got killed last night,' and I said, 'No!' So, I immediately called Modeen and I was up and went over there, you know, that day."[9]

Joel Dorn was home in Philadelphia when he received the awful news: "I heard about it the next morning because I was in Philly when it happened, so I might have been home midweek. I remember I got a call early in the morning from a guy I knew in Philly who said, 'I'm sorry to hear about your friend.' I said, 'What do you mean?' He said, 'King Curtis has been murdered.' Man, I called everybody living."[10]

Aretha Franklin's brother Cecil remembered sadly: "It was a devastating loss,' said Cecil. 'King Curtis had proven to be the best conductor Ree had ever known. He was fast to pick up her cues and keys. He was a dynamic musician himself, both in the studio and onstage. He gave her that snap that every great rhythm singer needs."[11]

Bernard Purdie also recalled Aretha's despondence over the loss of her friend: "It was a sad, sad time. And the strange part is that Aretha didn't even want his name mentioned; it was like she couldn't take the sadness. If someone happened to say anything about King, she went into her shell. I understood. She couldn't handle it. When Aretha was around, it was better to act like it had never happened."[12]

Purdie had invited Curtis and Modeen to his place in the Pocono Mountains in Pennsylvania for a cookout on August 13, and he was driving into town to pick up supplies. As described in his autobiography:

> He [Purdie] heard a series of King Curtis recordings on his car radio, being played one after another. He was enjoying the music and thinking to himself how great it was for Curtis to get such airplay, when the disc jockey took a station break with, "We'll return with our tribute to the late King Curtis after this."
>
> Purdie doesn't remember how he drove his car to the shoulder of the highway, but it must have been an alarming maneuver. A number of motorists stopped their cars and approached his car to find Purdie muttering, "He's dead! He's dead!" The motorists asked him who was dead. Purdie couldn't answer. He just started crying.[13]

Still very emotional about her loss when I spoke with her years later, Modeen remembered all the massive confusion she had experienced, and how grateful she had been for the strength of Aretha Franklin and Ruth Bowen:

> It was very difficult for me at that time to keep up with his instruments and most everything. See, we had bought a condo together, which is where we lived (150 West Ninety-Sixth Street). The mansion where we were going to live is where he was killed. It was not finished, but Curtis had put a full studio on that lower level where that swimming pool was, and most of his instruments and things were there. At our home, he had horns, you name it, but we did have people that were in his den [everywhere] and you can't keep up with them. My kids of course were teenagers, and I got them there as soon as I could, and Aretha Franklin, she was a *jewel*, and Ruth Bowen. These people didn't go home; they stayed with me. Aretha shopped at Saks and bought my dress for the funeral, the hat, everything, she just took care of it.[14]

Modeen continued to feel deeply indebted for such constant and loving support: "The day of the funeral, she [Aretha] prepared food; she was like a real jewel—her and Ruth Bowen. I don't know what I would have done without them, because it was like I was dazed; I didn't know what had happened. I knew what had happened but had not accepted it yet. Jerry [Wexler] put security there and had security around the clock, because it was crazy, people were calling making threats on my life. I was never able to figure out who would come up with something like that."[15]

During this time of total despair, Ruth Bowen and Aretha Franklin provided Modeen with a gift that can only be shared between dear friends: the welcome tonic of a good laugh. Bowen broke into appreciative laughter when she recalled Aretha saying to Modeen: "'You need a dress for the funeral.' She went to get Modeen a dress—and it had a big split up the front; you know Aretha."[16] Modeen chimed in with a gentle smile:

> You know how Aretha dressed. Well, this dress that Aretha had bought me for the wake, it had a split. Just a black sheath dress, very smart, something I would have bought—but not for a wake. The dress I wore the night of the wake. The doorbell rang, and I went to the door, and the police—because we were having threats—and I walked to the door with this wool dress on, beautiful dress—nice and simple, with a slit up the front. He [the police officer] looked at me and said, "You don't look like anybody in mourning."[17]

"At least we always found something to laugh about," Ruth said with a rueful smile. "We tried to blow it out of our minds. He was so missed, and all of our lives had to reorganize and get a hold of things and try to get Mo together to live her life."[18]

The angst-inducing death threats against Modeen were quickly followed by idle chatter, including rumors of gambling debts and drug deals gone bad—the gamut of uninformed and unsubstantiated speculation and slander regarding what may have led to King Curtis's death. To my question about this and all other reports, Modeen firmly and quickly responded:

> I signed the checks. I cashed his checks. Yet, if he went out there and was gambling, he used his American Express card, and you know who paid it? Me. He had *no* debt. Not only that, he had just signed a big contract with Atlantic—he wasn't that kind of a gambler. All I know is that he was with Atlantic and there was never any real money problems with Curtis. Curtis was probably making more money than he had ever made. He was a gambler, but he wasn't that kind of a gambler. If Curtis went to Vegas, he lost five thousand dollars. I don't ever remember his losing ten thousand dollars. I used to say to him, "That's it." I would

say to him, "I can't cover it," because I had no money (because I would put it in the stocks). I would do that to control his money.

If he had that kind of a problem, I would have been the first one to know it because the contract that people got from him for his work was my signature and the checks were signed by me. I wrote his checks, I wrote the band checks, and plus he had money in his account. You can put that to rest, because believe me that was not one of the problems. If he had that kind of a problem, he could have gone to Jerry [Wexler]. Jerry would have given him anything in the world, especially if he had somebody on his back and he said, "these people are going to kill me if I don't give them twenty-five thousand dollars," or whatever. They would have written him a check from Atlantic Records.[19]

Ahmet Ertegun immediately contacted Bernard Purdie to arrange the necessary musical support for Curtis's funeral service on Wednesday, August 18. Atlantic Records would summarily close that day. St. Peter's Church, reserved for only the crème de la crème of New York music society, would host the ceremony. Purdie hurriedly organized the Kingpins at

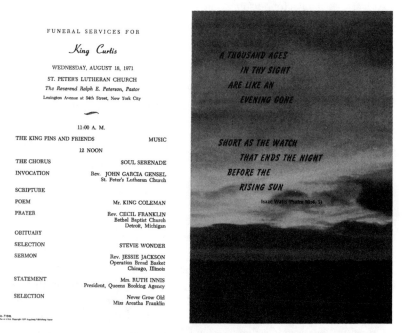

Funeral service program for King Curtis. *Courtesy of Modeen Brown.*

eleven a.m. outside the church the day of the funeral to bid farewell to their leader, playing an hour-long version of Curtis's signature hit, "Soul Serenade." Additional musicians, going to the funeral themselves, sat in from time to time over the next sixty minutes to perform their own contribution to the heartfelt musical send-off of their friend. A performance and a memorial truly befitting a King.

Outside the church, Aretha Franklin left an emotional message of comfort on a sign for everyone, which read, "Soul is feeling depth, the ability to reach someone. It's being part of what today is all about. It's not cool to be Negro or Jewish or anything else. It's just cool to be alive, to be around."[20]

Along with the outpouring of love and support for Modeen came the continued ugly, sobering reality that was Ethelyn. The day of the funeral, a car shared by the Rev. Jesse Jackson picked up Modeen at the Ninety-Sixth Street home. As it arrived at the curb at St. Peter's Church, Jackson and Modeen disembarked from their car and went inside. Close behind, in a separate car, came Ethelyn with eleven-year-old Curtis Jr. in tow. Ethelyn was appalled at the circumstances and vented her displeasure to *Jet* magazine: "I was surprised at the action of the Rev. Jesse L. Jackson. Being a clergyman and all, I resented him walking into the church with a woman that was not Curtis's wife and I was there."[21] Despite the legal separation agreement she had signed with Curtis in 1964, Ethelyn still considered herself to be Curtis's legal spouse (and, on paper, she still was). She also expected the appropriate level of decorum and respect that was due his "wife."

When Ethelyn learned that Modeen and Rev. Jackson exclusively would sit in the left front pew in front of Curtis's casket, she snatched Curtis Jr. and stormed from the church, anger mixed with humiliation written all over her face. She told a reporter from *Jet* magazine covering the ceremony that she was upset "because they showed disrespect for me as the lawful wife [by seating] me in the pew on the right side, while they sat her [Curtis's girlfriend, Modeen Broughton] in a pew on the left side in front of the casket."[22]

Jerry Wexler quickly dispatched an Atlantic staffer to chase Ethelyn down. After much beseeching that she at least allow Curtis Jr. to attend the service, she begrudgingly acquiesced. Curtis Jr. returned to the church, sitting in the left front pew alongside Modeen. As the two sat together, the little boy asked Modeen if he could see his father one last time before the service. Modeen gently escorted the youngster back behind the chapel to where Curtis's casket lay, opened the lid, and allowed the boy to say a very private goodbye to his father.

Back inside the church, the service commenced.

Stevie Wonder performed Dick Holler's 1968 song, "Abraham, Martin and John," adding to it with "Abraham, Martin, John … and now King Curtis"[23] When he reached the newly added fourth verse, he brought the crowd to tears by singing to the congregation, "Anybody here seen my old friend King Curtis?" Aretha Franklin's father, the Rev. C. L. Franklin, spoke and tried to reassure the inconsolable crowd by preaching that the Lord promised "He will not leave you comfortless. And we will all understand better by and by."[24]

The Rev. Jesse Jackson tried to bring some semblance of peace to the funeral service by saying, "The kind of hope that King Curtis blew into the human soul was the hope that is the spiritual force which is the enemy of despair, the source that allows Black people in America to still be alive."[25]

The impresario King Coleman spoke and said, "Death is just another step along life's way, no more than a gateway to a new and better day. Parting from our loved ones is much easier to bear when we know that they are waiting for us to join them there. For it is on the wings of death that the living soul takes flight, into the Promised Land and where there shall be no night."[26]

Ruth Bowen spoke, and then the Queen of Soul herself, Aretha Franklin, sang a sorrowful goodbye to her bandleader, dear friend, unofficial big brother with "Never Grow Old," her very first single for the J. V. B. and Checker labels.

Bonnie Bramlett grew quiet the minute the subject of Curtis Jr. came up during our interview, but she did say that she remains very appreciative of the love that Stevie Wonder extended to little Curtis at his father's funeral: "That was the *saddest* funeral. That little boy. Do you know that Stevie

Wonder gave him his harmonica [after the service]? Oh, Stevie Wonder went and handed him the harmonica and that little boy just sat there, so soft and gentle," she wistfully recalled. "He [Curtis Jr.] blew that harmonica."[27]

The funeral procession then left the church, wending its way east to Pinelawn Memorial Park on Long Island, final resting place to such luminaries as Count Basie and John Coltrane, as well as many others of the New York City music society. Once Curtis's casket was interred, slowly, one by one, everyone in the devastated congregation turned away and went slowly back home, still lost in their own personal memories of King Curtis.

Everyone, that is, save the disconsolate remaining "M'skeeters" posse of Delaney Bramlett and Duane Allman, who lingered together long after all had said their tearful prayers and goodbyes and left.

"Man, we just sat down there and cried," an emotional Delaney quietly murmured. "Me and Duane just sat there and cried and cried. We'd lost our great friend."[28]

Long live the King.

Chapter 18

In the Wake of Tragedy

S hortly after his death, both Atlantic Records and Aretha Franklin took out full-page ads in *Billboard*, *Cashbox*, and *Record World* magazines, grieving their personal loss in a very public way with soul-stirring tributes to their beloved King Curtis. Atlantic's August 28, 1971, *Billboard* ad read: "OUSLEY, KING CURTIS: We mourn the loss of our cherished friend and valued artist King Curtis. His life was devoted to his music. We will always miss him. Atlantic Recording Corporation."[1] Aretha followed, in *Billboard*'s September 4, 1971, issue with: "It is with a great deal of admiration I will always remember my dear friend and conductor KING CURTIS. His wonderful smile and friendship shall always be treasured among my most precious memories."[2]

A short two weeks after the death of King Curtis, on August 26, 1971, Duane Allman and the Allman Brothers band returned to New York City, performing a live concert for WPLJ radio station. At a break between songs, just before the band jumped into "You Don't Love Me," with Curtis's death still weighing heavily on his mind, a heartbroken Duane spontaneously decided to pay homage to his friend with his own heartfelt and personal memorial to the audience.

"About King Curtis, that was one of the finest cats there ever was, he was just right on top of it, gettin' next to young people, y'know? It's a shame. If y'all—if y'all get the chance, listen to that album he made out at Fillmore West—boy, it's incredible, it's unbelievable, the power and the emotional stature the man had. He's an incredible human being. Boy, I hope that, well, whatever it was, who did it, knows what he did, it was a terrible thing. The funeral, boy, Aretha sang and Stevie Wonder played—they played 'Soul Serenade.' All the ... [Duane breaks off into the first nine bars of Curtis's popular song] You ever hear that?"

A few in the audience respond with polite applause of recognition.

Duane continued: "Y'all probably a little bit young. It's fantastic. We'll do some of that—yeah, I know where we'll do it."[3]

Duane and the band immediately jump into "You Don't Love Me." The frenetic pace of the song seems to calm Duane, a medicinal release of energy helping to lift, temporarily, the weight of the deep sadness in his heart, getting him back to his familiar, comfortable musical roots. A little over eight minutes into the song, Duane slows the band, reaching a sorrowfully deliberate transitional phase.

Mirroring the incendiary, meteoric rise of King Curtis with the pace of "You Don't Love Me," Duane then stops, as if signifying Curtis's life and career being stopped in its tracks. Duane then achingly begins his memorial to Curtis, leading everyone into his own version of "Soul Serenade." As Curtis's saxophone could literally sing and speak the lyrics of songs he covered, so too does Duane Allman's guitar take on an almost saxello-like quality as he lovingly recreates his own uniquely personal interpretation of his friend's popular song.

Tenderly, Duane plays the first nine bars of the song again, and the audience responds by clapping along to the beat of the sweet melody, adding what they can to comfort Duane as he openly mourns his mentor and friend.

Just as the tune and crowd begin to settle in together to the mellow beat, Duane's guitar suddenly pierces the air and cries out in a moving, heartfelt solo, transitioning from saxello-like sound to razor-sharp electric guitar, taking his anguish to an entirely different height and shaking the head of his guitar skyward in anger. In this defining moment of his friendship with King Curtis, Duane purges his pent-up sorrow, shock, and disbelief. The crowd freezes, hypnotized in the moment as Duane delivers his angry, screaming eulogy for Curtis.

Rolling Stone magazine's David Fricke asked Butch Trucks, the Allman Brothers drummer, if the memorial was planned:

> No, that just popped up. But from the time he [Duane] came back from the funeral, up to that show, he talked about Curtis a lot, about the funeral—and about mortality. I think Duane understood that the way he lived life, he wouldn't live a long one.
>
> That day, on the air, was the first time we knew we were doing a tribute or, actually, "You Don't Love Me." I don't recall a set list. But if we had one, "You Don't Love Me" wasn't on it. Duane was at the microphone, talking about King Curtis. You can hear him: "Have you guys all heard 'Soul Serenade?'" He played a bit on guitar, then you could almost see a light bulb go off in his head. He stopped and started playing that riff [*hums the opening lick of 'You Don't Love Me'*].
>
> We knew what was coming then, although we didn't know when or exactly how. Duane played "Soul Serenade" a little slower than I was expecting. I was ready to kick into something more up tempo. But Duane was still so torn up by the fact that King was dead. It ripped him apart. When he came back from the funeral, that's when Duane started talking about his own funeral. He really did.[4]

A mere eight weeks after Duane Allman's royal tribute to his fallen friend, King Curtis, Atlantic Records once again suffered an excruciating loss. On October 29, 1971, Allman died in a motorcycle accident in his hometown of Macon, Georgia. Jerry Wexler choked through the eulogy at the funeral: "I did the eulogy at his funeral, and I was terrible because I was so broke-up I was hysterical. It was just a bunch of noise."[5]

Delaney Bramlett, after losing his second dear friend in the brief span of eleven weeks, was asked to sing one of Duane's favorite songs, "How Great Thou Art." Overcome with grief, Delaney declined. When hearing of Delaney's initial refusal to sing, his friend Jerry Wexler, consoled, "Listen … if I have to go up there and do it, you do too … "[6] Delaney sang his heart out.

"King," as he was most commonly addressed by so many who knew him, was gone. But now it seemed like everything was gone. Not just Curtis's life, but a few years later, and maybe not coincidentally, the soul music era also went by the wayside, having run its course. Long gone were Sam Cooke, Otis Redding, and many other industry stalwarts. Aretha Franklin majestically carried on, but the music industry was changing rapidly. Curiously, one of the great cultural representatives of this monumental time of change, soul music, became a casualty, morphing into the psychedelic offshoot of funk towards the end of the 1970s.

King Curtis's assailant, twenty-six-year-old Juan Montanez, was indicted by a grand jury and charged with second-degree murder. He was denied bail at his initial hearing. He was allowed to plea bargain down to a charge of second-degree manslaughter and entered a plea of guilty to the crime on December 3, 1971. He was sentenced on March 2, 1972, by the Honorable Gerald Culkin to serve a prison term not to exceed a maximum of seven years in Sing Sing prison in Ossining, New York.[7] He was assigned prisoner number 72-A-0137 and was paroled "for good behavior" on February 17, 1978, after having served six years.[8] According to *New York Daily News* writer David Hinckley, "he was released and hasn't popped up in the news since then. While he was in prison, he learned the trade of lens grinding, so who knows, maybe today he's making bifocals somewhere."[9] Montanez still lives in New York. When I contacted him for any comments, he hung up the phone without a word.

When asked what he missed most about Curtis, Joel Dorn lamented: "Some of the best fun was just hanging out when Curtis, Duane [Allman], and I were in New York at the same time. It was just fun".[10] Dorn valued Curtis not only for his friendship and musical talents, but for his counsel, for Curtis was savvy to the inner workings of Atlantic Records, which Dorn left in 1974:

> In the end, it was who was running the show—it was Ahmet's joint. I had been hassling Wexler to leave and he [Curtis] said, "Stay here and all your problems will be fixed—just keep your mouth shut." I got a lot of hassles, so I just picked up and split. The place was changing. The Atlantic that I fell in love with was pretty much gone and I never had

really adapted to the change, because I kind of liked it when the Dodgers were in Brooklyn and I liked it when Atlantic was on Sixtieth Street, so it was time for me to go. I had a little success and in the beginning of the '80s I bottomed out. It took me four to five years to catch another wave, so it was an interesting experience. I learned quite a few of life's lessons, but I sure wish Curtis was alive now because I would like to be an old guy with him—same with so many people—it would be a hoot now. The guys that are left now, Fathead [Newman], Les McCann, we are great friends now—we have so much fun—all the craziness is over pretty much, and I would like to have known Curtis now.[11]

Joel Dorn died on December 17, 2007, at age sixty-five.

Saxophone player Trevor Lawrence, who in the late 1960s played briefly with King Curtis and the Kingpins, still mourned the loss of his mentor and friend decades later:

Obviously, that death was shocking and terrifying … I just feel very sad right now even thinking about that. Man, I tell you something, I just hate to even think about it. Modeen and Curtis, he really loved that woman, by my recollection. They were really just so close and so nice to me. Modeen, she was always very nice to me, I don't even know why [laughs]. They were just the classiest, the nicest successful people that I had ever met. I really loved those people. And it was such a—oh God, just a terrible experience for everyone. That's all I can say. I think Curtis was a great man to be around. I mean, he really was. He really mapped my life out for me.[12]

Lawrence continues to perform around the world.

RCA Victor producer and *Billboard* reporter Bob Rolontz felt he couldn't overstate the industry's loss: "He got that hit 'Memphis Soul Stew' and then a couple of other things, then he had become a well-respected figure in the business so that he was leading bands and did a lot of work with Alan Freed, so that I would say right before he died he was really close to being one of the probably major figures of pop music."[13] Rolontz died on June 14, 2000, at age seventy-nine.

Isaac Hayes lamented, "It was such a tragedy, such a shame what happened to King Curtis and the way he left this world. It really broke my heart."[14] Isaac Hayes died on August 10, 2008, at age sixty-five.

Producer Jimmy Douglass was speechless when he learned of Curtis's death: "He said to me, when we getting on his bike that day, 'You know, Jimmy'—I swear to God, I swear to God he said this to me, I may not have paraphrased it exactly right, but it came down to this—'You know Jimmy, if I die today, I'm happy as hell,' he says. 'If I ain't got somethin', it's 'cuz I don't want it, or I don't know it exists. I have everything I want.'"[15]

Alas for the despondent Douglass, he was too upset to attend the funeral: "I got a call from Jerry Wexler and he said, 'Jimmy, Curtis is dead,' and I went, 'That's impossible, I just left him!' I was too young to process it. I mean, I didn't even attend the funeral because I couldn't process it. I didn't know anybody had died, yet, in my whole life. Let alone somebody who promised me the world. I'm talking about a seventeen-year-old kid who was fucking devastated."[16] To add insult to injury, Douglass also had to work the following day:

> I had a session booked the next day with Donny Hathaway to mix the Voices of East Harlem (he was producing it). So Donny walks off the elevator and he's talkin' about the weather, he's talkin' about this, and he's talkin' about that, and I looked at him and said, "Yo, you heard about Curtis, right?" And he said, "Yeah, man, that's a real drag, man." And he picked one of the songs and he said, "We're going to start with this one song right here first." I sat there and mixed five tunes that day with that man. With my heart, my fucking stomach in my toes. Emotionally, I was dying inside, and I just sat there and worked, 'cuz there was nobody else to talk to or ask about it; what are you going to do? And that was the day I grew up.[17]

Douglass also had to finish Curtis's last album, *Everybody's Talkin'*, and not without a few regrets. Douglass remembered Jerry Wexler calling and asking him:

> "Who's closer to him [Curtis] than anybody? You are, so you have to finish this up." And I'm co-producer on that album. And I went ahead and finished all the songs the way that I saw fit. I wish I would have used all the same players he did; that was a mistake. I didn't use his crew, because I had different visions of what a crew was. And they really all got really pissed at me. I didn't get it. That's all that I can say to you. I didn't get it. You know, as most kids don't get it, I didn't

get, like, what that was. Dude, these are his people he's figured out all
these years. Even if you think what they do isn't "cutting edge" like
you want it to be, these dudes are dope [talented] as fuck! They're our
men. And they will help guide you to finish the record that *he* wanted
finished, not the record that *you* think you wanted to finish. These are
all money lessons.[18]

Douglass apparently was a very attentive student of King Curtis's production
education at Atlantic Records, for it spawned his marvelous fifty-year career
in music. He's been nominated for eleven Grammy Awards, winning four
times, and continues to work with the preeminent artists in music, from Led
Zeppelin and AC/DC to Jay-Z and Kanye West.[19]

Fellow Atlantic producer Gene Paul was just as distraught:

I was in the shower. And my wife came in and told me that somebody
had stabbed Curtis. And I nearly fell in the shower. Curtis was—the
other side of Curtis was (laughing)—he didn't take any shit. He came
up the hard way. And made it very big. And well. And deserving.
And the other side of him is, when he saw the guy sitting on the steps he
got pissed and he didn't like it. And he walked over to the guy and had
him move, and—I think it was a blade he took out and just took him
out. Listen, we all have our shit. Nobody's perfect. And Curtis wouldn't
hurt a fly. But when it's on his doorstep and it looks bad, it's wrong, all
of this stuff. He took a little move, and it was the wrong move. But the
beautiful part of Curtis you could never forget, Curtis did so much for
the music world that people don't really—I mean some people know,
some "inside" people know, but what he did was just remarkable"[20]

Evidently, Gene Paul was also a good student of the game. He received a
Grammy Award for Roberta Flack's "Killing Me Softly" along with nine
other Grammy Awards, with thirty total nominations in fifteen different cate-
gories over his career.[21] And he still keeps in touch with Jimmy Douglass:

Jimmy Douglass calls up every once in a while.; We'll do some mastering stuff for him. He'll call up, and we'll start the mastering sessions
and just talkin' about the days at Atlantic and it will go on for hours.
We all just absolutely loved it. And one of the great parts about it was
we knew it was what it was. We appreciated it, we respected it, and
working with all the people—humbled. Completely humbled.

Curtis should be recognized not only for what he did, musically—my God how great he played—but what he did for all the other efforts that took place. He put the big band together for Aretha, the same thing. He, it was him that stabilized that whole rhythm section. From him, came the Atlantic rhythm section. And again, what he started way back in the sixties, that rhythm section that came out of there. It was Cornell, Richard Tee, Bernard Purdie, Chuck Rainey—that whole spin was just a phenomenal rhythm section. And a lot of that came from Curtis. He would just play and they just loved playing with him.

I mean Joel and I, [business partner and former Atlantic engineer] Joel Kerr and I, have talked about many of these sessions over and over the years. And we've looked at each other and our key phrase is, "We would have paid them to work there." That's how good it was.[22]

Ahmet Ertegun continued to have difficulty reconciling his friend's death up until his own death on December 14, 2006, at age eighty-three: "He certainly was the nicest, most wonderful person that I have ever known. I loved him like a brother."[23]

Jerry Wexler mourned the loss of his dear friend as well as the fact that Curtis's premature death took an incredible talent from this world: "So many memories ... shooting pool at my house in Long Island with Curtis and Tony Joe White ... fishing for sail off the Big "A" in the Gulf Stream ... his woman, Modeen, grilling steaks at four a.m. in their apartment on Central Park West after a session ... hanging out in Harlem after the gig at Small's' ... parties at Ahmet's with King blowing behind Esther Phillips. Curtis was noble, ballsy, and streetwise like nobody I ever knew."[24] Wexler died on August 15, 2008.

Aretha Franklin remained the regal Queen of Soul for decades after Curtis's death. She has said of Curtis, though she has never felt comfortable discussing him since his death: "King Curtis was a soul superhero, and I miss him still."[25] The Queen of Soul died on August 16, 2018, at age seventy-six.

Her longtime booking agent, Ruth Bowen, championed this book and tried valiantly on numerous occasions to get Aretha to interview with me (as did Modeen, who had always been close to Aretha). Being Aretha's booking agent and confidante for over forty-five-years was still not enough influence to convince Aretha. Ruth died on April 21, 2009, at the age of eighty-four.

Norman Dugger, the waifish ball of energy in Curtis's life as both a friend and his valet/personal assistant/rehearsal manager, transitioned from King Curtis's side to lend the same infectious enthusiasm and professionalism with Aretha Franklin over the next thirty-eight years. He died on November 5, 2016, at the age of seventy-six.

Immediately after King Curtis's death, Sam Moore's debut solo album for Atlantic Records was shelved. Officially, this may have been because the album had not been completely mixed, but more to the truth, it may have been due to Moore's all-encompassing drug addiction and his unreliability at the time. Either way, without Curtis's heavy-handed, loving support and studio creativity driving the project forward, Atlantic "lost" the master tapes to Sam Moore's solo album, only for them to be "rediscovered" and released *thirty-four years later*, due solely to the dogged pursuit of Sam and his wife, Joyce Moore. Sam Moore has released a second solo album, a production of duets produced by Randy Jackson, featuring the likes of Vince Gill, Mariah Carey, Eric Clapton, and Bekka Bramlett (Delaney and Bonnie Bramlett's talented daughter). He still has as much energy as ever.

Atlantic producers Tom Dowd and Arif Mardin continued to lend their tremendous studio talents to scores of musicians, successfully producing music up until their deaths in 2004 and 2006, at age seventy-seven and seventy-four, respectively.

Bernard Purdie was for a time assigned by Ahmet Ertegun to become the new leader of the Kingpins, but Curtis's creative energy and the emotional glue that held the group together were gone. Without the cohesiveness that Curtis brought to the group, they soon disbanded.

Gone, too, was King Curtis's savvy ability to help people at Atlantic Records navigate the company's political waters. King Curtis was the peacekeeper at Atlantic as no one knew better than Purdie. In his autobiography, Purdie's memories are described of clashing with Jerry Wexler when asked to "'play like Panama Francis.' Purdie would have none of that and told Wexler so in the session. Purdie told Wexler if he wanted Panama Francis, he should call him for the job. Wexler shut the session down, which was extraordinary, considering the probable expense involved."[26] King Curtis, as he had with producer Joel Dorn, attempted to navigate and ease the high emotions of the moment: "King Curtis was Purdie's rabbi and a musician whom Purdie held in the highest esteem. Purdie loved Curtis like an older brother and there was a great affection between them. Curtis talked to Purdie about the incident with Wexler and chided him for being so direct with him in the session, telling him he needed to be more diplomatic."[27]

Bernard Purdie is alive and well, enjoying recognition as one of the great drummers of all time, and he still records and performs. In an interview with author Jim Payne, he gave great kudos to his predecessor, King Curtis and the Noble Knights drummer Ray Lucas: "He was like an acrobat—so light on his feet. He danced on the pedals. He could take sticks and make them sound like brushes. He could be the quietest person in the world and be in the groove, and when he had to be fatback, he had no problem. And he had no problem swinging either."[28] Ray Lucas was seventy-two, alive and well in 2012 in his interview with Modern Drummer's Jim Payne. Based on my research, he appears to still be living in New York City.

Cornell Dupree formed a new band, Stuff, and then moved on to play and record on other projects as well. He is still regarded as one of the great lead guitar players in the music industry. When David Sanborn recorded his interpretation of King Curtis's song "Soul Serenade" for his 1992 album, *Upfront*, he called Cornell Dupree to record the guitar licks (as well as Kingpins Richard Tee to cover the organ). When asked why Sanborn sought him out specifically to play on the album, Dupree laughingly remembered, "I recorded with him because no one could play that lick, so they called me."[29] Cornell Dupree died on May 8, 2011, at age sixty-eight.

Both Chuck Rainey and Jerry Jemmott, mainstays at bass guitar in live and recorded performances for so many different iterations of King Curtis's bands over the years, continue to perform and record. Rainey was only too happy to chat with me about King Curtis: "What a pleasure to talk about King Curtis. I'm always glad to talk about Curtis, he was like another father to me."[30] The day after he had heard of Curtis's murder from Norman Dugger, Jemmott had a vision:

> In my kitchen. He [Curtis] was hovering above the kitchen cabinets. It just blew my mind. I mean I was like, "Holy ... ," you know. I mean for me it was just crazy because we never hung out. It was just about the music, and then I find that he's dead; the morning after, he's in my kitchen.
>
> It turned my life around in terms of the whole idea of spirituality and realizing there is a spirit world. It awakened me to a whole realm of existence which I would have never seen any other way. And that's when I went on to a spiritual journey to find my own spirituality, to find a connection, a way I can tap into the spirituality: yoga and then eventually I got into the occult sciences—astrology, numerology, you know—trying to get these questions answered: why, where. And then I eventually landed with the Richard Davis Institute, who does shows through true Buddhism, where I've been for the last thirty-five years. So, it was because of that initial presence of King Curtis in my house the day after he passed away that my life entirely changed.[31]

In 1972, after the excruciating deaths of King Curtis and Duane Allman, one after the other, Delaney Bramlett fell apart, both personally and professionally. One day he was driving over with Bonnie to Jerry Wexler's Long Island home to play guitar with his best buddies, the other two M'skeeters, and soon after, he had lost his two dearest friends in the space of a few months. Delaney didn't record for a year after his friends' deaths. But when he finally got back into the studio with producer Ike Turner, what Jerry Wexler heard on the studio tapes was, according to Wexler, "dog meat."[32] With Delaney in the throes of a horrible drug habit, he and Bonnie divorced. Over the years, Delaney survived a second divorce and health problems that nearly claimed his life, ultimately succumbing later to health complications. He died on December 27, 2008, at age sixty-nine.

One can only imagine the heavenly reunion the Three M'skeeters of Atlantic Records have enjoyed since then. Dear friend Jerry Wexler is certainly right there by their side. And to be sure, he has his tape recorder close by and turned on, not missing any recording opportunities this time.

Bonnie Bramlett landed more solidly on her feet than her ex-husband, releasing her first solo album in 1973. While on tour with Stephen Stills in 1979, she famously punched Elvis Costello in the face at a bar in Columbus, Ohio, after hearing him insult James Brown and Ray Charles. She also became a semi-regular cast member on Rosanne Barr's ABC television series, *Roseanne*. Bonnie Bramlett continues to sing and perform.

Curtis Jr. went back to live with his birth mother, Ethelyn, and Modeen never saw him again. He was approached by Dennis O'Keefe for Dennis's King Curtis documentary, but he declined to be interviewed. Some sources say Curtis Jr. fell into drug usage and died in June 1994.[33] Chuck Rainey had also heard that Curtis Jr. fell on hard times: "He lived on the street. And a big guy like his dad, but he lived on the street. And he didn't have a place to stay."[34]

Ethelyn Ousley is reported to still be living in New York City at a care facility. She could not be reached for comment.

And Modeen? In 1975 she married a politician, George Brown, the first Black lieutenant governor in Colorado history, and lived happily with her husband for the next thirty years, until his death in 2006. She travels often to visit her beloved children and grandchildren. But Curtis is never, ever far from her thoughts: "I have *never* had so much fun with one man. He was the love of my life."[35]

I want to be free,
To fly away and sing,
To the world about my soul serenade
My soul serenade
When you're not around,
There's a lonely sound
In my soul serenade

"Soul Serenade," by King Curtis and Luther Dixon

Epilogue

F ame and recognition have continued to follow King Curtis long after his death. In 1972 he was nominated posthumously for a Grammy Award for Best R&B Instrumental Performance for *Everybody's Talkin'*, the album of songs cut in Miami in August 1969 at Atlantic Record's South-Criteria Studios and later at the Atlantic recording studios in New York. The following year Curtis and Champion Jack Dupree were also nominated for the 1973 Best Ethnic or Traditional Recording category for their *Blues At Montreux* album.

Long overdue, King Curtis was finally inducted into the Rock and Roll Hall of Fame (as a sideman, the first year for that new category) in 2000. The influence of King Curtis on the pop, soul, rhythm and blues, and yes, jazz music of his era, as well as the repercussions of his death for the many that knew and loved him, continues to be felt.

Lenny Pickett, sax player in the Tower of Power and present music director of the *Saturday Night Live* band, told author Peter Grendysa: "King Curtis had that [vocal approach] completely nailed down. And he was always such a facile player. I think he got bagged as being an R&B player but always wanted to be thought of without such a narrow focus; many of his instrumental records have some very hip, jazz-oriented playing on them, and he was certainly capable of a lot more than playing solos on R&B singers' records. He described the art form, which is why he's one of the most imitated sax players of our day."[1]

Clarence Clemons, sax player for Bruce Springsteen and the E Street band, recalled to *DownBeat* magazine: "I heard King Curtis, he turned me on, and it was then that I decided I wanted to play tenor. His sound and tone were so big on those sessions he did and his feeling was right from the heart. Here was a guy who gave me something."[2]

Years later, when working on Aretha Franklin's "Freeway of Love," producer Narada Michael Walden asked Clemons to play the saxophone solo. Clemons said: "I was absolutely thrilled, because I felt as if I was actually taking the King's [Curtis's] place and also standing where the King stood— 'Long Live the King.' I was so deeply honored, thrilled to feel like I was taking King Curtis's place along Aretha Franklin's side and doing everything for the solo in 'Freeway of Love.' It was the highlight of my life."[3] Clemons died on June 18, 2011, at age sixty-nine.

Keyboardist Bobby Whitlock may have best summed up the feelings held throughout the music industry when he told me:

> He was just an open … a happy soul. When someone is open like that, really genuine, kids and animals gravitate towards them, like other happy, open souls. He was just right at the breaking point, where he would have been more than a cult figure. He was getting to the point where, had he lived, he would have been a Miles Davis kind of person. He would have been at the forefront of everything. His name would have been synonymous with saxophone, that's what impact he would have had. Because he was that genuine—that smile, now, that you see with him, that was as genuine as it gets. The big man. A great big man with a great big soul. A big instrument that he played—wow, he could make that little old saxophone say more than I ever heard."[4]

Whitlock continues to record and perform.

My first exposure to King Curtis was back in 1994 when I heard David Sanborn play "Soul Serenade" at a concert, and the song hit me like a lightning bolt. Sanborn had recorded the song on his 1992 album *Upfront* and now makes it a regular song in his live performances. Unfortunately, David has never met King Curtis, as he lamented to me:

> King Curtis was a magnet, and my great regret is I never got a chance to meet him. Because I remember where I was when I found out that he got killed. I was in California with the [Paul] Butterfield band at a place called the Golden Bear [in Huntington Beach]. And Trevor Lawrence, who was a saxophone player from New York, who was in the band at the time, who was very close to King Curtis, told me about that. And I was going to meet him because he was going to introduce me to him when we got back to New York.[5]

I've been asked by many why I wrote this book. Surprisingly to some people, my answer to this broad-based question has consistently been one simple word: justice. Once I started researching the life of Curtis Ousley, I quickly recognized the immense influence he contributed, successfully crossing over so many genres of music spanning nearly three decades. And precious few have ever heard of his name outside the music industry. Couple this with learning the specifics of his assailant's seemingly meager prison sentence, and I was consumed with anger over the injustice of it all.

Some might proffer a legitimate argument that Curtis's instigation of the confrontation with Juan Montanez was a valid reason for the reduction in charges. And to that point, concerns voiced early on by songwriter Doc Pomus to Curtis and that were passed on as well to Joel Dorn still carry an eerie and heart-wrenching echo: "Curtis had a horrible temper," said Dorn. "Doc Pomus was always telling him, when he would get mad, 'Watch yourself, man, that temper's gonna kill ya.' And he was right. He ended up dying when he couldn't let shit go. If somebody did something he didn't like, he didn't care who it was."[6]

My outrage was also heightened because King Curtis's untimely death had ripped him from the consciousness of the general public. He would be quickly dismissed by many as nothing more than a footnote to the careers of the Coasters, Buddy Holly, the Beatles, Jimi Hendrix, Duane Allman, Aretha Franklin, and many other greats of his generation. His impact on the lives of so many musicians and producers, past and present, much less his contribution to some of the most amazing music of the soul, R&B, pop, and jazz of the 1950s, '60s and early '70s, would never be fully recognized due to a simple, silly, maddening act of random violence. I don't think it's a stretch to say that, when he was killed, King Curtis was one of the most influential musicians of his generation, poised on the threshold of superstardom.

My goal has been to get King Curtis what I thought was some desperately long-overdue exposure and—no pun intended on Aretha Franklin's legendary work—respect. Along the way, I have been rewarded more than tenfold for my efforts. My initial anger and sense of injustice has been quickly replaced by something wonderfully unexpected: friendship.

Because of this project (and my obsession with it), I've met tremendous people and made some amazing new friends, both in the States and abroad. To a person, everyone who was interviewed for this work was delighted to contribute. Jimmy Douglass nearly brought me to tears when he described how cathartic it was for him to discuss King Curtis with me: "And I'm kinda going back there now, talkin' to you. When you called, I was like, "Oh my God, I've been dying to say something about this for my whole life."[7]

My greatest pride is in knowing that, as a result of my personal odyssey pursuing this book, I was able to reunite some very old and very dear friends who haven't heard from each other for over thirty-five years. Both Jerry Wexler and Delaney Bramlett had long given up hope of ever speaking with Modeen Brown again. They didn't know if she was alive or dead, much less how to track her down. As I was about to commence my interview with Jerry (the initial interview that energized me for the next twenty years) and before I could ask my very first question, he interrupted with, "Have you found Modeen?"

"No," I replied, "Not yet."

Deeply disappointed, Jerry wistfully replied, "She's *critical* to the story. If you ever find her, please let her know I would love to talk with her."[8]

When interviewing Delaney Bramlett, he was no less hopeful: "Man, I would *love* to talk to Modeen. If you hear from her, give her my love and have her call me."[9]

The author with two spectacular women: Modeen and his wife, Teresa, on his wedding day, January 21, 2012. *Courtesy of Greg Guederian.*

Not too shortly after my initial chat with Delaney, I was thrilled to finally locate Modeen (thanks to the able detective work of Dennis O'Keefe). I had her call Delaney and Jerry, who were both overjoyed to be reunited with their long-lost friend. No less elated was Modeen, who before they died had a chance to chat with or visit both Jerry and Delaney on numerous occasions, renewing their friendships and celebrating the life of King Curtis.

Appendix A

Recommended Listening

Album (LPs)	Label	Catalog #
The Coasters Greatest Hits **(The Coasters)** Poison Ivy / Along Came Jones / Down In Mexico / The Shadow Knows / I'm A Hog For You / Charlie Brown / Yakety Yak / Zing! Went The Strings Of My Heart / That Is Rock And Roll / Young Blood / Sweet Georgia Brown / Searchin'	Atco	33-111
Have Tenor Sax Will Blow (1959) **(King Curtis)** Midnight Ramble / Linda / The Shake / Jaywalk / Lil Brother // Peter Gunn // The Groove / Snake Eyes / Cuban Twilight / Birth of the Blues / Chili	Atco	33-113/SD 33-113
The New Scene of King Curtis (1960) **(King Curtis)** Da Duh Dah / Have You Heard / Willow Weep For Me // Little Brother Soul / In A Funky Groove	New Jazz	NJLP 8237

Album (LPs)	Label	Catalog #
Soul Battle (1960) **(Oliver Nelson, King Curtis,** **Jimmy Forrest)** Blues At The Five Spot / Blues for M.F. (Mort Freda) / Anacruses / Perdido / In Passing	Prestige	PRLP7223
Soul Meeting (1960) **(King Curtis)** Soul Meeting / Lazy Soul / All The Way // Jeep's Blues / What Is This Thing Called Love? / Do You Have Soul Now?	Prestige	PRLP 7222
Arthur Murray's Music For Dancing **The Twist! (1961)** Jersey Bounce-Twist / Twistin' Time / Honeysuckle Rose / The Peppermint Twist / The Huckle-Buck / The Arthur Murray Twist // Stompin' At The Savoy / The Twist / 12th Street Twist / Let's Twist Again / Alright Okay, You Win / The Fly	RCA Victor	LSP-2494
Trouble In Mind (1962) **(King Curtis)** Trouble In Mind / Jivin' Time / Nobody Wants You When You're Down And Out / Bad Bad Whiskey / I Have To Worry // Woke Up This Morning / But That's Alright / Ain't Nobody's Business / Don't Deceive Me / Deep Fry	Tru-Sound	TRU15001
Soul Twist (1962) **(King Curtis)** Soul Twist / Twisting Time / What'd I Say / I Know / Sack O' Woe Twist / Camp Meetin' // Wobble Twist / Irresistible You / Big Dipper / Twisting With The King / Midnight Blue	Enjoy	ENLP-2001
Shirelles and King Curtis **Give a Twist Party (1962)** **(the Shirelles and King Curtis)** Mama, Here Comes The Bride / Take The Last Train Home (Instrumental) / Welcome Home Baby / I've Got A Woman / I Still Want You / Take The Last Train Home (Vocal) / Love Is A Swinging Thing / Ooh Poo Pah Doo / New Orleans / Mister Twister / Potato Chips	Scepter	SRM-505/ SPS-505

Album (LPs)	Label	Catalog #
Country Soul (1962) **(King Curtis)**	Capitol	ST 1756

Any Time / Wagon Wheels / Home On The Range / Your Cheatin' Heart /
Brown Eyes / Night Train To Memphis // Raunchy / I'm Movin' On /
High Noon / Tumbling Tumbleweeds / Tennessee Waltz / Walkin' The
Floor Over You

Live at the Harlem Square Club, 1963 **(Sam Cooke)**	RCA Victor	LP 1-5181

Feel It / Chain Gang / Cupid / Medley: It's All Right, For Senti-
mental Reasons / Twistin' The Night Away / Somebody Have
Mercy / Bring It On Home to Me / Nothing Can Change This Love /
Having a Party

Soul Serenade (1964) **(King Curtis)**	Capitol	T 2095/ ST2095

Tequila / Night Train / Java / Harlem Nocturne / Honky Tonk / Soul Twist //
Memphis / Watermelon Man / Soul Serenade / Swingin' Shepherd Blues /
My Last Date (With You) / Wiggle Wobble

Plays The Hits Made Famous By **Sam Cooke (1965)** **(King Curtis)**	Capitol	T2341/ ST2341

Ain't That Good News / Bring It On Home To Me / Having A Party /
Good Times / You Send Me / Shake Shake / Tennessee Waltz / Chain
Gang / A Change Is Gonna Come / Cupid / Send Me Some Lovin' /
Twistin' The Night Away

That Lovin' Feelin' (1966) **(King Curtis)**	Atco	33-189/ SD33-189

The Shadow of Your Smile / Michelle / Cryin' Time / I Left My Heart
in San Francisco / Moonglow / Spanish Harlem / You've Lost That
Lovin' Feeling / What Now My Love / And I Love Her / Make the
World Go Away / Girl From Ipanema / On Broadway

Album (LPs)	Label	Catalog #
Live At Small's Paradise (1967)	Atco	33-198/SD
(King Curtis)		33-198

Tough Talk / Philly Dog / Preach / Blowin' in the Wind / Medley:
Peter Gunn, Get Along Cindy // Pots and Pans / The Shadow of Your
Smile / Road Runner / Something on Your Mind / Soul Theme

King Curtis Plays the Great Memphis	Atco	33-211/
Hits (1967)		SD-33-211
(King Curtis)		

Knock on Wood / Good to Me / Hold On! I'm Comin'' / When
Something Is Wrong with My Baby / Green Onions / You Don't
Miss Your Water // Fa-Fa-Fa-Fa-Fa (Sad Song) / In the Midnight
Hour / The Dog / I've been Loving You Too Long / Last Night /
Jump Back

| **King Size Soul (1967)** | Atco | 33-231/ |
| **(King Curtis)** | | SD33-231 |

Ode to Billie Joe / A Whiter Shade of Pale / For What It's Worth / To Sir,
With Love / Memphis Soul Stew / When a Man Loves a Woman / I Never
Loved a Man (the Way I Love You) / Life For Life (Vivre Pour Vivre) /
C.C. Rider / I Was Made to Love Her

| **Sax In Motion (1968)** | RCA Victor | CAS2242 |
| **(King Curtis)** | Camden | |

Jersey Bounce / Honeysuckle Rose / The Huckle-Buck / Stompin' At The
Savoy / Alright, Ok. You Win // 12th Street Rag / Movin' On / Rockabye
Baby / I'm With You / Open Up

| **Sweet Soul (1968)** | Atco | SD 33-247 |
| **(King Curtis)** | | |

Theme From Valley of the Dolls / Soul Serenade / I Heard It Through
the Grapevine / Sweet Inspiration / By the Time I Get to Phoenix /
Spooky / Honey / Up Up and Away / The Look of Love / Sittin' By the
Dock of the Bay

Album (LPs)	Label	Catalog #
Best of King Curtis (1968)	Atco	SD 33-266
(King Curtis)		

Harper Valley PTA / Ode to Billie Joe / Soul Serenade / I Heard It
Through the Grapevine / Sittin' on the Dock of the Bay / Memphis
Soul Stew // Spanish Harlem / Jump Back / Something on Your
Mind / You've Lost That Loving Feeling / Makin' Hay / I Was Made
to Love Her

Instant Groove (1969)	Atco	33-293
(King Curtis)		

Instant Groove / Hey Joe / Foot Pattin' / Wichita Lineman / Games People
Play / Sing A Simple Song / The Weight / La Jeanne / Green Apples / Somewhere / Hold Me Tight / Hey Jude

The Best Of (1969)	Prestige	PRST7709
(King Curtis)		

Jivin' Time / Harlem Nocturne / Hot Saxes / Sweet Georgia Brown /
The Party Time Twist // The Hully-Gully Twist / When The Saints Go
Marching In / Firefly / Honky Tonk / Long Way From St. Louis

Get Ready (1970)	Atco	SD 33-338
(King Curtis)		

Get Ready / Sugar Foot / Floatin' / Bridge Over Troubled Water /
Soulin' // Teasin' / Something / Promenade / Let It Be / Someday We'll
Be Together

Live At Fillmore West (1971)	Atco	SD 33-359
(King Curtis)		

Memphis Soul Stew / A White Shade Of Pale / Changes / Whole Lotta
Love / I Stand Accused / Changes / Ode To Billie Joe / Mr. Bojangles /
Signed Sealed Delivered I'm Yours / Soul Serenade

Album (LPs)	Label	Catalog #
Don't Fight the Feeling: The Complete Aretha Franklin & King Curtis Live at Fillmore West (2005) **(Aretha Franklin and King Curtis)**	Rhino Handmade	RHM2 7890

Intro / Knock On Wood / Whole Lotta Love / Them Changes / A Whiter Shade of Pale / My Sweet Lord / Ode to Billy Joe / Mr. Bojangles / Soul Serenade / Memphis Soul Stew / Signed, Sealed, Delivered (I'm Yours) / Respect / Call Me / Mixed Up Girl / Love The One You're With / Bridge Over Troubled Water / Eleanor Rigby / Make It With You / Don't Play That Song / You're All I Need To Get By / Dr. Feelgood / Spirit In The Dark / Spirit In The Dark (Reprise) / Knock On Wood / Them Changes / Whole Lotta Love / A Whiter Shade of Pale / I Stand Accused / Soul Serenade / Memphis Soul Stew / Respect / Call Me / Love The One You're With / Bridge Over Troubled Water / Share Your Love With Me / Eleanor Rigby / Make It With You / You're All I Need To Get By / Don't Play That Song / Dr. Feelgood / Spirit In The Dark / Spirit In The Dark (Reprise) / Knock On Wood / Whole Lotta Love / Them Changes / A Whiter Shade of Pale / Ode to Billy Joe / Mr. Bojangles / Soul Serenade / Memphis Soul Stew / Respect / Call Me

| **Everybody's Talkin' (1972)** **(King Curtis)** | Atco | SD 33-385 |

Groove Me / You're the One / Honky Tonk / Love the One You're With / If I Were a Carpenter / Everybody's Talkin' // Ridin' Thumb / Alexander's Ragtime Band / Central Park / Wet Funk (Low Down and Dirty) / Ridin' Thumb-Jam

| **Blues at Montreux (1973)** **(King Curtis and Champion Jack Dupree)** | Atlantic | SD 1637 |

Junker's Blues / Sneaky Pete / Everything's Gonna Be Alright / Get With It / Poor Boy Blues / I'm Having Fun

| **Dreams (1989)** **(Allman Brothers)** | Polygram | 839 417-2 |

You Don't Love Me / Soul Serenade, Song 1, Disc 3

Appendix B

King Curtis Billboard Pop and R&B Singles Charts Success

Year	Title	Pop Chart[1]	R&B Chart[2]
1962	Soul Twist	17	1
	Beach Party	60	—
1963	Do the Monkey	92	—
1964	Soul Serenade	51	—
1965	Spanish Harlem	89	—
1966	Something on Your Mind	—	31
1967	Jump Back	63	—
	Ode to Bille Joe	33	6
	For What It's Worth	87	—
	I Was Made to Love Her	76	49
1968	(Sittin' on) the Dock of the Bay	84	—
	Heard It through the Grapevine	83	—
	Harper Valley P.T.A.	93	—
1969	Instant Groove	—	35
1970	Get Ready	—	46
1971	Whole Lotta Love	64	43

Appendix C

Top 10 Must-Listen King Curtis Songs

1) "Soul Serenade"

   What many consider to be Curtis's signature song while at Capitol Records. His initial 1964 version is sweet, dreamy, and bright, played with a saxello. Interestingly enough, he recorded the song again in 1968 for Atlantic Records using a tenor sax and slowing the tempo, creating a surprisingly melancholy, bluesy work, very different from the original.

2) "Memphis Soul Stew"

   One of Curtis's most creative songs and his anthem while at Atlantic Records. He took particular advantage of the American Studios backing musicians in Memphis, perfectly mixing in all their respective talents. The song boils over with energy and excitement.

3) "Junker's Blues" (King Curtis with Champion Jack Dupree)

   Less than two months before his death, Curtis and his band delivered a breathtaking live performance (with literally no rehearsal) with Champion Jack Dupree in Montreux, Switzerland. "Junker's Blues" is a stunning exhibition of Curtis's ability to follow a difficult artist while creating a perfect interpretation of snorting, honking, and groaning throughout the song. His saxophone takes on an almost human quality sassing back and forth to Dupree. One of my favorites.

4) "Soul Twist"
Curtis's first number 1 hit. He stutters and stops, blaring back and forth with his band, creating a wonderful, swinging tune. He's at some of his brassy best here, with nice support from Billy Butler on guitar and Ernie Hayes on organ.

5) "Games People Play"
Curtis's only Grammy Award–winning song. While even Curtis did not expect this instrumental cover of Joe South's hit (whose original composition also won a Grammy the same year) to be particularly successful, it's a solid song where Duane Allman contributed some nice slide guitar.

6) "Trouble in Mind"
The title track from his 1961 Tru-Sound album. Curtis displays some exemplary guitar work along with an adequate singing voice. It's his melancholy, raspy saxophone, however, that breathes life into the song and gives it its haunting mood.

7) "Teasin'" (King Curtis with Eric Clapton)
The only song King Curtis recorded with Eric Clapton. Clapton continues to refer to this recording as one of his favorites, because he felt it was simply perfect. Curtis's saxophone and Clapton's guitar share an extraordinary synthesis and mesh into a single voice. It's unusual and hypnotic.

8) "Hold On! I'm Comin'"
From his *King Curtis Plays the Great Memphis Hits* album. You could pick any number of Stax Records hits recorded on the album and be content. This cover of the Sam and Dave classic has nice support from the Sweet Inspirations (Cissy Houston, Myrna Smith, Sylvia Shemwell, and Estelle Brown), who consistently backed Aretha Franklin at Atlantic Records. Atlantic Records vice president Jerry Wexler's favorite King Curtis album.

9) "Knock on Wood"

From the King Curtis album *Live at Fillmore West*, this was recorded in conjunction with the *Aretha Live at Fillmore West* album. It gives an excellent view of not only King Curtis in a live setting but the tight integration he shared with his band, the Kingpins. This up-tempo version of the Eddie Floyd hit helps you understand why all Curtis's band members felt an almost religious synergy with their bandleader and bandmates.

10) "Night Train"

Back in Fort Worth, Texas, when Curtis was just starting his professional career as a teen, this is how he ended every performance at Aaron and Robbie Watkins's Paradise Club. You can easily envision Curtis jumping up on the bar and walking back and forth, honking away to his rabid audience. Finishing an evening like this, there's no wonder people stormed the Paradise Club whenever young King Curtis was performing.

Appendix D

Top 10 King Curtis Accompaniments

1) "Respect" (Aretha Franklin)

   This cover of Otis Redding's song exploded onto the 1960s landscape, creating one of the great feminist anthems of all time. Curtis's solo at the song's break, based on Sam and Dave's "When Something Is Wrong with My Baby," shouts Aretha's charge on behalf of women out loud.

2) "Yakety Yak" (the Coasters)

   The breakthrough song that made King Curtis a worldwide star. Everyone that heard this song wanted to know, "Who is that saxophone player?" Curtis created a clever down-on-the-farm "chicken-scratch" solo that caught everyone's attention.

3) "Twistin' the Night Away" (Sam Cooke / King Curtis)

   From Cooke's raucous *Live at the Harlem Square Club, 1963* album. Sam and Curtis banter back and forth, with Curtis responding to Cooke's histrionics with roiling solos. The magnetic connection between the two is undeniable.

4) "Only You Know and I Know" (Delaney & Bonnie with the Allman Brothers and King Curtis)

   Recorded at A & R Studios in New York City for WPLJ radio on July 22, 1971, this is the last live recording of King Curtis. The interaction between Delaney, Bonnie, Duane Allman, and King Curtis is infectious. There are a number of King Curtis solos that highlight this Dave Mason–written song. Not unlike the synergy King Curtis generated with Sam Cooke on the *Live at the Harlem Square Club, 1963* album, you can feel the electricity between Curtis and Delaney & Bonnie.

5) "I Cried a Tear" (LaVern Baker)

   One of numerous LaVern Baker songs King Curtis played on. "I Cried a Tear" was her most successful hit (reaching number 2 on the Billboard R&B chart in 1959), and Curtis lends a sorrowful saxophone solo at the break in the tune.

6) "Reminiscing" (Buddy Holly)

   Buddy Holly invited King Curtis to write and record with him at Buddy's studio in Clovis, New Mexico, in September 1958, and this is one of the two songs recorded between the two. In spite of penning this song, Curtis was omitted from the writing credits when the song was launched in 1963 (long after Holly's death). A wonderful call-and-response between Buddy and Curtis, with a nice solo by Curtis.

7) "It's so Hard" (John Lennon)

   King Curtis and John Lennon became friendly during the Beatles 1965 tour. So when Curtis was sought out by famed "Wall of Sound" producer Phil Spector to play on Lennon's *Imagine* album, Lennon quickly agreed to Spector's choice. Curtis opens the song with a short solo and jumps into the remainder of the song here and there.

8) "Blues for M. F. (Mort Fega)" (Oliver Nelson, King Curtis, Jimmy Forrest)

   From the album *Soul Battle*, a great illustration of King Curtis's under-estimated ability to hang with established jazz saxophonists. Liner notes author Tom Wilson opines: "King Curtis continues to surprise the jazz fans who don't know about his jazz capabilities with a solo generally marked be adeptness and vitality, but particularly notable for beautiful phrasing which sustains an idea from the 24th to the 36th bar of his effort."[1]

9) "River Boat Dock" (Washboard Bill)

This Washboard Bill song, recorded in September 1956, gives a glimpse into some of Curtis's earliest work as a backing musician in the recording studios of New York City. The twenty-two-year-old leads off the song with a powerful solo, blowing blues into his lengthy performance and setting the tone for Washboard Slim's guitar.

10) "You Don't Love Me / Soul Serenade" (Allman Brothers)

While not a King Curtis–performed song, it is still incredibly important. This was recorded on August 26, 1971, a brief thirteen days after King Curtis's murder. It is heart-wrenching to hear Duane Allman's eulogy for his friend, and even more so when the song gets to the "Soul Serenade" section where Duane lets his guitar express the level of his grief in a way that, verbally, he can't. His performance is spine-tingling and will leave a lump in your throat. Whenever I had significant challenges working on this book, I would play this song and Duane would restore my focus and revive my energy.

Endnotes

After the first listing of each interview performed by the author, subsequent listings give the interviewee's surname followed by the word "interview."

Preface

1. Sid Bernstein, interview with the author, July 5, 2002.

Chapter 1

1. Dennis O'Keefe, director, "Soul Serenade: The King Curtis Ousley Story (as told by those who knew and love him)," 1987. Incomplete documentary film. All quotations based on transcript provided by director.
2. Mike Hennessey, "King Curtis: His Last Interview," *Record Mirror*, August 8, 1971, 5.
3. *Ibid.*
4. O'Keefe, "Soul Serenade."
5. *Ibid.*
6. Hennessey, "King Curtis."
7. Gayle W. Hanson, "Terrell, Isaiah Mulligan [I. M.] (1859–1931)," *Handbook of Texas*, Texas State Historical Association, https://www.tshaonline.org/handbook/entries/terrell-isaiah-milligan-im.
8. Hennessey, "King Curtis."
9. Joseph Muranyi, liner notes for *Have Tenor Sax, Will Blow*, King Curtis, Atlantic Records, 1959.
10. O'Keefe, "Soul Serenade."
11. Ray Sharpe, interview by Adam Komorowski, *BOSS* 12, November 1986, 6.
12. O'Keefe, "Soul Serenade."
13. Hennessey, "King Curtis."
14. O'Keefe, "Soul Serenade."
15. *Ibid.*
16. Hennessey, "King Curtis."
17. *Ibid.*
18. O'Keefe, "Soul Serenade."
19. *Ibid.*

Chapter 2

1. Ralph Cooper, *Amateur Night at the Apollo: Ralph Cooper Presents Five Decades of Entertainment* (Harper Collins, 1990), 72.
2. O'Keefe, "Soul Serenade."
3. *Ibid.*
4. *Ibid.*
5. *Ibid.*
6. Garvin Bushell, *Jazz from the Beginning* (University of Michigan Press, 1988), 118.
7. Tyree Glenn Jr., interview with the author, April 8, 2004.
8. *Ibid.*
9. Dale Wright, liner notes for *Old Gold*, Tru-Sound, TRU 15006, December 1961.
10. Glenn, interview.
11. *Ibid.*
12. *Ibid.*

Chapter 3

1. Mickey Baker, interview with the author, August 24, 2005.
2. Jerome "Doc" Pomus, liner notes for Jerome "Doc" Pomus, *It's Great to Be Young and in Love*, Whiskey, Women, And ..., RBD 713, December 25, 1999, 2–3.
3. Joel Dorn, interview with the author, May 15, 2004.
4. Baker, interview.
5. *Ibid.*
6. *Ibid.*
7. *Ibid.*
8. *Ibid.*
9. Barbara Castellano, interview with the author, September 9, 2005.
10. Castellano, interview with the author, September 9, 2005.
11. Major Robinson, "New York Beat," *Jet*, July 9, 1953, 65.
12. Major Robinson, "New York Beat," *Jet*, August 12, 1954, 65
13. Major Robinson, "New York Beat," *Jet*, September 30, 1954, 65.
14. Major Robinson, "New York Beat," *Jet*, August 12, 1954, 63.
15. Castellano, interview.
16. Baker, interview.
17. Major Robinson, "New York Beat," *Jet*, February 9, 1956, 65.
18. Castellano, interview.

Chapter 4

1. King Curtis, interview by Charlie Gillett, part 1, "KC Interviewed," *The Sound #4*, June/July 1985, 21–24. First part of transcription of 1971 interview.
2. Ahmet Ertegun, interview with the author, December 13, 2001.
3. Ahmet Ertegun, *What'd I Say*, (Welcome Rain, 2001), 268.
4. Bob Rolontz, interview by Roy Simonds, "Interview with Bob Rolontz," *The Sound #6*, October/November 1985, 7–9.
5. Cited in Roy Simonds, *King Curtis: A Discography*, Version 4.25, self-published, December 2008. 2.
6. Rolontz, Simonds interview.
7. Ertegun, interview.
8. Rolontz, Simonds interview.
9. Jerry Wexler, interview with the author, January 30, 2001.
10. *Ibid.*
11. King Curtis, Gillett interview, part 1, 25.
12. Peter Grendysa, liner notes for *Blow Man Blow!*, King Curtis, Bear Family Records, 1993, 6.
13. Castellano, interview.
14. Baker, interview.
15. Castellano, interview.
16. Baker, interview
17. Castellano, interview.
18. Peter Guralnick, *Sweet Soul Music*: *Rhythm and Blues and the Southern Dream of Freedom* (Little, Brown & Co., 1986), 55.
19. *Ibid.*, 55–56.
20. Jerry Wexler, *Rhythm and the Blues: A Life in American Music* (St. Martin's Press, 1993), 70.
21. Mike Stoller, interview by Rob Hughes and Roy Simonds, "Stoller," *BOSS* 8, March 1986, 15.
22. Bill Millar, *The Coasters* (W. H. Allen, 1975), 90.
23. *Ibid.*, 92.
24. *Ibid.*
25. *Ibid.*
26. *Ibid.*
27. Ertegun, interview.
28. King Curtis, Gillett interview, part 1, 26.
29. Wexler, interview.

30. Carl Gardner, *Yakety Yak I Fought Back: My Life with The Coasters* (Authorhouse, 2007), 72.
31. King Curtis, Gillett interview, part 1, 26.
32. *Ibid.*
33. Baker, interview.

Chapter 5

1. King Curtis, Gillett interview, part 1, 25–26.
2. Ertegun, interview.
3. Mort Shuman, interview by Stuart Colman, *Echoes* radio show, Radio London broadcast, October 26, 1986, transcribed by Roy Simonds in *BOSS* 12, November 1986, 8.
4. O'Keefe, "Soul Serenade."
5. Major Robinson, "New York Beat," *Jet*, September 25, 1958, 63.
6. Ellis Amburn, *Buddy Holly: A Biography* (St. Martin's Griffin, 1995), 84.
7. Bobby Keys, *Every Night's a Saturday Night: The Rock and Roll Life of Legendary Sax Man Bobby Keys* (Counterpoint, 2013), 11.
8. *Ibid.*
9. *Ibid.*, 22.
10. Amburn, *Buddy Holly*, 185.
11. Waylon Jennings, *Waylon: An Autobiography* (Chicago Review Press, 2012), 54–55.
12. Perry Meisel, *The Cowboy and the Dandy* (Oxford University Press, 1998), 17.
13. Major Robinson, "New York Beat," *Jet*, November 19, 1959, 64.
14. Muranyi, liner notes.
15. *Ibid.*
16. MyHeritage.com, "Curtis Ousley and Ethelyn Butler," New York City Marriages, 1950–2017.
17. Baker, interview.
18. Shirley Alston Reeves, interview with the author, April 12, 2008.
19. Nat Hentoff, liner notes for *The New Scene of King Curtis*, King Curtis, New Jazz NJ 8237, April 21, 1960.
20. Jason Ankeny, review of *Azure* by King Curtis, Allmusic.com, https://www.allmusic.com/album/azure-mw0000582649.
21. Earl Scruggs, interview by Jerome John, "Earl Scruggs Still Picking at 80," *Tuscaloosa News*, April 8, 2004, 6D.

22. Geoffrey Himes, "Earl Scruggs Stays Fresh through Long Career," *Chicago Tribune*, September 16, 2001, https://www.chicagotribune.com/news/ct-xpm-2001-09-16-0109160340-story.html.
23. Wexler, *Rhythm and the Blues*, 248–49.
24. Josh Alan Friedman, *Tell the Truth Until They Bleed: Coming Clean in the Dirty World of Blues and Rock and Roll* (Backbeat Books, 2008), 190.
25. Norman Dugger, interview with the author, May 23, 2005.
26. *Ibid.*

Chapter 6

1. Simonds, *King Curtis*, 59.
2. Rob Hughes, email to John Broven, November 27, 2021. Subsequently forwarded to author.
3. Joe Goldberg, liner notes for *Trouble In Mind*, King Curtis, Tru-Sound Records, TRU-15001, April 25, 1961.
4. *Ibid.*
5. Roy Simonds, back cover notes for *Live In New York*, King Curtis, JSP Records, JSP 8812, 2008.
6. Jim Payne, "R&B Drumming Legend Ray Lucas: Props from Peers," *Modern Drummer*, May 29, 2012, 59.
7. *Ibid.*, 60.
8. Valerie Wilmer, "Bobby Robinson: Legend of the Backstreets," *Melody Maker*, November 18, 1978, 47–48.
9. *Ibid.*, 47.
10. *Ibid.*
11. *Ibid.*, 48.
12. *Ibid.*
13. *Ibid.*
14. John Johnson Jr., Joel Selvin, and Dick Cami, *Peppermint Twist: The Mob, the Music, and the Most Famous Dance Club of the 1960s* (Thomas Dunne Books, 2012), 137.
15. Johnson Jr., Selvin, and Cami, *Peppermint Twist*, 136–37.
16. Major Robinson, "New York Beat," *Jet*, March 22, 1962, 64.
17. Johnson Jr., Selvin, and Cami, *Peppermint Twist*, 137.
18. Major Robinson, "New York Beat," *Jet*, December 21, 1961, 63.
19. Sharpe, Komorowski interview, 6.
20. Eddie Kirkland, interview by Norman Darwen, *BOSS* 15, April/May 1986, 4–5.
21. *Ibid.*, 5.

Chapter 7

1. Cornell Dupree, interview with the author, February 16, 2002.
2. *Ibid.*
3. *Ibid.*
4. *Ibid.*
5. Chuck Rainey, interview with the author, April 30, 2008.
6. King Curtis, Gillett interview, part 1, 26.
7. *Ibid.*
8. Sam Cooke, *Live at the Harlem Square Club, 1963*, RCA LP 1-5181, 1963.
9. Guralnick, *Sweet Soul Music*, 166.
10. Sam Moore, interview with the author, April 30, 2002.
11. Peter Guralnick, *Dream Boogie: The Triumph of Sam Cooke* (Little, Brown & Co., 2009), 451.
12. *Ibid.*
13. Curly Palmer, interview with the author, April 26, 2008.
14. *Ibid.*
15. *Ibid.*
16. *Ibid.*
17. *Ibid.*
18. *Ibid.*
19. *Ibid.*

Chapter 8

1. King Curtis, Gillett interview, part 1, 3.
2. Payne, "R&B Drumming Legend Ray Lucas," 60.
3. *Ibid.*
4. Jimmy Smith, interview with the author, April 28, 2008.
5. *Ibid.*
6. *Ibid.*
7. *Ibid.*
8. *Ibid.*
9. *Ibid.*
10. Bruce Eder, "King Curtis Plays the Hits Made Famous By Sam Cooke," https://www.allmusic.com/album/plays-the-hits-made-famous-by-sam-cooke-mw0000899479.
11. David Cavanaugh, liner notes for *King Curtis Plays the Hits Made Famous by Sam Cooke*, Capitol Records, ST 2341, 1964.

12. *Ibid.*
13. King Curtis, interview by Charlie Gillett, part 2, "KC Interview Pt. 2," *The Sound #5*, August/September 1985, 1–5. Second part of transcription of 1971 interview.
14. Arif Mardin, interview with the author, June 3, 2003.
15. Modeen Brown, interview with the author, October 1, 2001.
16. *Ibid.*
17. *Ibid.*
18. *Ibid.*
19. *Ibid*
20. *Ibid.*
21. *Ibid.*
22. *Ibid.*
23. *Ibid.*
24. *Ibid.*
25. Dupree, interview.
26. Brown, interview.
27. Dupree, interview.
28. Brown, interview.
29. Bobby Elliot, interview with the author, August 30, 2007.

Chapter 9

1. For a full account of Bernstein's career, see Sid Bernstein, *It's Sid Bernstein Calling* (Jonathan David, 2002).
2. Bernstein, interview.
3. *Ibid.*
4. *Ibid.*
5. "King Curtis at Shea Stadium NYC 1965," youtube.com/watch?v=Vn1RAjnb1TA. Filmmaker unknown.
6. Dupree, interview.
7. *Ibid.*
8. Rainey, interview.
9. *Ibid.*
10. Payne, "R&B Drumming Legend Ray Lucas," 60.
11. John Fraim, "Saxophonist Gene Walker on the 1966 Beatles Tour," *My People* (blog), https://mayorarnett.blogspot.com/search?q=beatles, 11-1-2010.
12. Payne, "R&B Drumming Legend Ray Lucas," 60.

13. Rainey, interview.

14. *Ibid.*

15. 15

16. Sharon Lawrence, *Jimi Hendrix: The Intimate Story of a Betrayed Musical Legend* (Harper Collins, 2005), 35.

17. Brown, interview.

18. Lawrence, *Jimi Hendrix*, 36.

19. Dupree, interview.

20. Payne, "R&B Drumming Legend Ray Lucas," 61.

21. Steven Roby and Brad Schreiber, *Becoming Jimi Hendrix* (Da Capo Press, 2010), 139.

22. Johnny Black, *Jimi Hendrix: the Ultimate Experience* (Thunder's Mouth Press, 1999), 39.

23. Roby and Schreiber, *Becoming Jimi Hendrix*, 142.

24. Brown, interview.

25. Dupree, interview.

26. Smith, interview.

27. Rainey, interview.

28. George Massey, interview with Cornell Dupree, April 13, 2010. Shared with author on cassette tape. Author's transcription.

29. Roby and Schreiber, *Becoming Jimi Hendrix*, 142–43.

30. *Ibid.*, 143.

Chapter 10

1. Bernard Purdie, telephone interview with the author, November 23, 2005.

2. *Ibid.*

3. Bernard Purdie, *Let the Drums Speak! The Life Story of the World's Most Recorded Drummer* (Pretty Media), 2014, 78–79.

4. Payne, "R&B Drumming Legend Ray Lucas," 61.

5. *Ibid.*

6. Wexler, interview.

7. Guralnick, *Sweet Soul Music*, 339.

8. Red Kelly, email conversation with John Broven, November 21, 2021. Forwarded to author.

9. *Ibid.*

10. Ruth Bowen and Modeen Brown, interview with the author, December 9, 2001.

11. *Ibid.*
12. Cissy Houston, interview with the author, March 10, 2010.
13. Gerri Hirshey, *Nowhere to Run: The Story of Soul Music* (De Capo Press, August 1994), 234.
14. Aretha Franklin and David Ritz, *Aretha: From These Roots* (Villard Books, 1999), 146–47.
15. Mardin, interview.
16. David Ritz, *Respect: The Life of Aretha Franklin* (Little, Brown & Co., 2014), 161.
17. Charlie Gillett, *Making Tracks: The History of Atlantic Records* (Panther Books, 1975), 168.
18. Ritz, *Respect*, 161.
19. *Ibid.*
20. Jerry Wexler, liner notes for *King Curtis Plays the Great Memphis Hits*, Atco Records, SD 33-211, 1967.
21. *Ibid.*
22. Isaac Hayes interview with the author, Naples Philharmonic Center, April 14, 2002.
23. Bowen and Brown, interview.

Chapter 11

1. Jerry Jemmott, interview with the author, April 2, 2008.
2. *Ibid.*
3. *Ibid.*
4. *Ibid.*
5. *Ibid.*
6. Bob Mehr, "Chips Moman: The Missing Man of Memphis Music," *The Commercial Appeal*, July 13, 2008, https://archive.commercialappeal.com/entertainment/chips-moman-the-missing-man-of-memphis-music-ep-396359660-324079771.html.
7. Gene Chrisman, interview with the author, October 2, 2012.
8. Roben Jones, *Memphis Boys: The Story of American Studios* (University Press of Mississippi, 2010), 58.
9. *Ibid.*, 87.
10. Bobby Wood, interview with the author, June 14, 2010.
11. Lyrics to "Memphis Soul Stew," Atco 6511, 67C-12768, Memphis, TN, July 5, 1967, Alfred Publishing.
12. Red Kelly, email conversation with John Broven, November 21, 2021. Forwarded to author.

13. Gene Chrisman, interview with the author, October 2, 2012.

14. Bobby Wood, interview with the author, June 14, 2010.

15. Jemmott, interview.

16. *Ibid.*

17. *Ibid.*

18. *Ibid.*

19. *Ibid.*

20. *Ibid.*

21. *Ibid.*

22. B-side of a 45 single with "Sittin' on the Dock of the Bay" on the A-side. Atco #6562, 67C-13570, 12-5-67.

23. Brown, interview.

24. Red Kelly, email conversation with John Broven, November 21, 2021. Forwarded to author. Although the date mentioned is listed in Roy Simmonds' *King Curtis Discography*, according to American guitarist Reggie Young's session logbook these sessions occurred on March 27–30.

25. Ertegun, *What'd I Say*, 171.

26. Mardin, interview.

27. *Ibid.*

28. Chrisman, interview.

29. Wexler, *Rhythm and the Blues*, 227–28.

30. *Ibid.*, 228.

31. Wexler, interview.

32. *Ibid.*

Chapter 12

1. Wexler, interview.

2. Mark Bego, *Aretha Franklin: The Queen of Soul* (St. Martin's Press, 1989), 113.

3. *Ibid.*

4. *Ibid.*

5. Phillip Leno Wright, *Free Mind Free Speech: Please!! May I Speak?* (Authorhouse, 2014), 31–33.

6. Wright, *Free Mind Free Speech*, 34.

7. Art Simmons, "Paris Scratchpad," *Jet*, September 26, 1968, 29.

8. Ed Ochs, "Soul Sauce," Billboard, September 21, 1968, 24.

9. Wright, *Free Mind Free Speech*, 40.

10. *Ibid.*, 41.
11. Wexler, *Rhythm and the Blues*, 252–53.
12. Ertegun, *What'd I Say*, 242.
13. Delaney Bramlett, interview with the author, July 3, 2002.
14. Eric Clapton, *Clapton: The Autobiography* (Broadway Books, 2007), 113–14.
15. D. Bramlett, interview.
16. *Ibid.*
17. *Ibid.*
18. Wexler, *Rhythm and the Blues*, 253.
19. *Ibid.*, 225.
20. *Ibid.*, 253.
21. Wexler, interview.
22. D. Bramlett, interview.
23. Galadrielle Allman, *Please Be with Me; a Song for My Father, Duane Allman*, (Spiegel & Grau, 2014), 237.
24. Bonnie Bramlett, interview with the author, October 3, 2015.
25. *Ibid.*
26. Allman, *Please Be with Me*, 237.
27. *Ibid.*
28. *Ibid.*
29. *Ibid.*
30. B. Bramlett, interview.
31. Allman, *Please Be with Me*, 237.
32. Brown, interview.
33. B. Bramlett, interview.
34. Brown, interview.
35. B. Bramlett, interview.
36. *Ibid.*
37. *Ibid.*
38. D. Bramlett, interview.
39. Mitch Lopate, "Delaney, Clapton, Allman and Friends: A Conversation with Delaney Bramlett," Swampland.com, Fall 2000, http://swampland.com/articles/view/title:delaney_bramlett.
40. Jemmott, interview.
41. Randy Poe, *Skydog: The Duane Allman Story* (Backbeat Books, 2006), 193.
42. Brown, interview.
43. Greg Allman, *My Cross to Bear* (William Morrow, 2012), 160–61.

44. Ben Fong-Torres, "Tales of Ike and Tina Turner: The World's Greatest Heartbreaker," *Rolling Stone*, October 14, 1971, 38.
45. Ertegun, *What'd I Say*, 226.

Chapter 13

1. Tom Dowd, interview with the author, March 31, 2002.
2. Ertegun, *What'd I Say*, 224.
3. Trevor Lawrence, interview with the author, July 20, 2015.
4. *Ibid.*
5. *Ibid.*
6. *Ibid.*
7. Brown, interview.
8. Dorn, interview.
9. Ray Coleman, *Clapton!* (Warner Books, 1985), 256.
10. Eric Clapton, interview by Tommy Vance, interview with Eric Clapton, BBC4, April 25, 1980. Radio broadcast. See also Eric Clapton and King Curtis performing "Teasin'" on Tommy Vance's radio show in 1980, https://www.youtube.com/watch?v=hGBvnI1WRg8.
11. *Ibid.*
12. Bobby Whitlock, interview with the author, August 15, 2005.
13. Bobby Whitlock, *Bobby Whitlock, a Rock and Roll Autobiography* (McFarland, 2011), 57–58.
14. *Ibid.*, 57.
15. *Ibid.*, 58.
16. D. Bramlett, interview.
17. *Ibid.*
18. Dupree, interview.
19. Brown, interview.

Chapter 14

1. Jerry Wexler, liner notes for *Jazz Groove*, Prestige Records, Prestige 24033, 1973.
2. Ertegun, *What'd I Say*, 268.
3. Moore, interview.
4. *Ibid.*
5. *Ibid.*
6. *Ibid.*
7. *Ibid.*

8. Vince Aletti, "Sam of Sam and Dave Meets King C," *Rolling Stone*, February 18, 1971, 6.

9. Moore, interview.

10. *Ibid.*

11. Aletti, "Sam of Sam and Dave," 6.

12. *Ibid.*

13. *Ibid.*

14. Moore, interview.

15. *Ibid.*

16. *Ibid.*

17. *Ibid.*

18. *Ibid.*

19. Bowen and Brown, interview.

20. *Ibid.*

21. *Ibid.*

22. *Ibid.*

23. Wexler, *Rhythm and the Blues*, 245.

24. Jemmott, interview.

25. *Ibid.*

26. Wayne Jackson, interview with the author, April 19, 2005.

27. Michael Lydon and Ellen Mandel, *Boogie Lightning: How Music Became Electric* (Da Capo Press, 1974, 180.

28. Bowen and Brown, interview.

29. *Ibid.*

30. Jemmott, interview.

31. Lydon and Mandel, *Boogie Lightning*, 162.

32. *Ibid.*, 163.

33. Bowen and Brown, interview.

34. *Ibid.*

Chapter 15

1. Jimmy Douglass, interview with the author, May 21, 2018.

2. *Ibid.*

3. *Ibid.*

4. *Ibid.*

5. *Ibid.*

6. *Ibid.*

7. *Ibid.*

8. Gene Paul, interview with the author, February 15, 2021.
9. *Ibid.*
10. *Ibid.*
11. Bowen and Brown, interview.
12. *Ibid.*
13. Ritz, *Respect*, 240.
14. *Ibid.*
15. Bowen and Brown, interview.
16. Dorn, interview.
17. *Ibid.*
18. Mike Hennessey, liner notes for *Blues at Montreux*, King Curtis and Champion Jack Dupree, Atlantic Records, 7 81389-2, June 17, 1971.
19. Dorn, interview.
20. Hennessey, *Blues at Montreux*, liner notes.
21. King Curtis and Champion Jack Dupree, "Sneaky Pete," *Blues at Montreux*, Atlantic Records, SD 1637, June 17, 1971.
22. Curtis and Dupree, "Get with It," *Blues at Montreux*.
23. Curtis and Dupree, "Poor Boy Blues," *Blues at Montreux*.
24. Curtis and Dupree, "I'm Havin' Fun," *Blues at Montreux*.
25. Bowen and Brown, interview.
26. Peppo Delconte, "Milan Caravan Stormy Scenes", *Billboard*, July 24, 1971, 46.
27. Ritz, *Respect*, 240–41.
28. Dugger, interview.
29. Brown, interview.
30. D. Bramlett, interview.
31. *Ibid.*
32. Lopate, "Delaney, Clapton, Allman and Friends."
33. Brown, interview.

Chapter 16

1. Merrill A. Roberts Jr., "The Week's Best Photos," *Jet*, August 5, 1971, 33.
2. O'Keefe, "Soul Serenade."
3. Douglass, interview.
4. Bowen and Brown, interview.
5. Dorn, interview.
6. Bowen and Brown, interview.

7. *Ibid.*

8. *Ibid.*

9. Mardin, interview.

10. Mitchell J. Hall, "The Good Luck Manhattan Mansion," *Active Rain* (blog), September 21, 2011, https://activerain.com/blogsview/2518488/ the-good-luck-manhattan-mansion.

11. Jerry Wexler, interview with the author, January 30, 2001.

12. Bowen and Brown, interview.

13. *Ibid.*

14. *Ibid.*

15. Dugger, interview.

16. *Ibid.*

17. *Ibid.*

18. *Ibid.*

19. Moore, interview.

20. Dugger, interview.

21. Bowen and Brown, interview.

22. *Ibid.*

23. *Ibid.*

24. *Ibid.*

25. *Ibid.*

26. *Ibid.*

27. *Ibid.*

28. *Ibid.*

29. *Ibid.*

30. *Ibid.*

31. *Ibid.*

32. *Ibid.*

33. *Ibid.*

34. New York City Police Department, Complaint Report against Juan Montanez, August 14, 1971.

35. New York City Police Department, Supplemental Complaint Report against Juan Montanez, August 16, 1971.

36. Bowen and Brown, interview.

37. *Ibid.*

38. *Ibid.*

39. Rainey, interview.

40. MyHeritage.com, US Social Security Applications and Claims, 1936–2007.

Chapter 17

1. D. Bramlett, interview.
2. *Ibid.*
3. *Ibid.*
4. B. Bramlett, interview.
5. O'Keefe, "Soul Serenade."
6. Ertegun, interview.
7. Ritz, *Respect*, 342.
8. Dupree, interview.
9. Rainey, interview.
10. Dorn, interview.
11. Ritz, *Respect*, 242.
12. *Ibid.*, 242–43.
13. Purdie, *Let the Drums Speak!*, 159.
14. Bowen and Brown, interview.
15. *Ibid.*
16. *Ibid.*
17. *Ibid.*
18. *Ibid.*
19. *Ibid.*
20. "King Curtis Buried; Aretha Leaves 'Cool' Message For All," *Jet*, September 2, 1971, 54.
21. *Ibid.*, 56.
22. *Ibid.*
23. "King Curtis Buried," 55.
24. *Ibid.*, 54.
25. *Ibid.*, 55.
26. *Ibid.*
27. B. Bramlett, interview.
28. D. Bramlett.

Chapter 18

1. *Billboard*, August 28, 1971, 11
2. *Billboard*, September 4, 1971, 44.
3. Duane Allman, "You Don't Love Me/Soul Serenade," Allman Brothers Band, *Dreams*, disc 3, Capricorn Records, June 20, 1989. Dialogue included before song begins (live studio recording).

4. Butch Trucks, interview by David Fricke, *Rolling Stone*, March 8, 2016, https://www.rollingstone.com/music/music-news/allman-brothers-butch-trucks-talks-epic-1971-radio-concert-230442/.
5. Wexler, interview.
6. D. Bramlett, interview.
7. The People of the State of New York v. John [Juan] Montanez, 4640-71 (Supreme Court of the State of New York, September 9, 1971).
8. Letter from James E. Sullivan, Superintendent, State of New York Department of Correction Services, Sing Sing Correctional Facility, Ossining, New York, April 16, 1987. Addressee illegible. Shared with author by Roy Simonds.
9. *Hittin the Web with the Allman Brothers Band* (blog), February 22, 2005, http://allmanbrothersband.com/modules.php?op=modload&name=XForum&file=viewthread&tid=25290. Page no longer available.
10. Dorn, interview.
11. *Ibid.*
12. Lawrence, interview.
13. Rolontz, Simonds interview, 8.
14. Hayes, interview.
15. Douglass, interview.
16. *Ibid.*
17. *Ibid.*
18. *Ibid.*
19. Jimmy Douglass (website), https://jimmydouglass.com.
20. Paul, interview.
21. G & J Audio (website), https://gandjaudio.com/about-us.html.
22. Paul, interview.
23. Ertegun, interview.
24. Wexler, *Rhythm and the Blues*, 249.
25. Gerri Hirshey, *Nowhere to Run*, 234.
26. Purdie, *Let the Drums Speak!*, 140.
27. *Ibid.*
28. Payne, "R&B Drumming Legend Ray Lucas," 58.
29. Dupree, interview.
30. Rainey, interview.
31. Jemmott, interview.
32. Wexler, *Rhythm and the Blues*, 263.

33. Toby Hero and Barbara Lochridge, interview with the author, Dec. 15, 2015.
34. Rainey, interview.
35. Brown, interview.

Epilogue

1. Grendysa, *Blow Man Blow*, liner notes, 2–3.
2. Clarence Clemons, interview by Don Palmer, *The Sound* #7, December/January 1986, 25.
3. Clarence Clemons, interview with the author, March 3, 2009.
4. Whitlock, interview.
5. David Sanborn, telephone interview with the author, December 19, 2008.
6. Dorn, interview.
7. Douglass, interview.
8. Wexler, interview.
9. D. Bramlett, interview.

Appendix B

1. Joel Whitburn, *Joel Whitburn's Top Pop Singles, 1955–2006* (self-published, 2007), 465.
2. Joel Whitburn, *Joel Whitburn's Top R&B Singles* (self-published, 1996), 248–49.

Appendix D

1. Tom Wilson, liner notes for *Soul Battle*, Oliver Nelson, King Curtis and Jimmy Forest, Prestige Records, PR 7223, September 9, 1960.

Bibliography

Interviews by Author

Baker, Mickey. Telephone interview. August 24, 2005.

Bernstein, Sid. Telephone interview. July 5, 2002.

Bowen, Ruth, and Modeen Brown. Interview at Bowen's home, Miami, FL. December 9, 2001.

Bramlett, Bonnie. Interview, Pinewood Social Club, Nashville, TN. October 3, 2015.

Bramlett, Delaney. Interview at his home, Hollywood Hills, CA. July 3, 2002.

Brown, Modeen. Interview in her home, Boca Raton, FL. October 1, 2001.

Castellano, Barbara. Telephone interview. September 9, 2005.

Chrisman, Gene. Telephone interview. October 12, 2012.

Clemons, Clarence. Telephone interview. March 3, 2009.

Dorn, Joel. Telephone interview. May 15, 2004.

Douglass, Jimmy. Telephone interview. May 21, 2018.

Dowd, Tom. Telephone interview. March 31, 2002.

Dugger, Norman. Interview in his home, Richmond, VA. May 23, 2005.

Dupree, Cornell. Interview in his home, Fort Worth, TX. February 16, 2002.

Elliot, Bobby. Email interview. August 30, 2007.

Ertegun, Ahmet. Telephone interview. December 13, 2001.

Glenn Jr., Tyree. Email interview. April 8, 2004.

Hayes, Isaac. Interview, Naples Philharmonic Center, Naples, FL. April 14, 2002.

Hero, Toby, and Barbara Lochridge. Telephone interview. December 15, 2015.

Houston, Cissy. Telephone interview. March 20, 2010.

Jackson, Wayne. Telephone interview. April 19, 2005.

Jemmott, Jerry. Telephone interview. April 2, 2008.

Lawrence, Trevor. Telephone interview. July 20, 2015.

Mardin, Arif. Telephone interview. June 3, 2003.

Moore, Sam. Telephone interview. April 3, 2002.

Palmer, Thomas "Curly."Telephone interview, April 26, 2008.

Paul, Gene. Telephone interview. February 25, 2021.

Purdie, Bernard. Telephone interview. November 23, 2005.

Rainey, Chuck. Telephone interview. April 30, 2008.

Reeves, Shirley Alston. Interview, The Philharmonic Center, Naples, FL. April 12, 2008.

Sanborn, David. Telephone interview. December 19, 2008.

Smith, Jimmy. Telephone interview. April 28, 2008.

Wexler, Jerry. Telephone interview. January 30, 2001.

Whitlock, Bobby. Telephone interview. August 15, 2005.

Wood, Bobby. Telephone interview. June 10, 2010.

Sources

Aletti, Vince. "Sam of Sam and Dave Meets King C." *Rolling Stone*, February 18, 1971.

Allman, Greg. *My Cross to Bear*. Harper Collins, 2013.

Allman, Galadrielle. *Please Be with Me; A Song for My Father, Duane Allman*. Spiegel & Grau, 2014.

Amburn, Ellis. *Buddy Holly: A Biography*. St. Martin's Griffin, 1995.

Ankeny, Jason. Review of *Azure*, King Curtis. https://www.allmusic.com/album/azure-mw0000582649.

Bego, Mark. *Aretha Franklin: The Queen of Soul*. St. Martin's Press, 1989.

Bernstein, Sid. *It's Sid Bernstein Calling*. Jonathan David, 2002.

Black, Johnny. *Jimi Hendrix: The Ultimate Experience*. Thunder's Mouth Press, 1999.

Bushell, Garvin. *Jazz from the Beginning*. University of Michigan Press, 1988.

Cavanaugh, David. Liner notes for *King Curtis Plays the Hits Made Famous by Sam Cooke*, King Curtis. Capitol, ST 2341, 1964.

Clapton, Eric. *Clapton: The Autobiography*. Broadway Books, 2007.

Coleman, Ray. *Clapton!* Warner Books, 1985.

Cooper, Ralph. *Amateur Night at The Apollo: Ralph Cooper Presents Five Decades of Great Entertainment*. Harper Collins, 1990.

Darwin, Norman. "Eddie Kirkland." *BOSS* 15, April/May 1986.

Delconte, Peppo. "Milan Caravan Stormy Scenes." *Billboard*, July 24, 1971.

Eder, Bruce. Review of *King Curtis Plays the Hits Made Famous by Sam Cooke*. https://www.allmusic.com/album/plays-the-hits-made-famous-by-sam-cooke-mw0000899479.

Ertegun, Ahmet. *What'd I Say*. Welcome Rain, 2001.

Fong-Torres, Ben. "Tales of Ike and Tina Turner: The World's Greatest Heartbreaker." *Rolling Stone*, February 18, 1971.

Franklin, Aretha, and David Ritz. *Aretha: From These Roots*. Villard Books, 1999.

Friedman, Josh Allen. *Tell the Truth until They Bleed: Coming Clean in the Dirty World of Blues and Rock and Roll*. Backbeat Books, 2008.

Gardner, Carl. *Yakety Yak I Fought Back: My Life with The Coasters*. Authorhouse, 2007.

Gillett, Charlie. *Making Tracks: The History of Atlantic Records*. Panther Books, 1975.

Gillett, Charlie. "KC Interviewed." *The Sound #4*, June/July 1985.

Gillett, Charlie. "KC Interviewed pt. 2." *The Sound #5*, August/September 1985.

Goldberg, Joe. Liner notes for *Trouble In Mind*, King Curtis. Tru-Sound, 15001, April 25, 1961.

Grendysa, Peter. Liner notes for *Blow Man Blow*, King Curtis. Bear Family, BCD 15 670 CI, 1993.

Guralnick, Peter. *Dream Boogie: The Triumph of Sam Cooke*. Little, Brown & Co., 2009.

———. *Sweet Soul Music: Rhythm and Blues and the Southern Dream of Freedom*. Little, Brown & Co., 1986.

Hanson, Gayle W. "Terrell, Isaiah Mulligan [I. M.] (1859–1931)." *Handbook of Texas*, Texas State Historical Association. May 1, 2007. Last updated December 28, 2020. https://www.tshaonline.org/handbook/entries/terrell-isaiah-milligan-im.

Henderson, David. *'Scuse Me while I Kiss the Sky: Jimi Hendrix: Voodoo Child*. Atria Books, 1978.

Hennessey, Mike. "King Curtis: His Last Interview." *Record Mirror*, August 8, 1971.

———. Liner notes for *Blues at Montreux*, King Curtis and Champion Jack Dupree. Atlantic, SD 1637, 1973.

Hentoff, Nat. Liner notes for *The New Scene of King Curtis*, King Curtis. New Jazz, NJLP 8237, April 21, 1960.

Hirshey, Gerri. *Nowhere to Run: The Story of Soul Music*. De Capo Press, 1994.

Hughes, Rob, and Simonds, Roy. "Stoller." *BOSS* 8, March 1986.

Jennings, Waylon. *Waylon: An Autobiography*. Chicago Review Press, 2012.

Johnson Jr., John, Joel Selvin, and Dick Cami. *Peppermint Twist: The Mob, the Music, and the Most Famous Dance Club of the 1960s*. Thomas Dunne Books, 2012.

Jones, Roben. *Memphis Boys: The Story of American Studios*. University Press of Mississippi, 2010.

Keys, Bobby. *Every Night's a Saturday Night: The Rock and Roll Life of Legendary Sax Man Bobby Keys*. Counterpoint, 2013.

Komorowski, Adam. "Ray Sharpe Interview." *BOSS* 12, November 1986.

Lawrence, Sharon. *Jimi Hendrix: The Intimate Story of a Betrayed Musical Legend*. Harper Collins, 2005.

Lydon, Michael, and Ellen Mandel. *Boogie Lightning: How Music Became Electric*. Da Capo Press, 1974.

Mehr, Bob. "Chips Moman: The Missing Man of Memphis Music." *The Commercial Appeal*, July 13, 2008, https://archive.commercialappeal.com/entertainment/chips-moman-the-missing-man-of-memphis-music-ep-396359660-324079771.html.

Meisel, Perry. *The Cowboy and the Dandy*. Oxford University Press, 1998.

Millar, Bill. *The Coasters*. W. H. Allen, 1975.

Muranyi, Joseph. Liner notes for *Have Tenor Sax Will Blow*, King Curtis. Atlantic, 1959, Atco, 33-113/SD 33-113.

O'Keefe, Dennis, dir. "Soul Serenade: The King Curtis Ousley Story (As Told by Those Who Knew and Loved Him)." 1987. Incomplete documentary film.

Palmer, Don. "Clarence Clemons." *The Sound* #7, December/January 1986.

Payne, Jim. "R&B Drumming Legend Ray Lucas: Props from Peers." *Modern Drummer*, May 29, 2012.

Poe, Randy. *Skydog: The Duane Allman Story*. Backbeat Books, 2006.

Pomus, Jerome "Doc." Liner notes for *It's Great to Be Young and in Love/Whiskey, Women, And ...*, Jerome "Doc" Pomus. RBD 713, December 25, 1999.

Purdie, Bernard. *Let the Drums Speak! The Life Story of the World's Most Recorded Drummer*. Pretty Media, 2014.

Ritz, David. *Respect: The Life of Aretha Franklin*. Little, Brown & Co., 2014.

Roby, Steven, and Brad Schreiber. *Becoming Jimi Hendrix: From Southern Crossroads to Psychedelic London, the Untold Story of a Musical Genius*. Da Capo Press, 2010.

Shumach, Murray. "King Curtis, the Bandleader, Is Stabbed to Death." *New York Times*, August 15, 1971.

Shuman, Mort. Interview by Stuart Colman. *Echoes* radio show. Radio London broadcast, October 26, 1986. Transcribed by Roy Simonds in *Boss 12*, November 1986, 6.

Simonds, Roy. Back cover notes for *Live In New York*, King Curtis. JSP, 1091, 2008.

Simonds, Roy. "Interview with Bob Rolontz." *The Sound* #6, October/
   November 1985.
Simonds, Roy. *King Curtis: A Discography*. Version 4.5. Self-published,
   2008.
Wexler, Jerry. Liner notes for *King Curtis Plays the Great Memphis Hits*,
   King Curtis. Atco, SD 33-211, 1967.
———. *Rhythm and the Blues: A Life in American Music*. St. Martin's
   Press, 1993.
Whitburn, Joel. *Joel Whitburn's Top Pop Singles, 1955–2006*. Self-published,
   2007.
———. *Joel Whitburn's Top R&B Singles, 1942–1995*. Self-published, 1996.
Whitlock, Bobby. *Bobby Whitlock, a Rock and Roll Autobiography*.
   McFarland, 2011.
Wilmer, Valerie. "Bobby Robinson: Legend of the Backstreets." *Melody
   Maker*, November 18, 1978.
Wilson, Tom. Liner notes for *Soul Battle*, Oliver Nelson, King Curtis, and
   Jimmy Forrest. Prestige, PR 7223, September 9, 1960.
Wolff, Daniel. *You Send Me: The Life and Times of Sam Cooke*. Quill William
   Morrow, 1995.
Wright, Dale. Liner notes for *Old Gold*, King Curtis. Tru-Sound, TRU 15006,
   December 1961.
Wright, Phillip Leno. *Free Mind Free Speech: Please!! May I Speak?*
   Authorhouse, 2014.

Index

I

M

Mandel, Ellen, 201
Mardin, Arif, 24, 109, 141–42, 156–58, 169, 193, 227, 255
Marvelettes, 80
Mason, Dave, 166
Massey, George, 131
McCartney, Paul, 211
McCracken, Hugh, 72, 84
McDuff, Jack, 75, 97–98
McNeely, Jay, 41
McPhatter, Clyde, 44, 53, 63, 85
Meisel, Perry, 58
"Memphis Soul Stew," 149–50
Mercury label, 71
Mickey and Sylvia, 53
Miller, Norman, 16
Mitchell, Blue, 76
Mitchell, Willie, 101
Modern label, 39
Modern Sounds in Country and Western Music, 87
Moman, Chips, 136–38, 147–48, 156
Montanez, Juan, 229–30
Montenegro, Hugo, 72
Montgomery, Bob, 57
Montgomery, Curtis. *see* Ousley, Curtis
Montgomery, Ethel, 1, 4
Montgomery, Gene, 10
Mooney, Art, 23
Moore, Danny, 97–98
Moore, Sam, 94–95, 132, 191–98, 230, 255
    Plenty Good Lovin': The Lost Solo Album, 197
Morrison, Van, 131
Muranyi, Joe, 7, 60

N

Napoleon, Joe, 22
Nelson, Oliver, 66, 179
New Burlesque Theatre, 15

Spector, Phil, 211
Spruill, Jimmy, 61
Stampley, Joe, 116
Star Date magazine, 39
Starliters, 80
Stax Records, 141, 148, 154, 165, 191–92, 194
Stewart, Jim, 136, 142, 147–48
Stidham, Arbee, 71
Stitt, Sonny, 12
Stoller, Mike, 27, 27, 45, 45–47, 47, 51
Stone, Jesse, 38–39, 42, 46
Stubbs, George, 78, 86
Sun Records, 147
Supremes, 69, 103, 106
    The Supremes:We Remember Sam Cooke, 106
swamp music, 165–66
Sylvia, 133–34

T

Taylor, Sam, 32, 39–40, 42, 109
"Tenor in the Sky," 19
Terrell, Ty, 46
That Lovin' Feeling, 109, 133
Thomas, Carla, 148
Thomas, Rufus, 102, 143, 148
Three Queen Booking Agency, 203
Tibbs Brothers, 42
Trouble in Mind, 73–74
Troy, Doris, 102
Tru-Sound label, 64, 72, 74–75, 77–78, 83
Turner, Big Joe, 43–44, 46, 53, 63, 102
Turner, Bo, 57
Turner, Ike, 176, 189
Turner, Tina, 176
Turner, Titus, 63, 160
Twist dances, 81–82

U

Uniques, the, 116